Vol. XC

W9-CLQ-158

# Bible Expositor and Illuminator

**SPRING QUARTER**                       **March, April, May 2018**

Editor in Chief: Todd Williams

Edited and published quarterly by
**THE INCORPORATED TRUSTEES OF THE
GOSPEL WORKER SOCIETY
UNION GOSPEL PRESS DIVISION**

*"CHRISTIAN LIFE SERIES"*
**UGP**
**UNION GOSPEL PRESS**

Rev. W. B. Musselman, Founder

Price: $4.65 per quarter*
$18.60 per year*
*shipping and handling extra*

ISBN 978-1-59843-677-8

# LOOKING AHEAD

The theme for this quarter of study is "Acknowledging God." We Christians often bemoan the fact that people in general do not acknowledge God as they should, but we also have to take a look at our own lives. Do we acknowledge God as we should? Perhaps the world does not acknowledge God because we do not acknowledge Him as we should.

How do we acknowledge God in our lives today? Our first unit of study helps answer that question by focusing on the importance of following God's ways rather than our own. In lesson 1, we look at God's command to Abraham in Genesis 22 to sacrifice his son Isaac. There we learn that God provides for us, which gives us assurance as we follow His ways.

In lessons 2, 3, and 4, we examine the completion of Solomon's temple, noting his prayer of dedication, the time of worship, and God's command to seek His face always. These lessons further unveil to us important elements in following God's ways.

To acknowledge God fully means we will come to a place of giving Him all glory and honor. In the second unit of study, we give glory and honor to the Lord Jesus as we remind ourselves that He has risen (lesson 5), that He appeared to many people after His resurrection (lesson 6), and that He now wants us, like Peter, to follow Him (lesson 7).

This unit of study concludes with the worship scenes in Revelation 4 and 5. In that magnificent setting, we will give glory to the Lord God Almighty (lesson 8) and will do so forever (lesson 9).

The final unit of study helps us understand that acknowledging God means we praise Him regularly. Lesson 10 turns our attention to Exodus 35 and II Corinthians 9 and the importance of a generous heart as one way of praising Him. Lessons 11 and 12 take us back to Leviticus, where we learn from the Feast of Firstfruits, the Sabbath Year, and the Jubilee Year how to praise the Lord.

The final lesson in this series, from Psalm 34 and Hebrews 2, leads us to rejoice in the Lord as a means of acknowledging Him. May these lessons help you acknowledge the Lord more and enable you to help others do the same.

—*Don Anderson.*

# Who Receives the Glory?

PAUL R. BAWDEN

The basketball game came down to the last few seconds. When one of the players got the ball, instead of passing it, he dribbled it, taking the last shot. He missed his shot, and his team lost the game. After the game, someone commented that it seemed odd that the player did not pass the ball to a more open player. The prevailing opinion was that he was a "glory hound." What does that term mean? It means that the player wanted to be in the limelight and receive all the honor. It was all about him and not the team he was on.

Such an attitude displays a misunderstanding of man's glory. First Peter 1:24 says, "For all flesh is as grass, and all the glory of man as the flower of grass. The grass withereth, and the flower thereof falleth away." Any glory that man has, then, is here today and gone tomorrow, just like man himself.

Is there glory that lasts for time and eternity? The answer is a definite yes! It is not found in finite man but in the infinite, eternal God revealed in the unchanging Word of God, the Bible.

When the work on the Old Testament tabernacle was finished, we read in Exodus 40: 34-35, "Then a cloud covered the tent of the congregation, and the glory of the Lord filled the tabernacle. And Moses was not able to enter into the tent of the congregation, because the cloud abode thereon, and the glory of the Lord filled the tabernacle." When Solomon later dedicated the temple, "the priests could not stand to minister by reason of the cloud: for the glory of the Lord had filled the house of the God" (II Chron. 5:14).

The word "glory" in the Old Testament has the idea of being heavy, meaning something that has incredible meaning and significance. When the glory of the Lord is mentioned, that is telling us something very significant about God. The Hebrew for "Lord" tells us that this is the self-existent, eternal God. Since the Lord is eternal, the glory of the Lord is eternal as well. When the glory of the Lord filled the tabernacle and temple, that was the revelation of the incredible, significant, awesome presence of the eternal God.

Certainly the biblical God has many characteristics, such as love, holiness, truth, justice, omnipotence, omnipresence, and omniscience; but the Lord's glory is really the manifestation of all His characteristics at one time. When the glory of Lord came to the tabernacle and temple, it was a display of His glorious presence that overwhelmed the people, for Moses could not enter the tent of the congregation, and the priests could not stand to minister by reason of the cloud, the glory of the Lord.

What happened to the glory of the Lord after the nation's disobedience in worshipping the creation rather than the Creator? Ezekiel 10 gives us the account of the glory of the Lord departing from the temple. The Lord's glory will not tolerate idolatry. Only when the Lord Jesus Christ returns to earth will the glory of the Lord fill the temple as it once did (chap. 43).

John penned these words in his Gospel, "The Word was made flesh, and dwelt among us, (and we beheld his glory, the glory as of the only begotten of the Father,) full of grace and truth" (1:14). The "Word . . . made flesh" is referring to the incarnation of Jesus Christ, the eternal Son of God. "Dwelt among us" could be translated, "tabernacled among us,"

(Editorials continued on page 186)

# Scripture Lesson Text

**GEN. 22:1** And it came to pass after these things, that God did tempt A'bra-ham, and said unto him, A'bra-ham: and he said, Behold, *here* I *am.*

**2 And he said, Take now thy son, thine only *son* I'saac, whom thou lovest, and get thee into the land of Mo-ri'ah; and offer him there for a burnt offering upon one of the mountains which I will tell thee of.**

3 And A'bra-ham rose up early in the morning, and saddled his ass, and took two of his young men with him, and I'saac his son, and clave the wood for the burnt offering, and rose up, and went unto the place of which God had told him.

**4 Then on the third day A'bra-ham lifted up his eyes, and saw the place afar off.**

5 And A'bra-ham said unto his young men, Abide ye here with the ass; and I and the lad will go yonder and worship, and come again to you.

**6 And A'bra-ham took the wood of the burnt offering, and laid *it* upon I'saac his son; and he took the fire in his hand, and a knife; and they went both of them to gether.**

7 And I'saac spake unto A'bra-ham his father, and said, My father: and he said, Here *am* I, my son. And he said, Behold the fire and the wood: but where *is* the lamb for a burnt offering?

**8 And A'bra-ham said, My son, God will provide himself a lamb for a burnt offering: so they went both of them together.**

9 And they came to the place which God had told him of; and A'bra-ham built an altar there, and laid the wood in order, and bound I'saac his son, and laid him on the altar upon the wood.

**10 And A'bra-ham stretched forth his hand, and took the knife to slay his son.**

11 And the angel of the LORD called unto him out of heaven, and said, A'bra-ham, A'bra-ham: and he said, Here *am* I.

**12 And he said, Lay not thine hand upon the lad, neither do thou any thing unto him: for now I know that thou fearest God, seeing thou hast not withheld thy son, thine only *son* from me.**

13 And A'bra-ham lifted up his eyes, and looked, and behold behind *him* a ram caught in a thicket by his horns: and A'bra-ham went and took the ram, and offered him up for a burnt offering in the stead of his son.

**14 And A'bra-ham called the name of that place Je-ho'vah–ji'reh: as it is said *to* this day, In the mount of the LORD it shall be seen.**

---

**NOTES**

4

# The Lord Will Provide

### Lesson: Genesis 22:1-14

Read: Genesis 22:1-24

TIME: 2050 B.C.                    PLACES: Beersheba; Moriah

---

**GOLDEN TEXT**—"Abraham said, My son, God will provide himself a lamb for a burnt offering: so they went both of them together" (Genesis 22:8).

---

## Introduction

The phrase "to acknowledge God" can have at least two different meanings. It can mean simply recognizing that God exists. That kind of acknowledgement is foundational, but it is certainly a low-level acknowledgement. We Christians must go beyond this foundational level and acknowledge that God is sovereign and that we are accountable to Him. Truly acknowledging God means we put ourselves under His authority, recognizing that He is our Creator who deserves our worship and obedience.

This week we begin a new series of lessons titled "Acknowledging God." In these lessons, we will examine Scriptures that point to God's greatness and our proper response to Him.

The first unit of this series focuses our attention on following God's ways as an essential component of acknowledging Him. If we are to acknowledge Him properly and fully, we must confess that His ways are right and commit ourselves to following His ways. In our first study, we examine Genesis 22, the account of Abraham's willingness to offer his son Isaac.

## LESSON OUTLINE

I. **GOD'S COMMAND TO ABRAHAM**—Gen. 22:1-2

II. **ABRAHAM'S OBEDIENCE TO GOD**—Gen. 22:3-10

III. **GOD'S PROVISION FOR ABRAHAM**—Gen. 22:11-14

## Exposition: Verse by Verse

**GOD'S COMMAND TO ABRAHAM**

GEN. 22:1 And it came to pass after these things, that God did tempt Abraham, and said unto him, Abraham: and he said, Behold, here I am.

2 And he said, Take now thy son, thine only son Isaac, whom thou lovest, and get thee into the land of Moriah; and offer him there for a burnt offering upon one of the mountains which I will tell thee of.

The events of Genesis 22 occurred "after these things" (vs. 1), referring to the events of chapter 21. Foremost among those events was the birth of Isaac (vss.1-7), the one through whom God promised to give Abraham his seed, and the departure of Hagar and Ishmael (vss. 8-21).

Against this backdrop, the events of Genesis 22 seem all the more striking. We are told that "God did tempt Abraham" (vs. 1). The word "tempt" does not mean God tempted Abraham to do wrong. That would be impossible since "God cannot be tempted with evil, neither tempteth he any man" (Jas. 1:13). The word "tempt" here means "to test" or "to prove."

God wanted to test Abraham to determine his level of obedience (cf. Gen. 22:12). In one sense this test must have been a supreme test of faith for Abraham since it involved Isaac, the son of promise, for whom he had waited so long. When God called his name, Abraham did not know what He was about to ask; nevertheless, he expressed his readiness to serve and obey when he responded, "Behold, here I am" (vs. 1).

God's command to Abraham must have astounded him. God told him to take his son Isaac and offer him as a burnt offering on one of the mountains in the land of Moriah. Had he heard God correctly? Abraham was familiar with burnt offerings, so he knew God was telling him to kill his son. How could that be since Isaac was his special son? He was special in two momentous ways:

Isaac was the miracle son God had promised to give Abraham and Sarah in their old age (Gen. 17:16-22; 18:9-15).

Isaac, not Ishmael, was the son through whom God would fulfill His promise to make Abraham a great nation (Gen. 12:1-3; 17:16-21; 21:12).

How could God fulfill His promise through Isaac if Abraham sacrificed him?

God had given Abraham his son, and now God was asking him to give his son back to Him. Though Abraham surely struggled in his emotions with this command from God, he nonetheless was obedient.

Before we delve further into this account, we need to address the question of whether God was telling Abraham to do something He would later expressly forbid—child sacrifice (Lev. 18:21; 20:3; Deut. 12:30-31; 18:10). First, we need to remember that God does no evil (Jas. 1:13); so we cannot accuse Him of doing something wrong. Second, God never intended for Abraham to slay his son. His command was only a test—a test to prove the sincerity of Abraham's faith.

## ABRAHAM'S OBEDIENCE TO GOD

**3 And Abraham rose up early in the morning, and saddled his ass, and took two of his young men with him, and Isaac his son, and clave the wood for the burnt offering, and rose up, and went unto the place of which God had told him.**

**4 Then on the third day Abraham lifted up his eyes, and saw the place afar off.**

**5 And Abraham said unto his young men, Abide ye here with the ass; and I and the lad will go yonder and worship, and come again to you.**

**6 And Abraham took the wood of the burnt offering, and laid it upon Isaac his son; and he took the fire in his hand, and a knife; and they went both of them together.**

**7 And Isaac spake unto Abraham his father, and said, My father: and he said, Here am I, my son. And he said, Behold the fire and the wood: but where is the lamb for a burnt offering?**

**8 And Abraham said, My son, God will provide himself a lamb for a burnt offering: so they went both of them together.**

**9 And they came to the place which God had told him of; and Abraham built an altar there, and laid the wood in order, and bound**

Isaac his son, and laid him on the altar upon the wood.

10 And Abraham stretched forth his hand, and took the knife to slay his son.

**The journey (Gen. 22:3-4).** Abraham showed his obedient faith by starting on the journey with his son Isaac, two of his servants, and wood for the burnt offering. The distance from Beersheba (21:32) to Mount Moriah (near Jerusalem) was about fifty miles. After three days of travel, he saw the place God had identified as the site of the offering. Many scholars believe it was the same location where the temple was built centuries later (cf. II Chron. 3:1).

**The faith (Gen. 22:5).** As they completed their journey, Abraham made an amazing statement of faith to his two servants: "I and the lad will go yonder and worship, and come again to you." Abraham believed not only that he would return but also that his son would return with him! Hebrews 11:19 gives us some insight on what Abraham was thinking. He believed "God was able to raise him up, even from the dead; from whence also he received him in a figure."

Abraham knew God's promises would be fulfilled through Isaac, and he also knew God had commanded him to slay his son. The only conclusion he could reach was that God would somehow raise his son from the dead, so both of them could come back to the servants. What a great demonstration of faith!

**The bearer (Gen. 22:6).** Abraham and Isaac started on their climb up the mountain alone, taking the wood, the fire, and the knife. Abraham laid the wood on his son to carry to the place of sacrifice. The parallel to Christ, who was compelled to carry the cross to His place of sacrifice, is striking in retrospect. Isaac carried wood that Abraham thought would be the means of his son's death.

**The conversation (Gen. 22:7-8).** As the two walked along, Isaac asked the obvious question. "Behold the fire and the wood: but where is the lamb for a burnt offering?" His question was a legitimate one, since at this point Isaac surely did not realize what his father had been commanded to do. Abraham's answer again shows his unwavering faith in God. "My son, God will provide himself a lamb for a burnt offering." Isaac appears to have been content with his father's response. The two of them continued on in what was most likely a quiet journey.

**The sacrifice (Gen. 22:9-10).** When the two reached the place God had identified, Abraham built the altar and placed the wood on the altar. Then he bound his son on the wood. We do not know what was going through the minds of the father and son, but surely Abraham must have had a considerable degree of trembling and fear. Still, he continued to follow through with God's command.

What about Isaac? He evidently accepted this matter from the Lord, for we have no record of any resistance. Such a response shows Isaac's faith in his father and in what God had said. Genesis 22:10 concludes this section by simply stating, "Abraham stretched forth his hand, and took the knife to slay his son." Abraham was not wavering in his obedient faith. He continued to believe God would somehow restore his son to life.

## GOD'S PROVISION FOR ABRAHAM

11 And the angel of the Lord called unto him out of heaven, and said, Abraham, Abraham: and he said, Here am I.

12 And he said, Lay not thine hand upon the lad, neither do thou any thing unto him: for now I know that thou fearest God, seeing thou hast not withheld thy son, thine only son from me.

13 And Abraham lifted up his

eyes, and looked, and behold behind him a ram caught in a thicket by his horns: and Abraham went and took the ram, and offered him up for a burnt offering in the stead of his son.

14 And Abraham called the name of that place Jehovah-jireh: as it is said to this day, In the mount of the Lord it shall be seen.

**The intervention (Gen. 22:11-12).** As Abraham was about to slay his son, the Angel of the Lord interrupted him: "Abraham, Abraham." Abraham made the same response he did in verse 1: "Here am I." He was still obediently following the Lord by faith. Abraham was prepared to slay his son, but we know he was very relieved to hear the voice from God again.

In Genesis 22:1-2, we read that God spoke to Abraham. In verse 11, we find that it is the Angel of the Lord who spoke to him. This connection shows us that the Angel of the Lord was not a created angel but none other than God Himself. Genesis 16:7 records the first appearance of the Angel of the Lord—when He met Hagar. (For further instances, see Genesis 31:11-13, Judges 6:11-22, 13:21-23, and Zechariah 3:1-2.)

In other appearances of the Angel of the Lord, He seems to be distinct from God (Gen. 24:7; II Sam. 24:16; Zech. 1:12-13). These passages can be harmonized with the earlier set by understanding the Angel of the Lord in them as the preincarnate Christ, who appeared to men and women in human form—a theophany (cf. Gen. 18:1-2; Num. 22:22-31; Judg. 2:1-4).

The Angel of the Lord is therefore most likely to be identified here as the preincarnate Christ Himself. He said to Abraham, "Lay not thine hand upon the lad, neither do thou any thing unto him" (Gen. 22:12). God had designed this test to prove Abraham's full devotion to Him. Abraham's actions revealed his heart and declared that he passed the

test. "For now I know that thou fearest God, seeing thou hast not withheld thy son, thine only son from me."

The acknowledgment that Abraham did not withhold his only son from God is riveting. It points ahead like a shining arrow to the time when God the Father would not withhold His only Son but gave Him up as sacrifice for our sins (John 3:16; Rom. 5:6-11; 8:32; I Cor. 5:7).

**The substitute (Gen. 22:13-14).** With a sense of relief, Abraham lowered his hand and spared his son. At the same time, the Lord drew his attention to a ram behind him caught by his horns in a thicket. This ram was the fulfillment of Isaac's question in verse 7 and Abraham's response in verse 8. Abraham gladly took the ram and offered it in place of his son (vs. 13). In grateful thanksgiving to God, he named the location where he offered the ram "Jehovah-jireh," which means "the Lord will see" or "the Lord will provide."

The idea of provision comes from the root meaning of "jireh," which is "to see." God in His infinite ability saw Abraham's need and provided a ram as a substitute for his son. (Even the English word "provide" shows this connection because it is a combination of two Latin words meaning "to see beforehand.")

Genesis 22:14 is the only place in Scripture where we find the name "Jehovah-jireh" used of God. Some other names of God can be discerned in the Hebrew text of passages throughout the Old Testament, although in most cases they are not readily apparent in the English text. A study of these names can yield insights into God's character and dealings with His people.

Genesis 22:14 ends with the statement "As it is said to this day, In the mount of the Lord it shall be seen." Long after Abraham's day, this location was known as the place where God saw the need of His servant Abraham and met that need. The mountain was

8

a reminder to the Israelites in the years to come that God saw their needs and provided for them.

Before we conclude this study, we should note several ways in which Isaac typified, or prefigured, the Lord Jesus Christ, who is our greatest provision.

• Isaac's birth was special because his parents bore him past the time of childbearing (Gen. 18:11). Christ's birth was special because He was born of a virgin (Matt. 1:23).

• In Hebrews 11:17, Isaac is called Abraham's "only begotten son," his one-of-a-kind, unique son. John 3:16 reminds us that God loved us to the extent that He gave His "only begotten Son." Christ was indeed a one-of-a-kind, unique Son.

• Abraham offered his son Isaac in response to God's command (Gen. 22:9-10). God the Father offered His Son, Christ, as a sacrifice for sins (Isa. 53:10).

• Isaac carried the wood that was to be used to offer him as a sacrifice (Gen. 22:6). Our Lord Jesus carried His cross to which He was nailed as our sacrifice (John 19:17).

• Isaac submitted without question to his father Abraham (Gen. 22:9). Jesus willingly submitted to His Father (Matt. 26:39).

• According to Genesis 22:5, Abraham evidently expected to slay his son and have him come back to life. Hebrews 11:19 tells us that in a sense Abraham did receive his son back from the dead. Christ Jesus died and rose again for our sins (I Cor. 15:3-4).

• In a slightly different sense, the lives of both Isaac and Christ involve substitution. God provided a ram as a substitute for Isaac (Gen. 22:13). Jesus Himself took our place of punishment for sin (Isa. 53:5). This comparison again highlights the concept of provision. God saw Abraham's need and provided a ram as a substitute in place of his son. God saw our need for salvation and provided His Son as our Substitute.

This truth of provision extends to our daily lives as well. God sees our situation. He knows everything about us (Ps. 139:1-16). He sees our needs and our hurts. He sees our failings and our pains. God sees what we are going through today. His heart is moved by our needs, and He provides for those needs. While Philippians 4:19 refers primarily to financial matters, its application reaches to every area of our lives.

Following in God's ways begins with a firm confidence that He will provide for us. Abraham had that confidence. Whatever you are facing today, meditate on the truth—God sees, and He will provide for you.

—Don Anderson.

# QUESTIONS

1. In what way did God "tempt" Abraham?
2. What special things about Isaac made it especially difficult for Abraham to obey God's command?
3. What did Abraham tell his two servants?
4. What did Abraham evidently believe God would do to Isaac?
5. What indications do we have that Isaac also was obedient to God's will?
6. Who spoke to Abraham from heaven, and what is the likely identity of that person?
7. How did God provide a substitute for Isaac?
8. What does "Jehovah-jireh" mean?
9. What are a few of the ways that Isaac prefigures Christ?
10. What provision do you need to trust God for today?

—Don Anderson.

# Preparing to Teach the Lesson

It might be difficult for the students in your class to believe, down deep to the point that it informs their every thought and decision, that God is the Supreme Ruler of the universe and that He will provide for His children. They are possibly used to seeing on the surface of their experience the idea that we are each in charge of our own individual lives and that we can provide for the important things of life. You have the high and holy responsibility in this lesson to help them understand that God will provide for both their spiritual and physical needs. This is where their religion (their beliefs as carried out in practice) and their understanding, thoughts, and activities in daily life connect.

## TODAY'S AIM

**Facts:** to see and understand how Abraham reacted to God's commands and provision.

**Principle:** to teach us to shape our thinking and reactions to life's circumstances in relation to God.

**Application:** to make it a habit of life and thought to watch for the Lord's provision in everything.

## INTRODUCING THE LESSON

This is the account of Abraham, that great man of faith, and the offering of his son Isaac—the son of promise and Abraham's heir. This was the son Abraham had when he and his wife Sarah were well past child-bearing age. God had promised this son and stated that Isaac was to father the line through which the Messiah would come.

## DEVELOPING THE LESSON

**1. The problematic command (Gen. 22:1-2).** God's command to Abraham was problematic on several levels. God had miraculously given him Isaac, and now Abraham's life was building around God's promise that this son would be the heir through whom blessing would come to the whole world. Abraham would be the father and patriarch of believers from then on throughout all time. Through him and through Isaac would come the Messiah, the Saviour of all believers.

And now God had told him to kill and offer Isaac as a burnt offering. God had never asked for human sacrifice and never would until the sacrifice of the Lord Jesus on the cross. But one day, God simply told Abraham to go do it.

We do not know all the thoughts that went through Abraham's mind. How could Isaac be the son of promise when he was dead? How could God give him a son and then ask him to kill the son he loved? Could God, would God, ask him to do something that looked and felt so wrong? Isaac was his promised son and his great hope.

We probably should not expect God to call us to do something this dramatic, but He may call us to do something way beyond our comfort zone. Just as Abraham would never have guessed that God would make this request, so we have no idea what God might call us to do.

**2. The patient response (Gen. 22:3-9).** Abraham did not ask for an explanation, although we certainly would not have blamed him for asking! He got up early and headed out to do what the Lord had said. It took three days to get to the place God designated, and Abraham still had no explanation. Isaac did not see how they were going to offer a sacrifice without a sacrificial lamb. Abraham patiently responded to Isaac's question with, "God will provide."

We all understand that there can be an irresponsible claim that "God will provide" by some spiritually irresponsible person. But, we should not put ourselves in a bad spot and then expect God to provide the way out of it. We can, however, learn from the patient carrying out of God's will by Abraham. He even went so far as to bind Isaac and put him on the altar to offer him up as a sacrifice to God! We have no idea what Isaac was thinking either, but he must have been exceedingly troubled.

When God asks us to do something, we must patiently carry out His wishes, even if it takes many years. You may teach a Sunday school class for years and see no results: keep teaching. You are serving the Lord by serving His people in a humble task. Keep serving. God will provide the results.

**3. The provided sacrifice (Gen. 22:10-14).** When Abraham started to kill the sacrifice (Isaac) on the altar, God stopped him. Abraham was mentally and spiritually prepared to obey God to the end, to the ultimate. Abraham's faith and obedience were complete. It was just like Paul's "I have kept the faith" (II Tim. 4:7). God did not require the ultimate sacrifice; He saw that Abraham was willing. God provided the ram caught by his horns in a thicket. It still required a little work by Abraham to get the ram out of the thicket and offer it as a sacrifice, but God had provided.

Again, we have only to be faithful. God will provide what He requests. It is rarely easy, but it is always good to trust the Lord. Remember, this wonderful experience of the Lord that Abraham had was possible only because Abraham believed and obeyed God, and Abraham entered into a special relationship with the Lord that few have ever had. God called out to him twice (Gen. 22:11) as He has few others ("Moses, Moses" in Exodus 3:4, "Saul, Saul" in Acts 9:4; cf. Matt. 27:46; Mark 15:34).

We may not have a special task given us, but we have all the clear commands of Scripture. We may not have a special circumstance wherein we must trust God to provide, but we do have all the ordinary tasks of life in which we can trust and obey Him and see His provision brought about. Whether it seems miraculous or rather ordinary, we can all see God's hand at work if we will only look with the eyes of faith.

## ILLUSTRATING THE LESSON

We must trust when we cannot see. This is the essence of prayer.

## CONCLUDING THE LESSON

It is all well and good to "ooh and aah" over Abraham and his faithfulness, but we have to come to grips with our own commitment to God and His promises. He has promised to save us by His grace and not by our works. If we believe Him, our daily habits will echo that belief and demonstrate that it exists (cf. Jas. 2:26). Our witness should include the way we trust God and do not worry about what people and even nations can do.

## ANTICIPATING THE NEXT LESSON

In our next lesson, we will study the wonderful prayer of Solomon at the dedication of the temple.

—*Brian D. Doud.*

# PRACTICAL POINTS

1. God expects us to listen for His voice and respond to His call (Gen. 22:1-2).
2. Following God's instructions requires planning and preparation (vss. 3-5).
3. Faith gives you the courage to obey God and trust that He will provide (vss. 6-8).
4. Faithful service to God requires willingness to make a sacrifice (vss. 9-10).
5. God provides what we need to carry out His plan (vss. 11-13).
6. We should always acknowledge God as our Provider and praise Him (vs. 14).

—*Valante M. Grant.*

# RESEARCH AND DISCUSSION

1. What kind of attitude should we possess when responding to the call of God?
2. How do we find the strength to obey God, even if it means losing something dear to us?
3. What roles do faith and trust play in obedience to God?
4. What is the significance of making sacrifices to God? Is it still necessary to make them today?
5. How does it affect our faith when God provides what we need?
6. How do we know that God accepts the sacrifices that we offer?
7. How does God respond to complete faith and obedience to Him (Gen. 22:17-18)?

—*Valante M. Grant.*

# ILLUSTRATED HIGH POINTS

**God did tempt Abraham**

God kept His promise and gave Abraham a son in his old age. Now He tested Abraham to see whether he loved God more than Isaac. Abraham passed this test with flying colors.

Our tests are usually less dramatic. A boy was on his way to Sunday school with two nickels, one for the offering and one for an ice-cream cone afterward. On the way, he dropped one down an open grate and said, "Oops, there goes the Lord's nickel!"

**Abraham rose up early**

Abraham was committed to obeying God, no matter what the outcome.

Someone wrote a paragraph about how some Christians are "lost in the woulds." They say, "I would come to Sunday school, but that's my day to sleep in," "I would stay for church, but we have to eat dinner early," or "I would give more to the church, but we have so many bills."

These people need to change their "woulds" into "wills," put Christ first in their lives, and give God their best.

**Thou hast not withheld thy son**

A young boy was seriously ill in the hospital. The medical staff had done everything they could, to no improvement. It was a frightening time for the parents. Only the wife and her mother were believers at the time.

Finally, there came a breakthrough, and the child improved and remains healthy today over fifty years later. The parents were grateful with God's answer to prayer. The mother, however, said, "You know, my son didn't start to improve until I told God I would let him go, if that was what He willed." As she gave her son to God, He gave him back.

—*David A. Hamburg.*

# Golden Text Illuminated

"Abraham said, My son, God will provide himself a lamb for a burnt offering: so they went both of them together" (Genesis 22:8).

When we read of the ultimate test that God put His servant Abraham through, we feel both dismay and admiration. We cringe at the thought that God might put us through a similar trial, but we admire the great faith that Abraham showed throughout his. Nowhere does his faith shine more brightly than in the statement recorded in our golden text.

Short of when he had to actually take knife in hand (Gen. 22:10), this was possibly the most painful moment in Abraham's ordeal. Isaac knew that they were on their way to offer a special sacrifice to the Lord. He may have only now worked up the courage to ask about the lack of a sacrificial animal (vs. 7).

Abraham had undoubtedly been dreading the moment when Isaac would find out that *he* was to be the sacrifice, and quite naturally would have put off disclosing that fact. His answer may sound evasive to us, but in reality it demonstrates the great faith that he was exercising.

Hebrews 11:17-19 tells us that Abraham acted in faith when he set out to obey God's command to offer up his son. He believed that God would keep His promise regarding the blessing through Isaac and would, if necessary, even raise him from the dead. This faith was seen earlier in Abraham's instructions to the servants to remain at the foot of the mountain: "I and the lad will go yonder and worship, and come again to you" (Gen. 22:5).

Abraham voiced the same faith in his answer to Isaac, stating it in different terms: "God will provide himself a lamb for a burnt offering." It is true that when Isaac was laid bound on the altar, he would have thought he was the provided lamb and may have considered the answer disingenuous. But Abraham was not merely putting him off. From the other statements in this passage and in Hebrews, we must assume that he genuinely believed the assurance he gave his son.

Of course, Abraham did not know the actual outcome in advance. He could not have known about the ram (Gen. 22:13). He did not know that the Lord was merely testing him. But he knew that God would ultimately provide, no matter what the two of them might have to go through.

But we cannot read this text without realizing that Abraham spoke truly of a far greater provision than he knew—or could have known even after the provision of the substitute for Isaac. When we read, "God will provide himself a lamb," we encounter one of the earliest and clearest foreshadowings in all the Old Testament of the greater Sacrifice to come.

God, who spared Abraham from going through with this most difficult test, did not spare Himself from putting His own Son through the full measure of grief. "He . . . spared not his own Son, but delivered him up for us all" (Rom. 8:32). God provided a Lamb, and it was costlier to Him than any cost He has ever asked any of His servants—or any human being anywhere—to bear. Isaac was spared through the substitution of a ram; we have been saved eternally through the substitution of the Lamb of God.

—*Kenneth A. Sponsler.*

# Heart of the Lesson

A favorite story my mother read to me when I was a child was about a little girl living on the mission field who, along with other missionary children, was asked to donate a toy for needy children. The little girl had two dolls. One she loved. After agonizing, she gave her beloved "Miss Bump" to the fund. She reasoned that God had given His best, His only Son, and she should do likewise.

God asked Abraham, father of the Jewish people, to give Him the thing Abraham most cherished: his son.

**1. Faith tested (Gen. 22:1-2).** God decided to test whether or not Abraham had enough faith in Him to be obedient. God asked him to sacrifice his son, his only son Isaac, the son Abraham loved, to God as a burnt offering at a location God would specify in the land of Moriah.

God knew how Abraham felt about Isaac. Isaac had been a miracle baby, born when Abraham was one hundred years old. Isaac was the son Abraham had longed for his entire married life.

Isaac also was the fulfillment of God's promise that Abraham would be the father of a great nation and bring blessing to all families of the earth. Sacrificing Isaac seemingly would undo God's promise to Abraham.

**2. Journey taken (Gen. 22:3-5).** Abraham's obedience was swift. He woke up early the next morning, saddled his donkey, chopped wood for a burnt offering, and fetched two servants and his son for the long walk.

The trip took three days. On the third day, Abraham could see the place they were to offer the sacrifice. Abraham told the servants to wait with the donkey while he and Isaac went farther to worship. Abraham's words show his faith: He told the men that he and Isaac would return to them. Abraham believed that somehow everything was going to turn out all right—that God was going to cause a miracle to happen. Hebrews 11:19 reveals Abraham believed God could even raise up Isaac from the dead.

**3. Obedience demonstrated (Gen. 22:6-10).** Isaac had seen burnt offerings; this was how his father worshipped God. But Isaac saw a difference between this occasion and those past. He asked, "Where is the lamb?" Abraham's carefully chosen words show his faith. He told Isaac that God Himself would provide the lamb.

Abraham built the altar and laid wood upon it. Next, he bound Isaac and laid him upon the kindling. Now Isaac knew. But he did not run away or resist. He submitted to his father, just as Abraham was submitting to his Heavenly Father. All was in place. Abraham reached for the knife.

**4. Substitute provided (Gen. 22:11-14).** At this critical moment, the Angel of the Lord—the preincarnate Christ—told Abraham to put down the knife. God said that now He knew Abraham feared Him. Abraham had passed the test.

Abraham looked up and saw a ram caught by its horns in a nearby thicket. He had not seen the ram earlier, but he knew why the ram was there. Abraham offered the ram on the altar in place of his son, and the two worshipped the Lord.

Abraham named the mountain "Jehovah–jireh," meaning "the Lord sees" or "the Lord provides." King David later designated this mountain as a place for Israel's sacrifices, and it was the site of the temples.

Are we willing, like Abraham, to stand with open hands before God? Like Abraham, do we trust God with the things we hold most dear?

*—Ann Staatz.*

# World Missions

The Bible says God has placed eternity in the hearts of men (Eccles. 3:11). Deep within each heart is the question, "Where is the Lamb?" He has also placed many redemptive revelations within cultures for those who are ready to ask that question.

Don Richardson, in his book *Eternity in Their Hearts* (Bethany House), shares stories of how God has prepared peoples for the gospel message by placing values or customs in their culture that resonate with the gospel when it arrives. Missionaries meeting primitive tribes for the first time have been shocked to hear that they had been waiting centuries for a stranger to arrive with a holy book and tell them the way to God. Others have found parts of the culture that provide avenues for gospel truths, such as the amazing true story of a tribe of cannibals in Richardson's book *Peace Child* (Bethany House). Once murderous and barbaric, when they heard the gospel using their sacred ceremony as the analogy, almost the entire tribe accepted Christ immediately.

God has placed such arrows leading people to Him in many other places and religions. Islam's Koran tells followers to read the gospels and study about Jesus (*Isa*) because He came from God and shows the way to heaven.

Buddha, who lived five hundred years before Christ, told followers they should look for the Holy One to come, who would be known by the marks in his hands and feet and a stab wound in his side.

These things within cultures and religions should give us hope that God has been and is preparing people's hearts to be ready for harvest.

He has been at work and is working today. One sources states that in 1970, there were 240,000 missionaries. In 2015, there were 400,000. Also in 1970, almost 45 percent of the world was considered unevangelized. By 2015, that number had dropped to 29.3 percent (www.abwe.org/sites/default/files/resources/documents/attachments/2016/05/message).

Yet there is much to be done. Though there are 78,000 evangelical Christians for every unreached people group in the world, only 1 percent of all church income goes to reaching those unreached people—the same amount Americans spent in 2011 on Halloween costumes for their pets. Eighty-six percent of adherents to other religions do not personally know a Christian.

That can change. Though there are more people today than ever before, there is also more opportunity for them to be reached like never before. The New Testament is available in a readable language for 94 percent of the world. Christian radio has the potential to reach 99 percent of the world. The Jesus Film has been viewed over 4 billion times and could be viewed by 99 percent of the world in a language they know. Young people from closed countries are coming to American colleges to study. Millions are coming to Christ through the Internet.

Some estimates say that in A.D. 100, the ratio of people to believers was 360 to 1. Now the number is less than 8 to 1. In A.D. 100, there were 12 unreached people groups to every 1 congregation of believers. Now there is 1 unreached group per 1,000 congregations. We have the ability and the resources to give the world the message it needs. God has provided Himself a Lamb.

Each of us should ask God how He wants us to share that message both locally and globally and then do it.

—*Kimberly Rae.*

# The Jewish Aspect

A headline in the September 9, 2010, edition of *The Sun* from San Bernardino County, California, reads, "Jews Celebrate First Day of 5771th New Year." The story continues to describe the blast from the shofar that announced the arrival of Rosh Hashanah.

Rosh Hashanah appears in the Hebrew Bible under the name *Yom Teruah,* that is, the Festival of Trumpets. It begins on the first day of Tishri, the first month on the Jewish civil calendar and the seventh month on the Jewish religious calendar. In America, the celebration generally falls in September or October.

The name "Rosh Hashanah" means "head of the year." Rosh Hashanah is a New Year's celebration and marks the beginning of the penitential period that ends with Yom Kippur ten days later.

The shofar, an instrument traditionally made from a ram's horn, plays a large part in the celebration. In most communities the shofar sounds one hundred times during Rosh Hashanah (Posner, "Why Do We Blow One Hundred Shofar Blasts on Rosh Hashanah?" www.chabad.org).

This week's Scripture lesson text, Genesis 22:1-14, also plays a prominent role in the celebration. The Jewish community reads this passage annually in the synagogue on the second day of Rosh Hashanah.

Genesis 22 relates the defining moment in the story of Abraham and Isaac. To the Jewish person, this portion is known as *Akedah,* or "Binding."

In the narrative, God told Abraham to offer Isaac as a sacrifice. However, as Abraham prepared to obey and raised the knife, the Angel of the Lord stopped him and directed his attention to a ram. Jewish sages teach that after Abraham obeyed, "God took the horns from this ram and made shofarot (plural for shofar)" (Reeves, *The Jewish Holidays,* AuthorHouse). Thus, the ideas of obedience and redemption became tied to the shofar.

Rosh Hashanah encourages the participant to look back over the past year, to consider any misdeeds, and to rectify all wrongs. During Rosh Hashanah, the Jewish person performs *teshuvah,* which means "to return" and is the word to describe repentance in Judaism.

Two ideals are meant to dominate this holiday. First, the individual should humble himself as he realizes that it is God who has power over life and death. Second, the individual should turn away from negative influences and return to God (Olitzky and Judson, *Jewish Holidays,* Jewish Lights).

One Jewish belief states that God is the Author of two books—the Book of Life and the Book of Death. Tradition holds that before Rosh Hashanah, God writes the names of the individuals who have acted righteously during the prior year in the Book of Life; they will live another year. However, He inscribes the names of those who have acted sinfully in the Book of Death. Most are "in between" and have their judgment suspended past Rosh Hashanah to Yom Kippur. This allows them time to repent.

In ancient times, Rosh Hashanah, the only Jewish festival without a fixed date, began at the new moon. The trumpet, or shofar, then announced its arrival.

First Thessalonians 4:16 reminds us that Christ's return in the clouds will be accompanied by "the trump of God." Rosh Hashanah, with its themes of repentance and the shofar, may well serve as a prophetic picture of the return of Christ.

—*Robin Fitzgerald.*

# Guiding the Superintendent

Jehovah-jireh is translated "the Lord will provide." One does not need to be around church people very long before they hear from someone, "The Lord will provide." This expression is usually used to encourage one who has experienced a loss of some kind.

Our lesson for this week examines this Old Testament name for God and what it means that God provides.

## DEVOTIONAL OUTLINE

**1. The test (Gen. 22:1-2).** The context for this account of the Lord's provision is God's trial of Abraham involving perhaps one of the strangest commands ever given to a human, and in particular to a father. God wanted to test Abraham by asking him to sacrifice his only son Isaac, the one he truly loved, as a burnt offering.

Here was the test: Who did Abraham love more—God or God's gift? Somewhere in your life as a believer, you will face this test: How much of your love for God is based simply on what you think you can get from Him? Is God more like a Santa Claus, or is He the God of the universe?

**2. The response (Gen. 22:3-8).** There was no reluctance or hesitation on Abraham's part. Abraham took a couple of his servants and his son and headed to the mountain for the sacrifice. What must have been going on in Abraham's head? Hebrews 11:19 gives this hint: "Accounting that God was able to raise him up, even from the dead." This is remarkable. Abraham expressed a belief in resurrection, even though he lived long before Christ.

Abraham had waited decades to have a son. His son was now at least in his upper teens. God had asked Abraham to sacrifice more than twenty-five years of his life. The test was all about his willingness to part with his dearest possession.

When they finally arrived within sight of the mountain, Abraham told his servants that he would go up there to worship. To worship means to bow down. Truly Abraham worshipped God—he bowed his will to God's will when it did not make much sense.

Isaac asked an obvious question: "Where is the lamb for a burnt offering?" (Gen. 22:7). Perhaps Abraham *did* realize how prophetic his words would be. John the Baptist would answer this question, "Behold the Lamb of God, which taketh away the sin of the world" (John 1:29).

**3. The intervention (Gen. 22:9-14).** With not a second to spare, the Angel of the Lord called out to Abraham, stopping him as he held the knife. It was never God's intention to sacrifice a human being. Only after Abraham had clearly revealed his love for God was he able to call the place Jehovah-jireh. The Lord will truly provide, but He wants us to regard Him as our dearest possession.

## AGE-GROUP EMPHASES

**Children:** This week's lesson text is a great one to help your children realize what it means for God to provide for their needs.

**Youths:** Isaac was probably in his teen years when this event occurred. Have your young people discuss what they think might have been going through Isaac's mind during this situation. The text reveals only that he was obedient to his father.

**Adults:** Most adults have certain possessions they hold dear. This lesson will help them realize that in the end God is really their only truly valuable possession.

—Martin R. Dahlquist.

# Scripture Lesson Text

**II CHRON. 6:12** And he stood before the altar of the LORD in the presence of all the congregation of Is'ra-el, and spread forth his hands:

**13 For Sol'o-mon had made a brasen scaffold, of five cubits long, and five cubits broad, and three cubits high, and had set it in the midst of the court: and upon it he stood, and kneeled down upon his knees before all the congregation of Is'ra-el, and spread forth his hands toward heaven,**

14 And said, O LORD God of Is'ra-el, *there is* no God like thee in the heaven, nor in the earth; which keepest covenant, and *shewest* mercy unto thy servants, that walk before thee with all their hearts:

**15 Thou which hast kept with thy servant Da'vid my father that which thou hast promised him; and spakest with thy mouth, and hast fulfilled *it* with thine hand, as *it is* this day.**

16 Now therefore, O LORD God of Is'ra-el, keep with thy servant Da'vid my father that which thou hast promised him, saying, There shall not fail thee a man in my sight to sit upon the throne of Is'ra-el; yet so that thy children take heed to their way to walk in my law, as thou hast walked before me.

**17 Now then, O LORD God of Is'ra-el, let thy word be verified, which thou hast spoken unto thy servant Da'vid.**

18 But will God in very deed dwell with men on the earth? behold, heaven and the heaven of heavens cannot contain thee; how much less this house which I have built!

**19 Have respect therefore to the prayer of thy servant, and to his supplication, O LORD my God, to hearken unto the cry and the prayer which thy servant prayeth before thee:**

20 That thine eyes may be open upon this house day and night, upon the place whereof thou hast said that thou wouldest put thy name there; to hearken unto the prayer which thy servant prayeth toward this place.

**21 Hearken therefore unto the supplications of thy servant, and of thy people Is'ra-el, which they shall make toward this place: hear thou from thy dwelling place, *even* from heaven; and when thou hearest, forgive.**

**NOTES**

# A Prayer of Dedication

## Lesson: II Chronicles 6:12-21

### Read: II Chronicles 6:1-21

TIME: 959 B.C.                                    PLACE: Jerusalem

---

**GOLDEN TEXT**—"O Lord God of Israel, there is no God like thee in the heaven, nor in the earth; which keepest covenant, and shewest mercy unto thy servants, that walk before thee with all their hearts" (II Chronicles 6:14).

---

## Introduction

When a disaster strikes, either natural or man-made, many people have an increased awareness of the Lord and acknowledge Him in ways they did not before the disaster. You may remember the days right after September 11, 2001, when people talked about the Lord and even gathered to pray. Sadly, however, such acknowledgement of God usually wanes in the days and weeks that follow.

What makes the difference between a shallow, passing acknowledgement of God and a steady, long-term acknowledgement of Him? The difference is commitment. One must enter into a genuine commitment to follow the Lord's ways, pursuing a heartfelt dedication to Him.

This study looks at a time in the Old Testament after Solomon had completed building the temple of the Lord. Solomon had followed the ways of the Lord in building the temple and then expressed his dedication to the Lord in a moving prayer, showing a genuine spirit of humility at this time.

## LESSON OUTLINE

I. HUMBLING HIMSELF BEFORE GOD—II Chron. 6:12-13

II. RECOUNTING GOD'S GREATNESS—II Chron. 6:14-18

III. MAKING PETITION OF GOD—II Chron. 6:19-21

## Exposition: Verse by Verse

### HUMBLING HIMSELF BEFORE GOD

**II CHRON. 6:12** And he stood before the altar of the Lord in the presence of all the congregation of Israel, and spread forth his hands:

**13** For Solomon had made a brasen scaffold, of five cubits long, and five cubits broad, and three cubits high, and had set it in the midst of the court: and upon it he stood, and kneeled down upon his knees before all the congregation of Israel, and spread forth his hands toward heaven.

Second Chronicles 2 through 5 records Solomon's work of building and furnishing the temple of God in Jerusalem. After its completion, a cloud filled the temple, "so that the priests could not stand to minister by reason of the cloud: for the glory of the Lord had filled the house of God" (5:14). After recounting the history of the building project (6:1-11), Solomon dedicated the temple.

Solomon's dedication took place near the bronze altar, the altar used for offering sacrifices. This altar was 20 cubits long, 20 cubits wide, and 10 cubits high (30 feet long by 30 feet wide by 15 feet high) (II Chron. 4:1). These measurements describe the base of the altar, which had a ramp going to the top where the sacrifices were made. The altar stood in the courtyard in front of the temple (II Kings 16:14).

For this occasion, Solomon constructed a special bronze platform in the middle of the outer court (II Chron. 6:13). The platform measured 5 cubits long, 5 cubits wide, and 3 cubits high (7½ feet by 7½ feet by 4½ feet). The king began the proceedings by standing on this platform in the presence of all the people of Israel and spreading out his hands toward God. He then knelt on the platform to offer his dedicatory prayer to God.

Solomon recognized the greatness and provision of God in the construction of the temple, and he showed his humility and acknowledgement of God by raising his hands to heaven and kneeling on the platform.

## RECOUNTING GOD'S GREATNESS

14 And said, O Lord God of Israel, there is no God like thee in the heaven, nor in the earth; which keepest covenant, and shewest mercy unto thy servants, that walk before thee with all their hearts:

15 Thou which hast kept with thy servant David my father that which thou hast promised him; and spakest with thy mouth, and hast fulfilled it with thine hand, as it is this day.

16 Now therefore, O Lord God of Israel, keep with thy servant David my father that which thou hast promised him, saying, There shall not fail thee a man in my sight to sit upon the throne of Israel; yet so that thy children take heed to their way to walk in my law, as thou hast walked before me.

17 Now then, O Lord God of Israel, let thy word be verified, which thou hast spoken unto thy servant David.

18 But will God in very deed dwell with men on the earth? behold, heaven and the heaven of heavens cannot contain thee; how much less this house which I have built!

God's faithfulness (II Chron. 6:14-15). Solomon began his dedicatory prayer by recounting God's faithfulness. He acknowledged that the Lord God of Israel was unlike any of the gods of the nations around Israel—whether their gods were in heaven or on earth.

Solomon further extolled the Lord as the one who keeps His covenant and mercy to those who walk before Him in obedience. The word "mercy" is the Hebrew word *hesed,* which speaks of God's loyal or covenant-keeping love to His people. Solomon's statement hearkens back to Moses' words in Deuteronomy 7:9: "Know therefore that the Lord thy God, he is God, the faithful God, which keepeth covenant and mercy with them that love him and keep his commandments to a thousand generations."

Solomon then highlighted the faithfulness of God by noting how He had kept His promise to his father, David. The specific promise Solomon had in mind related to the building of the temple of the Lord and to the establishment of an eternal kingdom through David's descendants (I Chron. 22:10).

King Solomon elaborated on God's faithfulness by saying that what He had spoken with His mouth He had fulfilled with His hand. God did what He said He would do. He had fulfilled His words that day in Israel. He was faithful to His promises.

We should note in this passage (II Chron. 6) the frequent use of the name LORD (vs. 12) or LORD God (vss. 14, 16, 17, 19). The name LORD (note the smaller capital letters "ORD" in the name, different from "Lord") is the translators' way of treating *yhwh,* the sacred and personal name of the Lord. This name is sometimes pronounced "Yahweh," of which "Jehovah" is a hybrid form. Out of respect and to avoid mispronunciation, the ancient Jews would not pronounce this name of God but spoke a word that meant "Lord." The translators chose to use the form "LORD" with its unique capitalization to render the sacred name Yahweh, which most likely refers to God's eternal existence and faithfulness to His covenant.

The other Hebrew word for the Lord is *adonai,* which is rendered as "Lord" with lowercase letters "ord." This name refers to God's control or lordship. Both names are used in Psalm 8:1. "O LORD our Lord, how excellent is thy name in all the earth! who hast set thy glory above the heavens." The two names together convey His personal name and His lordship over all creation.

### God's promise (II Chron. 6:16-17).
Solomon then entreated the Lord to continue to fulfill His promise relating to the throne of Israel. The promise made to David was that "there shall not fail thee a man in my sight to sit upon the throne of Israel."

We first find this promise given to David in II Samuel 7 when Nathan the prophet told David, "And when thy days be fulfilled, and thou shalt sleep with thy fathers, I will set up thy seed after thee, . . . and I will establish his kingdom. He shall build an house for my name, and I will stablish the throne of his kingdom for ever" (vss. 12-13). Some of David's descendants were punished for their sinfulness, but the Lord never rejected David's line as the true rulers of Israel.

Of special significance is the fact that Jesus Christ was of the line of David (Rom. 1:3); He will someday sit on the throne of Israel. This promise is the basis of premillennial faith, which sees a future for Israel with a restored Davidic throne (Acts 13:32-34) in a literal one thousand-year millennium.

A recurring phrase in II Chronicles 6 is "thy servant David" (vss. 15-17). Though David was Solomon's father, Solomon chose to speak of him to God as "thy servant." This phrase highlights the respect and honor given to David.

While God promised to continue David's line forever, His blessing on the kings in that line depended on their obedience to God's law. "Yet so that thy children take heed to their way to walk in my law, as thou hast walked before me" (II Chron. 6:16). In verse 17, Solomon reiterated his plea for the Lord to keep His promise to David.

### God's immensity (II Chron. 6:18).
Solomon recognized that though he had built the temple as a dwelling place for the Lord, such a building, no matter how glorious, could not contain Him (cf. 2:6). In this connection, theologians refer to God's attribute of immensity. Immensity is related to omnipresence, but it seems to go beyond omnipresence. To say God is immense means He cannot be measured. And if He cannot be measured, then He cannot be confined to one spatial area, in this case the temple. He fills every part of everything. He even transcends His universe!

The point of Solomon's statement is

his amazement that one who is immeasurable and immense and who fills everything will actually dwell with mankind on earth. That understanding of God is amazing, but it is true. God's dwelling with people on earth would come to its fullest expression in the birth of Jesus Christ who "was made flesh, and dwelt among us" (John 1:14). Jesus Christ is truly "Emmanuel . . . God with us" (Matt. 1:23).

## MAKING PETITION OF GOD

**19 Have respect therefore to the prayer of thy servant, and to his supplication, O Lord my God, to hearken unto the cry and the prayer which thy servant prayeth before thee:**

**20 That thine eyes may be open upon this house day and night, upon the place whereof thou hast said that thou wouldest put thy name there; to hearken unto the prayer which thy servant prayeth toward this place.**

**21 Hearken therefore unto the supplications of thy servant, and of thy people Israel, which they shall make toward this place: hear thou from thy dwelling place, even from heaven; and when thou hearest, forgive.**

**A petition to be heard (II Chron. 6:19-20).** Even though Solomon acknowledged that the Lord is immeasurably great and reigns far above His creatures, still he was bold enough to ask Him to hear "the cry and the prayer" he offered to God. Notice in this text how Solomon referred to himself as "thy servant" and addressed God, "O Lord my God." This form of address to God includes His personal name (Lord) and the name *elohim*, which declares His deity.

Solomon intensified his appeal by connecting the temple he had built with his petition to be heard. He first declared the importance of the temple as the place where God had put His name. This association shows that God's character and reputation were closely intertwined with the temple and was the reason for God to hear his prayers.

The concept of God putting His name at a location goes back to Deuteronomy 12. God instructed the Israelites when they entered the Promised Land to destroy all the places where the pagan nations had worshipped and worship Him only at "the place which the Lord your God shall choose out of all your tribes to put his name there, even unto his habitation shall ye seek, and thither thou shalt come" (vs. 5). That place originally was the tabernacle where God would meet with His people (Exod. 33:7-11).

By the time period of II Chronicles 6, the tabernacle was no longer the place where God put His name. That place was now Solomon's temple, which became the focal point in God's program (vss. 34, 38).

Since the temple was so important, Solomon asked God to give His attention to the temple day and night and to hearken to the prayer that Solomon, His servant, was directing toward that place. It is noteworthy that centuries later, Daniel faced Jerusalem as he prayed (Dan. 6:10).

**A petition for forgiveness (II Chron. 6:21).** Solomon continued his appeal for God to hear the prayers he and his people would make toward this place. (Note that five times in verses 19-21, Solomon asked God to hear His people's prayers.) Solomon had earlier acknowledged that God was immense and could not be contained in a place (vs. 18). Yet he also understood that heaven was God's dwelling place. Both concepts of God are accurate.

The most important plea Solomon made is found at the end of II Chronicles 6:21: "When thou hearest, forgive." Solomon knew that the Israelites would disobey the Lord. Later in his prayer, he observed, "For there is no man which sinneth not" (vs. 36). Accordingly, he specifically asked the Lord to be open to their prayers of forgiveness.

In the rest of this chapter Solomon identified several scenarios in which he asked God to hear, intervene, and forgive His people. He culminated his appeal by focusing on what we know as the captivity of Israel in the years to come. (Moses prophesied it in Leviticus 26:33, 44-45.) When they would face that situation and turn back to the Lord, Solomon asked God, "Hear thou from the heavens, even from thy dwelling place, their prayer and their supplications, and maintain their cause, and forgive thy people which have sinned against thee" (II Chron. 6:39).

Solomon knew it was important to dedicate the temple he had built for God. Such a magnificent structure where the infinite God had put His name needed an appropriate dedication.

We do not worship at a temple today. Rather, we believers are the temple of God. "What? know ye not that your body is the temple of the Holy Ghost which is in you, which ye have of God, and ye are not your own?" (I Cor. 6:19). Likewise, our bodies, which the infinite God indwells, should have an appropriate dedication. That dedication is described in Romans 12:1: "I beseech you therefore, brethren, by the mercies of God, that ye present your bodies a living sacrifice, holy, acceptable unto God, which is your reasonable service."

Our dedication to the Lord is not a one-time event but rather should be a daily practice for us. We should acknowledge daily that we belong to God and dedicate everything we do to Him. How do we make such a continual dedication? "And be not conformed to this world: but be ye transformed by the renewing of your mind, that ye may prove what is that good, and acceptable, and perfect, will of God" (Rom. 12:2).

A good practice for all believers is to take some time each day, preferably in the morning, to tell the Lord we want to present our bodies as "a living sacrifice" to Him, which is the only reasonable thing we can do in view of His mercy toward us. We should pray, "Lord, I acknowledge that You made me; You saved me, and You own me. Today again I dedicate myself to You to follow Your ways. I present myself to You for whatever You want."

—Don Anderson.

# QUESTIONS

1. What immediately preceded Solomon's dedication of the temple?
2. In what ways did Solomon show his humility and reliance on God?
3. What is the significance of the names "LORD" and "Lord"?
4. How are both of these names meaningful to us?
5. What appeal did Solomon make about God's promise to David?
6. How do we understand both God's immensity and His awareness and concern for our lives?
7. How did Solomon bolster his appeal to God to listen to his prayers?
8. What was the important truth about the place where God would put His name?
9. What was Solomon's main petition to the Lord?
10. What are steps you can take to dedicate yourself to the Lord?

—Don Anderson.

# Preparing to Teach the Lesson

Lessons on prayer are usually popular because many of us would rather learn about prayer than actually pray. We also love to hear dramatic stories about how someone prayed and God provided a spectacular answer. Most of our prayers will probably seem small and the answers not too notable to many people. Prayer can be hard work, and how to get it right may always be a mystery to some of us.

The challenge of today's lesson is to get your students to see that their prayers are important to God and that He actually uses them in the grand overall plan He has for His people. Talking to God also benefits the one praying and is the answer to the call of God to draw near to Him.

## TODAY'S AIM

**Facts:** to see the setting, the substance, and the supplication in Solomon's prayer on this occasion.

**Principle:** to recognize that prayer is a unique activity in which we can engage.

**Application:** to make our daily lives practically one continuous prayer.

## INTRODUCING THE LESSON

Our study today on the prayer of Solomon at the dedication of the temple in Jerusalem is enlightening, instructional, and beneficial to our own personal prayer lives and for our corporate prayers. Throughout Scripture God repeatedly calls on His people to pray to Him and forbids them to pray to anyone else.

The simplest definition of prayer is "talking to God." Whether they are offered out loud or thought out silently, God hears our prayers. Our lives as His children start with our prayer of faith, accepting Christ as our Saviour. Our spiritual lives continue with confession of sins, prayer for God's guidance, requests for daily needs, thanks for everything, and rejoicing in the good things He gives us. Hopefully, at the end of our earthly lives, we will offer to Him a prayer of thanks for His blessing on our lives and commend ourselves to His care as we pass from this life to go to be with Him, as faith becomes sight.

## DEVELOPING THE LESSON

**1. The setting of Solomon's prayer (II Chron. 6:12-13).** This was a great time for prayer, at the completion of building the temple. God had instructed David as to just how to do it, and Solomon had faithfully followed what David had passed on to him (I Chron. 28:11-21. Before the temple was put into service, it was appropriate to dedicate it.

There are many events in the life of a believer or a congregation of believers that prayer is the appropriate response to. It is a shame to waste such an opportunity by failing to pray.

Solomon had prepared a place to offer this prayer of dedication. He was elevated above the crowd where he could be seen and heard by everyone. They could thus participate by agreeing with Solomon in prayer in their hearts while he prayed. Do you see how inadequate it would be to offer this prayer silently? Kneeling in reverence and humility before God and reaching out his hands toward God was also the best, and maybe the only correct, way for Solomon to pray at a time like this.

**2. The substance of Solomon's prayer (II Chron. 6:14-18).** Solomon began by remembering God's faithfulness to His promises. He reminded God of His promise to David, which God had now fulfilled with the completion of the temple. Then Solomon reminded God (and everyone else) that God had also promised that men from David's descendants would always rule over Israel as long as they were faithful to God. This was a place in the prayer where it became personal for Solomon.

Then Solomon asked a deep theological question: Would God actually dwell in this man-made building? Solomon understood that God is infinitely large and could not be contained in His fullness in the temple in Jerusalem. Yet His name and character were to be remembered by all mankind there, and in a special sense His presence would be revealed there.

**3. The supplication in Solomon's prayer (II Chron. 6:19-21).** We often think of prayer as asking God for things. What Solomon asked was that God would continually be open and receptive to the prayers offered to Him in this place. Solomon asked that God would hear and forgive His people when they prayed at the temple or even toward it if they were far away.

We are reminded here that the answer to our prayer for salvation, and for every other matter, depends on the grace and mercy of God. On our part, we have but to ask. Did James not say that we have not because we ask not (Jas. 4:2-3)? God's answer did not depend on the intellect of Solomon (the wisest man ever) or his works, although he had just finished building this wonderful temple. The answer to Solomon's prayer was rooted in God's faithfulness to His promises.

## ILLUSTRATING THE LESSON

The world sees nothing in our praying, but God sees great value there.

LITTLE SEEN BY THE WORLD

PRAYER IS SEEN BY GOD

## CONCLUDING THE LESSON

How many prayers do you think have been offered by people since the beginning—trillions and trillions? God has heard and remembers each and every one.

We may think of answers to prayer in three basic general categories: yes, no, and wait.

The answer to a prayer may sometimes be "wait" because only God knows the best time for the best answer. The prayer of Solomon that we are studying was prayed only once on a very specific occasion, and the answer was immediate. We may need to pray a certain prayer often and over a long period of time before we get an answer.

We are instructed in Scripture to "pray without ceasing" (I Thess. 5:17), or pray all the time. We are told we are to be "giving thanks always for all things unto God" (Eph. 5:20). We are to be talking to God all the time about everything in humility and thankfulness for His grace and mercy.

## ANTICIPATING THE NEXT LESSON

Our next lesson highlights the beautiful subject of worship.

—Brian D. Doud.

# PRACTICAL POINTS

1. God's power is sovereign. Even kings and rulers bow down before Him (II Chron. 6:12-13).
2. When we honor God's covenant, He always keeps His promises (vss. 14-15).
3. Sometimes it takes multiple generations to complete a task for God (vss. 16-17).
4. It is an honor for the presence of God to dwell in our house of worship (vs. 18).
5. We should reverence the house of God.
6. The house of God is a place of refuge, forgiveness, and healing (vss. 19-21).

—*Valante M. Grant.*

# RESEARCH AND DISCUSSION

1. What is the purpose of a dedicated house of worship? Is it necessary?
2. What characteristics are necessary to build an acceptable house for God?
3. How should we respond to someone who has been chosen by God to start or to complete a job for Him?
4. Is God's presence limited to the house of worship?
5. How can we recognize the fulfillment of a promise that God made to a previous generation?
6. How can we identify and function in our roles in God's plan?
7. How do we invoke the presence of God into our place of worship and keep it there (II Chron. 6:20-21)?

—*Valante M. Grant.*

# ILLUSTRATED HIGH POINTS

**Kneeled down**

King Solomon prayed a beautiful prayer as he and the nation dedicated the newly constructed temple as a house of prayer (cf. Isa. 56:7). He also asked God to forgive the people and nation if they fell into sin (II Chron. 6:22-40). Sadly, Solomon apparently abandoned his commitment to God and allowed his many wives to turn his heart after false gods (cf. I Kings 11:4).

**There is no God like thee**

In the retail world, one needs to be wary of knockoffs—items that look like the real thing but are only cheap imitations.

In the world, we are often told that the God of the Bible is the same as Allah, Buddha, Confucius, or whatever. Nothing could be further from the truth. God Almighty is the only true Living God. He is absolutely unique in His Person and work. John 3:16 expresses it perfectly. God loved (and still loves) the world. How did He show it? By sending Jesus to suffer and die in the place of sinful man so that he may be forgiven!

**Heavens cannot contain thee**

As a young boy in Sunday school, I was told that heaven existed beyond what I could see in the sky. I could not comprehend that, so I figured there was a big box that included everything that existed.

Soon I realized that if there was such a box, there had to be something beyond it. So I envisioned a larger box that housed the first box, then another box that housed the first two.

At this point I gave up and admitted to myself that this was not the answer. God was simply beyond my comprehension. Seven decades later, I still agree.

—*David A. Hamburg.*

# Golden Text Illuminated

"O Lord God of Israel, there is no God like thee in the heaven, nor in the earth; which keepest covenant, and shewest mercy unto thy servants, that walk before thee with all their hearts" (II Chronicles 6:14).

It is often said that public prayers should not be used as a vehicle for preaching to others. This is true if the preaching consists of voicing pet peeves or riding personal hobbyhorses. But the Bible is filled with public prayers that proclaim truth. Solomon's prayer at the dedication of the temple is no exception.

The prayer, which runs from II Chronicles 6:14 to the end of the chapter (vs. 42), is largely a plea for forgiveness for anticipated future sins on the part of God's people and for deliverance from the variety of afflictions those sins would bring (vss. 21-42). Solomon knew his people's propensity for falling away from devotion to the God who loved and provided for them. Ironically, he would be one of the first to do so later in life. But at this moment, the words he spoke were altogether true and unblemished.

Although all the pleas that Solomon voiced point indispensably to God's holiness, grace, and mercy, they are founded upon basic truths uttered at the beginning of the prayer. The golden text contains the groundwork that Solomon laid in proclaiming the kind of God that Israel had come together at the temple to worship.

The first thing to be emphasized about God was His utter incomparability. "There is no God like thee." The Old Testament makes this point over and over (Exod. 15:11; Deut. 4:35; II Sam. 7:22; Ps. 86:8; Isa. 40:25; 46:9, to cite just a few). It was one of the basic truths Israel needed to learn and be reminded of repeatedly.

The Lord's incomparability has no bounds. There is none like Him "in the heaven, nor in the earth." Even the most hard-bitten pagan would not have made such a claim for any of the gods he bowed down to. It is human nature to try to make God something less than He is and more like familiar things, but this tendency must be resisted at all costs. God is not just another part of creation; He is totally above it and unique.

But this incomparable God also relates to people personally. He keeps "covenant"; that is, He is faithful to keep His promises. He is not like the pagan gods, who say one thing and do another. He does not keep His word only at convenience, as so many people do.

God's character is also marked by mercy. Pagan gods could be capricious and cruel, but God shows mercy and kindness in His dealings with His people—"thy servants, that walk before thee with all their hearts." We might at first think that such people do not need mercy, but no one who walks closely with God would ever be so proud as to think God's mercy and grace were not needed every moment. And it is only by God's mercy that we are enabled to walk before Him in the first place.

Unlike Solomon and the Israelites, we do not have a temple to dedicate to the Lord. If we are Christ's and have the Holy Spirit, we *are* God's temple, and we can dedicate our lives to Him every day. We can do this fully confident that He is a faithful God who will keep every promise He has made to us.

—Kenneth A. Sponsler.

# Heart of the Lesson

Before I begin the three-hour drive home after visiting my parents, my mother, father, and I stand in a circle in the living room, arms around each other's shoulders, and pray for a safe journey. Prayer always has been part of our family life. Prayer also was important to national life in ancient Israel.

After spending seven years building a temple to replace Moses' tabernacle, Solomon gathered the entire nation for a dedication service in Jerusalem.

**1. Preparation for prayer (II Chron. 6:12-13).** Solomon stood on a tall, bronze platform he had built in the temple court, facing the people with his hands spread. Then he dropped to his knees. Instead of asking the people to worship him as many rulers throughout the ages have done, Solomon lifted his arms toward heaven. He showed humility and respect for God as he prepared to pray. Posture is important in prayer; it reflects our heart attitude.

**2. Words of worship (II Chron. 6:14-15).** Solomon honored God by saying no other god in the heavens or on the earth is like the God of Israel. God is unique because He is a covenant-keeping God. He keeps the promises He makes to His people. Solomon cited the temple dedication as an example of God keeping a promise to his father, David.

God also is unique because He shows mercy. Mercy means God refrains from giving people what they deserve. God shows this mercy to His servants—those who seek to obey Him with all their hearts.

**3. Words of petition (II Chron. 6:16-21).** God had promised King David a dynasty if his descendants continued to obey God's law as he had done. A man from David's line perpetually would sit on the throne of Israel. Solomon asked God to keep this promise He had made to David.

Solomon paused in his prayer to reflect again on God's majesty. Solomon questioned if God really would dwell with men. Heaven—even the highest heavens—could never contain God. If the heavens could not contain God, Solomon said, how could this temple he had built contain God?

Yet this temple was the place God had chosen to put His name. It was the place where God would meet with His people.

As he prayed, Solomon termed himself the Lord's servant and referred to the Lord as his God. Solomon expressed his own faith in God; he was not relying on his father's faith as he led the nation.

Solomon asked that God's eyes would be upon the temple day and night. He wanted God always to be aware of it. He wanted to be sure God agreed to hear his prayers as he prayed toward the temple.

For a third time, Solomon asked God to hear his prayers. But this time he extended that request to include the nation's prayers. He asked God to hear His people's requests and to forgive them.

The request for forgiveness provides a clue as to the nature of the people's prayers. They were confessions of their failure to keep God's law and pleas for God's mercy and forgiveness. Solomon, at the temple dedication, desired that his people follow their God. When they faltered, he wanted to be sure God would forgive them and restore them.

Solomon's example teaches the importance of opening our hearts to God even with others present, especially those we nurture. Do our children ever "catch" us on our knees?

—Ann Staatz.

# World Missions

Foreigners. Does this have a negative connotation? When we think of the word "foreign," it might conjure up synonyms such as strange, confusing, or separate. We might envision foods we would never want to eat, customs that seem rude, or incomprehensible ideas of life, family, and values.

The natural human tendency is to be drawn toward the familiar and avoid the unfamiliar. We tend to more readily trust people like us and have a harder time connecting with those who are different.

Ironically, when we think of foreign missions, we tend to consider the missionaries who go as our own and the people in the countries where they serve as the foreigners. In truth, to the nationals of that country, it is the missionaries who are foreign! Nationals may distrust foreigners among them, fearing they have come to convert them to their own culture and ways, which might be seen as immoral, aggressive, or unholy.

The above reasons are why national workers are such a gift from God to missions. God has shown Himself to men and women all around the world, and He is keeping His covenant and showing mercy to nationals who walk before Him with all their hearts. And many are reaching their own people.

K. P. Yohanan, an Indian missionary whose ministry has reached millions in his country, says there are 285,000 national missionaries in the world today, making up two-thirds of the global missionary force. Yet national missionaries are sadly neglected when it comes to world funding.

Bob Finley, author of *Reformation in Foreign Missions* (Christian Aid), claims that indigenous missionaries do 90 percent of pioneer mission work, but only receive 10 percent of mission funding. Conversely, foreign missionaries do 10 percent of pioneer mission work, but receive 90 percent of mission funding.

As a former missionary, I know that missionaries from the West require a great deal more money than national missionaries. Though we lived on less than many of our American friends, we were unbelievably rich compared to a national missionary. Our home cost around $150 per month to rent, our food was more, our travel costs were very high, and we "needed" luxuries like toilet paper and medication and diapers.

Beyond that, we had to spend a great amount of time doing non-evangelistic work—language study, building relationships, trying to make openings for the gospel, and brainstorming ways to get beyond misconceptions of why we were there and what we really hoped to accomplish.

National missionaries do not need years of language study, lists of rules about where to put their hands and feet, or special passports. They have access to many places Western missionaries are no longer allowed. They are accepted in ways a foreigner may never be. And they often naturally know better what scriptural truths will most impact their own people.

Missionaries should still go from anywhere God sends them to anywhere God sends them. However, let us not neglect the valuable group of warriors called by God to reach their own people. Let us be sure to include national missionaries in our missions focus. They too are our brothers and sisters in Christ, serving to expand the kingdom. Let us help them.

—Kimberly Rae.

# The Jewish Aspect

"Sukkot Festival in Jerusalem," a headline from a prominent news source proclaims. Under the caption, an ultraorthodox Jewish girl looks out of a temporary hut built for the Jewish holiday (www.upi.com).

In this week's lesson, we see Solomon dedicating the first temple. The dedication took place during the holiday of Sukkot (II Chron. 5:3).

For thousands of years, the Jewish people have celebrated Sukkot, also called the Festival of Tabernacles (or Feast of Booths). Modern Jews continue to fulfill the biblical command of Leviticus 23:34-36 by participating in this holiday.

The festival of Sukkot begins on the fifteenth day of the Jewish month of Tishri and ends on Tishri 21. Tishri generally falls in September or October.

In the past, two major ideas dominated the holiday. First, the celebration marked the joyful time of the fall harvest. Second, Leviticus 23:40-43 commands each family to build and live in a hut known as a "sukkah" during the festival.

A sukkah is a temporary structure of at least two and a half walls and a roof. Tradition requires that the roof of the sukkah be made of natural materials such as leaves, branches, or straw and that it must have enough open spaces so that the stars can be seen at night. Participants decorate the sukkah with carpets, tapestries, nuts, corn, or wreaths.

Today, Jewish people are encouraged to sleep, read, study, and talk in the sukkah, but only if it can be done comfortably. The rabbis believe that you should rejoice in the sukkah, not suffer in it. As a result, modern Jews might relax or eat in the sukkah but then go into their houses to sleep.

The Jewish people build the sukkah to represent the huts their ancestors built in the desert after being redeemed from Egyptian bondage. God's sheltering presence marked the desert period as He sustained His people with food and water. The sukkah reminds people of the beauty of God's sheltering presence.

Once a year, Jewish people move into the temporary structure of a sukkah as a reminder that real comfort, safety, and security are found in the shelter of God rather than in worldly possessions. Michael Strassfeld, a Jewish author says, "[It is] under the wings of the Shekinah that one can find real security and shelter—not our homes" (*The Jewish Holidays,* William Morrow).

Solomon chose the holiday of Sukkot to dedicate the first temple to God. Several centuries later, the Israelites celebrated Sukkot after they finished rebuilding the altar and prior to the construction of the second temple (Ezra 3:4).

In addition, there are some who argue that Jesus' birth actually occurred during Sukkot (Scheifler, "On What Day Was Jesus Born?" biblelight.net). The temple was created to house God's presence. As Christians, we understand that Jesus, as flesh and blood, also housed God's presence.

Sukkot stands as an important holiday for both Jews and Christians alike. The holiday anticipates the messianic end of days when the Messiah will return to take His rightful place. Zechariah 14:16-19 tells us that at that time both Jew and Gentile will go to Jerusalem to worship and celebrate Sukkot. As Leviticus 23:41 commands, the holiday will be celebrated forever.

—Robin Fitzgerald.

# *Guiding the Superintendent*

King David was a man of many dreams. However, he was never able to see the realization of his key desire. David wanted to build a great temple for his God. Instead, God told David that He would establish a house, not vise versa. The promise was clear. David's "house" (that is, his descendants, his lineage) would be established forever, and the task of building God's house would fall to David's son (II Sam. 7:1-17).

The lesson this week concerns David's son Solomon dedicating the temple he built to his God. Notice throughout the prayer that Solomon's focus is not on the temple of God but on the God of the temple.

## DEVOTIONAL OUTLINE

**1. Solomon's preparation (II Chron. 6:12-13).** Solomon had a small metal platform built and placed in the middle of the court before the temple. In front of all the people, he knelt before God in humility and raised his hands in worship.

**2. God is faithful to His promises (II Chron. 6:14-17).** A key purpose for prayer is not to remind God of what we want but for us to remember who God is. Solomon began his prayer of dedication by remembering that "there is no God" like the Lord in the entire universe. He had been faithful to His people by remembering His promises.

Solomon saw this great temple as a fulfillment of God's promise to his father David.

**3. God is present and hears prayer (II Chron. 6:18-21).** From the beginning (cf. 2:6), Solomon was aware that God could not be confined to one place on earth, even this magnificent temple.

The people of Israel faced ever-present idolatry, which tended to confine God to just one place. Solomon's prayer contradicted the notion of local deities common to pagan worship.

Solomon knew that God, being infinite, could not be confined to a geographical location. Nevertheless, He had appointed a place for His worshippers to meet with Him. Solomon knew that Israel's God, who cannot be limited to one building, was still very interested in being present with His human creation.

Solomon entreated God to hear every prayer offered from the temple. To emphasize this plea, three times Solomon implored God to hear his prayer. Not only did he appeal to God's hearing, but he asked that God's "eyes may be open upon this house day and night" (II Chron. 6:20).

Solomon began his prayer emphasizing God's mercy (II Chron. 6:14) and ended his prayer seeking His forgiveness (vs. 21). This is a great pattern for our prayers. Prayer begins with realizing that all we have is due to God's mercy and not to anything we have done. Prayer ends with the knowledge that we are forgiven people.

## AGE-GROUP EMPHASES

**Children:** To help the students grasp who the God they serve is, have them list as many characteristics of God as they can find in this week's text.

**Youths:** Teens are starting to formulate their own ideas about God. Based on this passage, ask this question of the class: How big is our God?

**Adults:** The doctrine of divine transcendence is one that many have trouble understanding. Have the class discuss how God can dwell in heaven and here with people at the same time.

*—Martin R. Dahlquist.*

# Scripture Lesson Text

**II CHRON. 7:1** Now when Sol'o-mon had made an end of praying, the fire came down from heaven, and consumed the burnt offering and the sacrifices; and the glory of the LORD filled the house.

**2 And the priests could not enter into the house of the LORD, because the glory of the LORD had filled the LORD's house.**

3 And when all the children of Is'ra-el saw how the fire came down, and the glory of the LORD upon the house, they bowed themselves with their faces to the ground upon the pavement, and worshipped, and praised the LORD, *saying*, For *he is* good; for his mercy *endureth* for ever.

**4 Then the king and all the people offered sacrifices before the LORD.**

5 And king Sol'o-mon offered a sacrifice of twenty and two thousand oxen, and an hundred and twenty thousand sheep: so the king and all the people dedicated the house of God.

**6 And the priests waited on their offices: the Le'vites also with instruments of musick of the LORD, which Da'vid the king had made to praise the LORD, because his mercy *endureth* for ever, when Da'vid praised by their ministry; and the priests sounded trumpets before them, and all Is'ra-el stood.**

7 Moreover Sol'o-mon hallowed the middle of the court that *was* before the house of the LORD: for there he offered burnt offerings, and the fat of the peace offerings, because the brasen altar which Sol'o-mon had made was not able to receive the burnt offerings, and the meat offerings, and the fat.

**8 Also at the same time Sol'o-mon kept the feast seven days, and all Is'ra-el with him, a very great congregation, from the entering in of Ha'math unto the river of E'gypt.**

9 And in the eighth day they made a solemn assembly: for they kept the dedication of the altar seven days, and the feast seven days.

## NOTES

# Worshipping in God's Temple

## Lesson: II Chronicles 7:1-9

### Read: II Chronicles 7:1-11

TIME: 959 B.C.                                          PLACE: Jerusalem

---

**GOLDEN TEXT**—"When all the children of Israel saw how the fire came down, and the glory of the Lord upon the house, they . . . worshipped, and praised the Lord, saying, For he is good; for his mercy endureth for ever" (II Chronicles 7:3).

---

# Introduction

Worship is a popular subject in churches today. Churches have worship services, worship leaders, worship teams, and worship songs. Schools have worship degrees, and Christian organizations have worship seminars.

We wonder, however, if much that passes today for worship is merely external or emotional. Worship is much more than singing (or listening) to music or feeling emotionally encouraged.

True worship is consciously thinking about God and His greatness. The Lord can certainly use the different parts of a service to promote worship, but in the end worship is a personal matter within each believer.

Sometimes worship may result in an outward expression, but we should not fall into the trap of thinking that worship always has to be shown outwardly.

As we pursue our study of how ancient Israel acknowledged God and followed in His ways, we discover that one of the elements of following God's way was true worship. Our study in II Chronicles 7 helps us get a clearer picture of how we should truly worship our great God.

## LESSON OUTLINE

I. WORSHIP BY PRAISING GOD—II Chron. 7:1-3

II. WORSHIP BY SACRIFICE AND MUSIC—II Chron. 7:4-7

III. WORSHIP BY ASSEMBLING—II Chron. 7:8-9

# Exposition: Verse by Verse

**WORSHIP BY PRAISING GOD**

**II CHRON. 7:1** Now when Solomon had made an end of praying, the fire came down from heaven, and consumed the burnt offering and the sacrifices; and the glory of the Lord filled the house.

2 And the priests could not enter into the house of the Lord, because the glory of the Lord had filled the

Lord's house.

**3 And when all the children of Israel saw how the fire came down, and the glory of the Lord upon the house, they bowed themselves with their faces to the ground upon the pavement, and worshipped, and praised the Lord, saying, For he is good; for his mercy endureth for ever.**

Second Chronicles 6 records Solomon's moving prayer as he dedicated the temple he had just built. Chapter 7 continues the events of the temple dedication by recounting the ways in which the king and the people worshipped God during the dedication.

**God's fire and glory (II Chron. 7:1-2).** When Solomon finished praying, God showed His acceptance of the king's actions in two ways—by sending fire from heaven to consume the sacrifices and by filling the temple with His glory.

Fire is a fitting symbol of the Lord because it speaks dramatically of His presence, His holiness, and His purity. God destroyed Sodom and Gomorrah through fire (Gen. 19:12-29). He met Moses in the burning bush (Exod. 3:1-22). He led the Israelites by a pillar of fire (Exod. 13:21-22). God descended on Mount Sinai in fire (Exod. 19:1-25). The Lord responded to David's offering with fire after he had sinned (I Chron. 21:26). This place was the same site where Solomon later built the temple (II Chron. 3:1). God sent fire from heaven in response to Elijah's prayer (I Kings 18:20-40).

In the New Testament, the Holy Spirit appeared on the Day of Pentecost as "cloven tongues like as of fire" (Acts 2:3). The Lord will test our works at the Judgment Seat of Christ by fire (I Cor. 3:13). The writer of Hebrews stated that "our God is a consuming fire" (12:29).

At the same time that the sacrifices were being consumed, the glory of the Lord filled the temple. This was the second time during the dedication service that God's glory filled the temple. It first happened when the ark was brought into the most holy place (II Chron. 5:7-14). God's glory took the appearance of a luminous cloud that signified His presence. God led His people in the wilderness by a cloud (Exod. 13:21-22). God's glory filled the tabernacle (Exod. 40:34-35). The glory of God later left the temple, showing His rejection of His people (Ezek. 10:1-22). In the millennial temple, the glory of the Lord will again be seen (Ezek. 43:5; 44:4).

**The people's response (II Chron. 7:3).** The Israelites were overwhelmed at the sight of the Lord's presence in the fire and in the cloud. The priests could not enter the temple to perform their service. The people fell to the stone pavement in awe and worshipped the Lord by praising God with these words: "For he is good; for his mercy endureth for ever." Surely this manifestation of the Lord convinced the Israelites that God existed and that He alone was worthy of worship.

These words of praise were used frequently in the Old Testament (cf. I Chron. 16:34; II Chron. 5:13; Ezra 3:11; Ps. 106:1; 107:1; Jer. 33:11). Their frequency shows that these words may have been a customary statement of praise from God's people.

Of special note is Psalm 136, which begins with the words "O give thanks unto the Lord." The psalmist then makes several statements about God's deliverance and care, such as "To him that smote Egypt in their firstborn" (vs. 10) and concludes each statement with the words "for his mercy endureth for ever." This psalm is usually thought of as an antiphonal psalm with one group making the first statement and a second group responding in praise.

Three words in II Chronicles 7:3 are noteworthy as an expression of praise. First, the Lord is *good*. To say the Lord is good means more than saying He does good things. His attribute of goodness means He is inherently good and is the source of all goodness. In Psalm 34:8, David penned the words "O taste and see that the Lord is good: blessed is the man that trusteth in him."

Second, the Lord has *mercy*. The word "mercy" refers to His covenant faithfulness to His people and is often translated "lovingkindness," as we noted in the last lesson. It points to His enduring, undeserved love for His own.

Third, the Lord's faithful love to His people endures *forever*. There will never be a time when He withdraws His loyal love from His people.

## WORSHIP BY SACRIFICE AND MUSIC

**4 Then the king and all the people offered sacrifices before the Lord.**

**5 And king Solomon offered a sacrifice of twenty and two thousand oxen, and an hundred and twenty thousand sheep: so the king and all the people dedicated the house of God.**

**6 And the priests waited on their offices: the Levites also with instruments of musick of the Lord, which David the king had made to praise the Lord, because his mercy endureth for ever, when David praised by their ministry; and the priests sounded trumpets before them, and all Israel stood.**

**7 Moreover Solomon hallowed the middle of the court that was before the house of the Lord: for there he offered burnt offerings, and the fat of the peace offerings, because the brasen altar which Solomon had made was not able to receive the burnt offerings, and the meat offerings, and the fat.**

The king and his people continued their worship by offering sacrifices to the Lord and praising Him through music.

**Worship by sacrifice (II Chron. 7:4-5).** The text tells us that Solomon offered 22,000 bulls and 120,000 sheep. How could the Israelites offer 142,000 animals at this time? No doubt a large number of priests had to be engaged in sacrificing all these animals. This huge number of animals shows the people's love for the Lord and their desire to exalt and worship Him.

**Worship by music (II Chron. 7:6).** Music played a big part in the people's worship of the Lord. The Levites used the musical instruments David had made for the purpose of praising the Lord. David was an accomplished musician himself (I Sam. 16:14-22) and saw the value of music in worshipping God. First Chronicles 15:16 states that "David spake to the chief of the Levites to appoint their brethren to be the singers with instruments of musick, psalteries and harps and cymbals, sounding, by lifting up the voice with joy."

In I Chronicles 23:5, we read that "four thousand praised the Lord with the instruments which I made, said David, to praise therewith." In this worship service, the priests stood opposite the Levites and responded with trumpets in an antiphonal arrangement as the Israelites stood in respect to the Lord.

**Worship by offerings (II Chron. 7:7).** In addition to sacrificing the bulls and the sheep (vs. 5), Solomon also offered burnt offerings, grain offerings, and the fat of peace offerings.

The burnt offering is described in detail in Leviticus 1:1-17 and 6:8-13. The burnt offering had to be a male without any defect from the herd or from the flock. The entire animal was to be consumed. The priests sprinkled the blood on the altar, indicating that this sacrifice was to acknowledge the people's sinfulness and a desire to renew a right relationship with the Lord. As the smoke from the cooked meat ascended to heaven, it was a "sweet savour unto the Lord" (1:9, 17).

The grain offering is described in Leviticus 2:1-16 and 6:14-23. This offering consisted of flour or grain that was offered to the Lord as an expression of thanksgiving to God. The grain offering, with its oil and frankincense, also was "a sweet savour unto the Lord" (2:2, 9).

Solomon also offered the fat of the peace offerings as described in Leviticus 3:1-17 and 7:11-36. The fat of the animal was not to be eaten but rather was to be offered as food (3:11), showing fellowship with the Lord.

These three offerings indicated the people's desire for a right relationship with the Lord, their thanksgiving to Him for what He had done, and their desire for fellowship with Him. Each of these offerings provided an aroma (a "sweet savour") that was pleasing to the Lord. In saying that the Lord smelled the aroma of the offerings, the Bible is simply using vivid human language to convey that God was pleased and accepted them as an indication of the people's worship and adoration.

Solomon presented so many offerings that the bronze altar he had made (II Chron. 4:1) was not sufficient to receive them. He therefore consecrated a special area in the middle of the courtyard to present these offerings. He likely had to utilize some additional altars constructed for this special event.

## WORSHIP BY ASSEMBLING

8 Also at the same time Solomon kept the feast seven days, and all Israel with him, a very great congregation, from the entering in of Hamath unto the river of Egypt.

9 And in the eighth day they made a solemn assembly: for they kept the dedication of the altar seven days, and the feast seven days.

An immense gathering (II Chron. 7:8). The worshipful dedication of the temple continued with a weeklong assembly of the people. The people came from "the entering in of Hamath unto the river of Egypt." These two geographical locations refer to the northern and southern boundaries of Israel. ("Hamath" likely indicates an area toward the Euphrates River [cf. Num. 13:21; 34:8], and the "river of Egypt" was a brook or wadi in northeastern Sinai.) In other words, the people came from all over Israel for this occasion.

A solemn assembly (II Chron. 7:9). The people spent a total of fifteen days in dedication and feasting. Apparently, they spent seven days in the temple dedication ("the dedication of the altar") and then continued for another seven days celebrating a second feast. The people then assembled once more on the eighth day of the second week before returning to their homes (vs. 10).

We understand the second week to be the Feast of Tabernacles because of the parallel account in I Kings 8:2. The Feast of Tabernacles, described in Leviticus 23:33-44, commemorated God's provision and protection of the Israelites in the forty years of wandering in the wilderness.

Based on other biblical references, we can probably date these two feasts on the Jewish calendar. Second Chronicles 5:3 tells us these events took place in the seventh month (September-October). The Feast of Tabernacles was from the fifteenth to the twenty-second of the month (Lev. 23:39); therefore, the earlier feast must have begun on the eighth day of the seventh month. Since the Day of Atonement occurred five days before the Feast of Tabernacles (vs. 27), then the first week of dedication must have included the Day of Atonement as well.

The parallel passage in I Kings 8:66 states that at the conclusion of these events, "On the eighth day he [Solomon] sent the people away: and they blessed the king, and went unto their tents joyful and glad of heart for all the goodness that the Lord had done for David his servant, and for Israel his people."

Second Chronicles 7 records how the people of God worshipped the Lord at the dedication of the temple. Their actions provide an excellent model of how we can worship our Lord today. Think back through the elements of the Israelites' worship, and note how we can apply those elements to our worship today.

• Worship by praising God. Praise should be a part of every believer's life. The book of Psalms, the praise book of Israel, concludes with this exhortation: "Praise ye the Lord. Praise God in his sanctuary: praise him in the firmament of his power. Praise him for his mighty acts: praise him according to his excellent greatness. . . . Let every thing that hath breath praise the Lord" (150:1-2, 6).

• Worship by sacrifice and music. We do not offer animal sacrifices today but rather spiritual sacrifices (I Pet. 2:5). Hebrews 13:15-16 describes our kind of sacrifices. "By him therefore let us offer the sacrifice of praise to God continually, that is, the fruit of our lips giving thanks to his name. But to do good and to communicate forget not: for with such sacrifices God is well pleased." Above all, we need to offer ourselves as living sacrifices (Rom. 12:1-2).

The Lord has also ordained music to be an important part of our worship. One of the marks of a Spirit-filled person is singing. "Speaking to yourselves in psalms and hymns and spiritual songs, singing and making melody in your heart to the Lord" (Eph. 5:19).

• Worship by assembling. We ought to worship the Lord privately and in our homes, but we must also worship Him corporately by assembling with fellow believers at church. Hebrews 10:25 emphasizes the importance of meeting with other believers. "Not forsaking the assembling of ourselves together, as the manner of some is; but exhorting one another: and so much the more, as ye see the day approaching."

—Don Anderson.

# QUESTIONS

1. Why is fire a fitting symbol for the Lord?
2. What other Scriptures use fire as a symbol of the Lord?
3. What was the glory of the Lord that filled the temple?
4. What other Scriptures speak of the glory of the Lord?
5. What was the people's response to the fire and the Lord's glory?
6. What did the large number of animal sacrifices show about the people's worship?
7. What part did music play in the dedication of the temple?
8. What were the three kinds of sacrifices, and what did they show about the people?
9. In what sense were the sacrifices a "sweet savour"?
10. What was the significance of the two weeks of observances?

—Don Anderson.

# Preparing to Teach the Lesson

Some of your students may have wondered at times why certain events are recorded in the Bible. They might have asked, "What is the relevance today of all this history and ceremony and pageantry?" This lesson and the next one should begin to answer this question, not just to your students' amazement but for their edification, faith, and instruction in righteous living.

We can enter into the joy of the Lord through passages of Scripture like these, as well as through more familiar verses. We must worship the Lord regardless of whether we see any special response to that worship. He is deserving of our highest praise and worship, and He is sovereign in the way He deals with us and honors our praise and worship.

## TODAY'S AIM

**Facts:** to see the significance of the Lord's response to Solomon's prayer at the dedication of the temple.

**Principle:** to see that God may also respond to our worship, although in a smaller and less dramatic manner, when we obey Him in worship.

**Application:** to worship God, expecting Him to respond in a way that honors Him and blesses His people.

## INTRODUCING THE LESSON

We do not often see immediate results from our worship services or God doing something in response when we worship Him. We do not worship God to get something out of Him but because of who He is and what He continually does in His world.

In the passage we are studying today, we do see God responding to the worship of His people with miraculous evidence of His presence. We do not expect God to respond to our worship in exactly the same way; that is, we do not expect God to send down fire from heaven and consume our offerings, which are usually in the form of cash and checks, not slain animals! We should not expect to see His glory fill our sanctuary as a bright light of awesome beauty and power. But is it not appropriate to consider what kind of response to our worship we should expect from God? Are we expecting any response at all from Him?

As far as we know, God has never repeated the response shown in this passage. It was a seal of His approval of the Israelites' offerings and worship at this special time.

## DEVELOPING THE LESSON

**1. The seal of God's approval of the Israelites' worship (II Chron. 7:1-3).** Everything was concluded in the building of the temple. All was in place, including the burnt offering sacrifice on the altar. Solomon had prayed in dedication of the temple to the worship of the Lord. God showed His approval of it all by sending down fire and consuming the offering. The glory of the Lord was so overpowering in the temple that the priests could not go into the house of the Lord.

This occasion was so miraculous and striking that we should think that it would have been retold and gloried in for generations. They had not been informed in any way that this would happen. No special prayers or formulas or works of any kind had been prescribed as the way to get this kind of response from God. They did not do something special to get something special to happen.

We may be belaboring the point, but we must remember that when people promote formulas to gain holiness or special access to God, or to get our prayers answered, we must avoid them and simply obey what God has actually said. To go beyond that is sacrilege. "Secret" and "special" methods will not avail in the throne room of God and will probably offend Him.

**2. The sacrifices of God's people as further worship (II Chron. 7:4-6).** The priests and Levites officiated in their prescribed places. It must have taken a whole army of priests to offer as many sacrifices as would have been necessary to serve the number of people ("a very great congregation" [vs. 8]) involved at this occasion.

**3. The sacrifices, feast, and solemn assembly (II Chron. 7:7-9).** The whole burnt offering was entirely burned up, but when one took part in many of the other sacrifices, it was done by eating a portion of the sacrifice, which was roasted, before the Lord, being mindful of His presence and the fact that the sacrifice was made to honor the Lord.

The solemn assembly was a gathering of God's people before Him.

## ILLUSTRATING THE LESSON

Psalm 51:17 reminds us that the sacrifices of God are a broken spirit and a contrite heart.

**WORSHIP GOD**

**WITH A BROKEN AND CONTRITE HEART**

## CONCLUDING THE LESSON

Our word "worship" actually comes from a combination of two words: "worth" and "ship." It means telling God what He is worth to us. Our worship of the Lord has to be informed by the Bible, which tells us that He is of supreme worth. He is the Creator and Sustainer of the universe. He is the Creator of our bodies and souls. He is God, Father of the Lord Jesus Christ, and the Author of all that is good. In Him alone are all truth, love, justice, and compassion. He alone has perfect understanding, righteousness, knowledge, and wisdom. God has announced to us that He is willing to save us from our sins, govern and guide our lives, and eventually bring us to heaven to live with Him in perfect love, harmony, and beauty.

In our text for today, we see how the people of Israel saw God's glory and fire from heaven consuming their sacrifices. They worshipped God at the newly finished temple. We must see God through the eyes of faith and worship Him in much humbler places. We can worship Him while working, driving our car, or mowing the lawn. Because we can approach Him in prayer, we can worship Him with all our lives and with every breath we take. We can even bring every thought captive to the obedience of Christ.

We leave, then, any response to our prayers to God. We do not need a temple. We need not bring animal sacrifices according to the law. We worship Him with a cleansed conscience and an obedient heart, knowing that He hears every prayer.

## ANTICIPATING THE NEXT LESSON

Our next lesson centers on the idea of seeking the Lord's face. God has promised great reward for worshipping Him in this way.

—*Brian D. Doud*

# PRACTICAL POINTS

1. True worship ushers the glory of the Lord into the congregation (II Chron. 7:1).
2. When God is moving, we should be still, in reverence of Him (vss. 2-3).
3. Good spiritual leaders set an example of worship for the congregation (vss. 4-5).
4. God deserves praise for His everlasting mercy (vs. 6).
5. We should reverence our church building as a place set aside for worship (vs. 7).
6. It is good to set aside time to celebrate our blessings from God (vss. 8-9).

—*Valante M. Grant.*

# RESEARCH AND DISCUSSION

1. Do we know when the glory of the Lord comes in and fills the congregation? How should we respond?
2. Is it important to offer God a sacrifice while in worship? Why or why not?
3. How do the actions of the leader influence the worship of the people (II Chron. 7:4-5)?
4. Compare and contrast an everyday worship experience with a worship experience within the congregation?
5. What are some benefits of joining a congregation to worship and bring offerings?
6. When we are dedicated to building the church, what can we expect to see in our own families (vs. 11)?

—*Valante M. Grant.*

# ILLUSTRATED HIGH POINTS

## They bowed . . . and worshipped

The Israelites saw God's fire and glory. If it had been today, thousands would have taken pictures with their mobile devices. All the Israelites could do was fall to the ground, worship, and praise God.

A ministry friend always urges Christians to be alert to what he calls "God sightings." These may include the deer we did not hit, the parking space right in front of the store when we are in a hurry, or the car breaking down, not on a deserted road, but in the driveway.

## Praised the Lord, saying

The children of Israel were shouting, "For he is good; for his mercy endureth for ever" (II Chron. 7:3). They were enthusiastic in praising God.

Every Sunday during the fall, thousands of Americans flock to stadiums and loudly express their love for their favorite football team. Some suggest that fan noise is the "twelfth man" on the team.

Truly many bow and "worship" at the altar of sports. They sacrifice huge sums of money, time, and energy for the game. Many are almost depressed when their team loses. Certainly, some of this is simple entertainment, but few show even half as much enthusiasm in worshipping the God of glory.

## Hamath unto the river of Egypt

The above phrase indicated the northern and southern boundaries of the land of Israel. Jerusalem was located in the middle, so it is conceivable that some had traveled two hundred miles. At twenty miles a day, it was a long trip.

The attraction, of course, was the temple. The people could return home with a great story.

—*David A. Hamburg.*

# Golden Text Illuminated

**"When all the children of Israel saw how the fire came down, and the glory of the Lord upon the house, they . . . worshipped, and praised the Lord, saying, For he is good; for his mercy endureth for ever" (II Chronicles 7:3).**

Last week, we looked at part of Solomon's prayer at the dedication of the temple. We read in II Chronicles 7:1 that when he finished praying, fire came down from heaven, consuming the sacrifices on the altar, and the glory of the Lord filled the temple. Verse 2 tells us that the priests could not even enter the structure because of the glory of God. Imagine that happening in your church!

The glory of God that was manifested here probably involved a supernatural light of intense brilliance and power. It would have been nearly (if not totally) impossible to look at. The New Testament reminds us that God dwells in light that "no man can approach unto" (I Tim. 6:16).

The Hebrew word for "glory" in our text, however, relates to weight or heaviness. So there may have been a sense of incredible weight or presence that the priests simply could not stand up under. When we truly experience God's glory, we will be flattened with awe (yet made whole rather than harmed).

The multitude of ordinary Israelites who were assembled outside reacted to this event with completely appropriate behavior. They bowed down and "worshipped, and praised the Lord." The full verse says that they actually put their faces to the ground as they bowed down. They were not following a prescribed ritual in doing this. It was a spontaneous response to the manifestation of God's glory before them. Worship does not require a specific posture, but bowing down or falling flat on one's face is a natural expression of what needs to be in the worshipper's heart. Worship is essentially a recognition of and response to who God is, especially regarding His incomparable greatness, holiness, and power. Worship acknowledges that God matters more than anything else; it is all (rightly) about Him.

The opposite of worship, perhaps, is not so much atheism or blasphemy as an attitude that treats God as inconsequential. It is seen in busy lives that try to fit God into a small slot in their schedules. God, however, cannot be contained. It is we who must fit into His schedule and His agenda.

Closely tied to worship is praise. In fact, they are like twins. The assembled Israelites praised God, focusing on two of His important attributes: "He is good" and "his mercy endureth for ever."

For modern readers, it seems almost axiomatic that God should be called good. But this was by no means a given among the peoples of ancient times. Pagan gods were often conceived of as anything but good; they were feared for their arbitrary cruelty and ill will toward humans. Israel learned early on, however, that goodness is one of the Lord's defining characteristics.

They also learned of His enduring mercy, both by precept and through experiencing it over and over again. The word the Israelites used is a rich one. It is often translated "lovingkindness" and points to the intimate, loving, and faithful relationship the Lord sought with His people. They often strayed from that relationship, but He never did.

—*Kenneth A. Sponsler.*

# Heart of the Lesson

When I was a student at a Christian college, I attended daily chapel services at a church near the campus. One dreary, overcast day, the speaker was talking about the Second Coming. Suddenly, light burst through the stained-glass windows, illuminating the sanctuary. An audible gasp filled the room. No, Jesus did not appear. But that experience gave me a hint of the wonder Israel felt when the nation beheld God's glory.

**1. Glory fills the temple (II Chron. 7:1-3).** Solomon had just finished his prayer dedicating the new temple when fire blazed down from heaven and consumed the burnt offerings and sacrifices on the temple altar. God had accepted those sacrifices and was pleased with them. All Israel witnessed this supernatural event—physical evidence that their God was the living God.

But even more moving was when God's glory filled the new temple. His glorious presence permeated the entire building. God loved His people. He had come to dwell with them.

God's glory was so overwhelming that the priests were unable to enter the temple to carry out their responsibilities. Meanwhile, the people spontaneously fell to the ground on their faces, worshipping. This will be our immediate response some day when we meet Jesus. Like the people of Israel, we will be unable to do otherwise, no matter how reserved or undemonstrative we are in this life.

**2. Israel worships (II Chron. 7:4-7).** King Solomon and all the people offered sacrifices to the Lord as part of their worship. Solomon offered 22,000 oxen and 120,000 sheep, a massive number of animals. These sacrifices looked forward to Jesus' future sacrifice on the cross for us.

The priests walked to their assigned posts, and the Levites followed. They carried musical instruments King David had made for praising God. The priests blew their trumpets, and all Israel stood. This phase of the temple dedication was a joyous musical celebration.

King Solomon dedicated the middle of the temple courtyard to God. This area was needed for burnt offerings and the fat of the peace offerings because the bronze altar was unable to handle the number of offerings King Solomon and the people were bringing to God.

**3. Celebrations cease (II Chron. 7:8-9).** The temple dedication was a seven-day celebration. The Feast of Tabernacles, another seven-day celebration, followed immediately. Israelites from every tribe and every part of the country arrived in Jerusalem to remember God bringing them out of Egypt to the Promised Land. During this week, they lived outdoors in shelters they built from tree branches.

The Feast of Tabernacles started and ended on a Sabbath. On the second Sabbath, the eighth day, the nation held a solemn assembly to close the feast. They made burnt offerings to the Lord and did no work.

The people had focused on the Lord for fourteen days, offering sacrifices, repenting, praising, singing, and acknowledging God's presence, work, and goodness in their lives.

Knowing God's attributes as the Bible describes them and seeing Him working in our lives should draw us to worship and to proclaim His goodness. Set aside time for worship. Worship can involve many aspects: music; giving; prayer; prostrating oneself (or practicing other prayer postures); and talking about God, His attributes, and His blessings to us.

—*Ann Staatz.*

# World Missions

Why was the Hindu priest knocking on his door in the middle of the night? The missionary, Raju (name changed for safety reasons), fought fear. He knew his work kept him at risk of being beaten by angry Hindu leaders, dragged away by outraged villagers, or worse.

Nevertheless, he welcomed the Hindu priest and his wife inside and served them tea and fruit. The priest, Lomash, asked whether Raju had had a prayer meeting earlier that night. When Raju said yes, the man exclaimed, "Then it is true!"

He told Raju an incredible story. Lomash had awoken from a vivid dream. In his dream, Raju and some other men were praying when four witch doctors came to his home with chains and sticks and rods to kill him. However, when they tried to enter Raju's yard, they could not. Some invisible force kept them back. Each time, they were knocked to the ground. Even their iron rods could not penetrate the force around Raju's home.

In the Hindu priest's dream, the witch doctors became very afraid. They realized Raju's God had power greater than their own. They ran away in fear.

The Hindu priest said the dream showed him that Raju's God is the true God. He and his wife wanted Him to be their God also.

Raju rejoiced, but more amazing news was to come. The next day, other villagers came and told him that the night before, during his prayer meeting, witch doctors had come to his home. "They came with rods and chains," the villagers said. "But for some reason, they could not hurt you. They ran away scared." The villagers wanted to know what mysterious power had protected Raju.

It had not been just a dream! Word spread about how the witch doctors could not withstand the power of the true God and how the Hindu priest and his wife had turned to God. So many people in the area wanted to know more, four more missionaries came to help share the good news.

The story is a beautiful one of power and people seeing the glory of God, but we must not forget that for that moment of glory and victory to happen, a young man had to be willing to risk his own life to share the gospel with the lost.

There is a cost to missions. Missionaries testify that God supplies their needs, but that often means they give up a life of comfort to experience needs only God can provide for. They see God at work, but that means they go into the darkness where the Light shines brightest.

Those who want to see the glory of God must be willing to obey the call to personal sacrifice. People who do not obey the call, who choose lives where they feel safe or have financial security, or do not have to give up much, forfeit getting to see the glory of God in many ways. If there are no needs, how can God provide in a way that shows His glory?

If those witch doctors had not come, intending to kill, how would the villagers have ever seen that God's power was greater?

In heaven, we will have all eternity for comfort and security and abundance. Right now, we are in a battle for the souls of mankind. Let us be willing to give our lives as living sacrifices so the world will see God's power and know Him to be the true God who can save them.

—*Kimberly Rae.*

# The Jewish Aspect

In 2015 the Temple Institute, a research organization in Jerusalem dedicated to preparing for the construction of the temple, released a three-dimensional architectural rendering of the third temple. Nearly two thousand years after the temple's destruction, this organization has begun preparations to make Israel's dream of a rebuilt temple a reality. In addition to the plans, the organization has now completed many items for the temple service including the menorah, the golden incense altar, and the golden table of showbread (templeinstitute.org).

Throughout history, the holy temple has been of utmost importance to the Jewish people. In this week's lesson, we see King Solomon dedicating the first temple to the Lord during Sukkot. Hundreds of years after Solomon dedicated the first temple, there was a rededication of the second temple in Jerusalem. This rededication resulted in the creation of another eight-day Jewish celebration known as Hanukkah.

Hanukkah commemorates this rededication of the second temple in Jerusalem, which took place during the second century B.C. In 167 B.C., the Syrian ruler Antiochus Epiphanes decided to force all people under his control to Hellenize, or adopt Greek culture. Sabbath worship and circumcision were outlawed, replaced by worship of Greek gods and sacrificing pigs (Strassfeld, *The Jewish Holidays*, William Morrow).

The Syrians came into the village of Modein to set up an altar. They commanded the Jews to sacrifice a pig on the altar as an act of submission. This was very insulting and detestable to the Jewish people.

As things began to escalate, a group of devout Jews left their possessions and moved to the desert. A band of soldiers pursued them, attacked them on the Sabbath, and killed one thousand people (I Maccabees 2:38). Because it was the Jewish Sabbath, the Israelites did not fight back.

Mattathias, a high priest from the tribe of Levi, heard of the massacre and began a revolt. Eventually, his son Judas took over as leader. Mattathias, Judas, Judas's brothers, and a small band of Jewish men fought the Syrians. The Syrian armies greatly outnumbered the Jews. However, the small group ultimately pushed back the Syrian warriors and reclaimed the temple.

After the temple was cleansed, the group decided to celebrate Sukkot. They had been in bondage during the time that the celebration should have taken place. Since they were rededicating the temple, they decided that it would be appropriate to celebrate the festival outside of the correct time frame.

Legend has it that when they got to the temple, there was only enough oil for one day. However, when they lit the candlestick, a miracle occurred. The oil, which should have burned for one day, lasted eight days.

The festival of Hanukkah occurs on the twenty-fifth of Kislev, which means it falls late in November or December. Josephus, a Jewish historian, called the festival "lights" (Schauss, *The Jewish Festivals*, Random House).

Some scholars believe that based on calculations from the time of the conception of John the Baptist, Jesus' conception probably fell on or around Hanukkah (Reeves, *The Jewish Holidays*, Authorhouse). If so, the "light festival," Hanukkah, provided a perfect entrance for the Light of the World.

—Robin Fitzgerald.

# Guiding the Superintendent

In spite of the fact that Solomon knew that God could never be confined to an earthly building ("Will God in very deed dwell with men on the earth?" [II Chron. 6:18]), God in a most dramatic way accepted Solomon's prayer, displaying His awesome power and holiness. Both king and people responded with great praise and sacrificing.

## DEVOTIONAL OUTLINE

**1. God's response (II Chron. 7:1-2).** To emphasize His acceptance of Solomon's dedicatory prayer, God responded in two ways. Fire came down from heaven, consuming the sacrifice. Then, His glory filled the temple to such an extent that the priests were incapable of entering.

This was not the first time that God had demonstrated His overwhelming presence to the people of Israel. God had manifested His presence powerfully at Sinai (Deut. 4:11; 5:22). He also displayed His power to Moses and Aaron and all the people in a similar manner when the tabernacle was dedicated (Lev. 9:24). Years later, God's fire would fall when His presence came to inhabit His new temple, the church (Acts 2:3-4). Warren Wiersbe put it this way: "Prayer went up, fire came down, and glory moved in" (*With the Word,* Nelson).

**2. The people's response (II Chron. 7:3-9).** There was only one way the people could respond to this display of God's glory, power, and presence. The people bowed with their faces to the ground and worshipped God. What better way to worship God than to praise Him: "For he is good; for his mercy endureth for ever."

To express their gratitude following this public praise of God, the king and all the people offered sacrifices to God. King Solomon joined in the great celebration of sacrifice with an offering that is almost beyond comprehension. He offered 22,000 oxen and 120,000 sheep! So massive was the offering that King Solomon consecrated an area in the middle of the temple courtyard to receive part of the sacrifice. The Levites who were musicians joined the priests in the festivities with more praise and music.

The feast (meaning the Feast of Booths) followed for seven days after the seven days for dedicating the altar, for a total of fourteen days of worship. The people came from the far corners of the country, from its extreme north (Hamath) to the river of Egypt in the far south. Before returning to their homes, the people gathered one more time to celebrate and worship their God. The great altar of the temple had been dedicated.

God demonstrated to Israel that He was indeed accessible through prayer, sacrifice, and praise. When one gets a clear picture of who God is, he can truly offer worship to God.

## AGE-GROUP EMPHASES

**Children:** Second Chronicles 7 contains the account of a great time of worship in ancient Israel. Have your children discuss what they can learn about worship from this account.

**Youths:** Have your students imagine themselves participating in this great time of celebration. Have them think through what the people might have been experiencing.

**Adults:** Some may see Solomon's massive offering as way too excessive. Part of biblical worship is expressing one's gratitude to God lavishly. What do your adults believe would be proper but not excessive gratitude offered to God?

—*Martin R. Dahlquist.*

# Scripture Lesson Text

**II CHRON. 7:12** And the Lord appeared to Sol'o-mon by night, and said unto him, I have heard thy prayer, and have chosen this place to myself for an house of sacrifice.

**13 If I shut up heaven that there be no rain, or if I command the locusts to devour the land, or if I send pestilence among my people;**

14 If my people, which are called by my name, shall humble themselves, and pray, and seek my face, and turn from their wicked ways; then will I hear from heaven, and will forgive their sin, and will heal their land.

**15 Now mine eyes shall be open, and mine ears attent unto the prayer** *that is made* **in this place.**

16 For now have I chosen and sanctified this house, that my name may be there for ever: and mine eyes and mine heart shall be there perpetually.

**17 And as for thee, if thou wilt walk before me, as Da'vid thy father walked, and do according to all that I have commanded thee, and shalt observe my statutes and my judgments;**

18 Then will I stablish the throne of thy kingdom, according as I have covenanted with Da'vid thy father, saying, There shall not fail thee a man *to be* ruler in Is'ra-el.

**19 But if ye turn away, and forsake my statutes and my commandments, which I have set before you, and shall go and serve other gods, and worship them;**

20 Then will I pluck them up by the roots out of my land which I have given them; and this house, which I have sanctified for my name, will I cast out of my sight, and will make it *to be* a proverb and a byword among all nations.

**21 And this house, which is high, shall be an astonishment to every one that passeth by it; so that he shall say, Why hath the Lord done thus unto this land, and unto this house?**

22 And it shall be answered, Because they forsook the Lord God of their fathers, which brought them forth out of the land of E'gypt, and laid hold on other gods, and worshipped them, and served them: therefore hath he brought all this evil upon them.

NOTES

# Seeking His Face

## Lesson: II Chronicles 7:12-22

Read: II Chronicles 7:12-22

TIME: 959 B.C.                    PLACE: Jerusalem

---

**GOLDEN TEXT**—"If my people, which are called by my name, shall humble themselves, and pray, and seek my face, and turn from their wicked ways; then will I hear from heaven, and will forgive their sin, and will heal their land" (II Chronicles 7:14).

---

## *Introduction*

Think of all the kinds of advisers people go to for counsel and direction. People seek out friends, talk show hosts, advice columnists, financial consultants, counselors, and psychiatrists. Even Christians seek out these kinds of people sometimes.

Seeking help from other people, especially trusted friends and counselors, is not wrong. God intends that we help one another. Sometimes, however, we are so concerned about seeking other people that we forget to seek the Lord.

Our present study focuses on seeking the Lord (II Chron. 7:14). This concept is so crucial that we find a reference to it more than twenty times in the Old Testament. For example, Psalm 105:4 exhorts, "Seek the Lord, and his strength: seek his face evermore."

What is seeking the Lord? It involves following after Him and His way when we face a decision or a problem. Our text in this study directs us to seek God's face, which adds a personal element to this instruction.

## LESSON OUTLINE

I. THE BLESSINGS OF SEEKING GOD'S FACE—II Chron. 7:12-18

II. THE CONSEQUENCES OF NOT SEEKING GOD'S FACE—II Chron. 7:19-22

## *Exposition: Verse by Verse*

### THE BLESSINGS OF SEEKING GOD'S FACE

**II CHRON. 7:12** And the Lord appeared to Solomon by night, and said unto him, I have heard thy prayer, and have chosen this place to myself for an house of sacrifice.

**13** If I shut up heaven that there be no rain, or if I command the locusts to devour the land, or if I send pestilence among my people;

**14** If my people, which are called

by my name, shall humble themselves, and pray, and seek my face, and turn from their wicked ways; then will I hear from heaven, and will forgive their sin, and will heal their land.

15 Now mine eyes shall be open, and mine ears attent unto the prayer that is made in this place.

16 For now have I chosen and sanctified this house, that my name may be there for ever: and mine eyes and mine heart shall be there perpetually.

17 And as for thee, if thou wilt walk before me, as David thy father walked, and do according to all that I have commanded thee, and shalt observe my statutes and my judgments;

18 Then will I stablish the throne of thy kingdom, according as I have covenanted with David thy father, saying, There shall not fail thee a man to be ruler in Israel.

Second Chronicles 7:12-22 follows the typical way an ancient Near Eastern covenant was structured by listing the blessings for compliance (vss. 12-18) and the consequences for disobedience (vss. 19-22). (Deuteronomy 27 through 28 is another example of this kind of structure.) First, we note the blessings for obedience, or in this case, seeking God's face.

**The Lord's appearance (II Chron. 7:12).** This verse states that God appeared to Solomon at night. It was the second time God had appeared to him. The first appearance is recorded in II Chronicles 1:7: "In that night did God appear unto Solomon, and said unto him, Ask what I shall give thee." That had taken place soon after the king's accession to the throne.

These appearances raise two questions: How did God appear to Solomon, and why were both times at night? The Lord may have appeared in a theophany (temporarily taking on a human form), but perhaps more likely

He simply gave some visible indication of His presence as He talked to Solomon. Maybe these two appearances were similar to the Lord's appearance to Samuel where the Lord "came, and stood, and called as at other times" (I Sam. 3:10). No matter how the Lord manifested Himself, we can be sure that Solomon recognized it was the Lord who appeared to him.

Interestingly, both appearances occurred at night, as was the case also with Samuel (I Sam. 3:3-10). Perhaps God chose the nighttime so that Solomon could give his full attention to the Lord. Even today the Lord often brings thoughts to our minds in the still of the night when other matters are not clamoring for our attention.

In this appearance the Lord assured Solomon that He had heard his prayer and accepted what he had done (II Chron. 6:12-42). He also affirmed that the temple was the special place of His presence and the only place for offering sacrifices.

**The Lord's remedy for judgment (II Chron. 7:13-14).** In these verses the Lord set out a scenario of potential judgment and then told Solomon what to do if that judgment were to come.

The potential judgment would be the Lord withholding rain, sending locusts to devour the land, and inflicting disease among the people because of their sin. These were not purely hypothetical consequences. Viewed even on just a human level, the outlined disasters were quite probable in light of the people's history of disobedience.

Even though judgment was likely, the Lord encouraged Solomon by outlining for him the remedy for the judgment. The remedy involved the people humbling themselves, praying, seeking the Lord's face, and turning from their wicked ways.

If the Israelites took these steps, God promised He would hear them, forgive their sin, and heal their land. The idea of healing their land probably conveyed restoration, which could mean restoring the abundance of the land or even restoring them to the land itself as was the case after the exile.

Second Chronicles 7:14 is sometimes used by pastors and Christian politicians to explain how we can turn a country back to the Lord. This verse certainly shows the principle that God will restore in response to obedience, but we need to be careful about applying it to the United States or to any other country.

God made this promise specifically to His covenant nation, the Israelites. This verse is not a promise to Christians or to whatever contemporary nation they live in. We should try to influence the spiritual direction of our country, but we should be careful of applying this promise directly to us.

One of the steps the Israelites were to take was to seek the Lord's face. That is an anthropomorphic expression, that is, one that speaks of divine realities in human terms. Seeking the Lord's face is essentially the same as seeking His presence. (The Hebrew word for "face" can be translated as "presence" because seeing someone's face means being in that person's presence.)

While the promise of II Chronicles 7:14 was made to Israel, today we should still seek the Lord's face, or His presence, in a personal and intimate relationship. We need to live so close to the Lord that we have a conscious awareness of His presence in our lives. We should have such a close relationship with Him that it is like looking in His face. David exhorted us to "seek the Lord and his strength, seek his face continually" (I Chron. 16:11).

**Blessings to Israel (II Chron. 7:15-16).** If Israel fulfilled the requirements of verse 14 and sought the Lord's face, God said He would respond in two ways. First, He would respond favorably to their prayers (vs. 15). Again using anthropomorphic expressions, the Lord said His eyes would be open and His ears attentive to the cries of His people.

Second, God said He would place His name, His eyes, and His heart in the temple, which He had chosen and sanctified. Each of these three things is significant. God's name stands for who He is—His character and being. God's eyes convey the idea that He will always look out for His people. He will always give them His full attention. God's heart speaks of His deep concern and care for His people. Furthermore, God's name, eyes, and heart would be in the temple unceasingly, indicating His constancy toward His people.

**Blessings to Solomon (II Chron. 7:17-18).** In addition to the blessings that would come to the nation, God also promised a specific blessing to Solomon if he continued to seek God's face and did everything God asked of him, just as his father, David, had done.

The specific blessing promised to Solomon was the establishment of his throne and the perpetuation of his dynasty. This promise to David is first recorded in II Samuel 7, where Nathan told David what God would do. "I will set up thy seed after thee, which shall proceed out of thy bowels, and I will establish his kingdom. . . . I will stablish the throne of his kingdom for ever" (vss. 12-13). Furthermore, the Lord said through Nathan, "And thine house and thy kingdom shall be established for ever before thee: thy throne shall be established for ever" (vs. 16). This promise is repeated in I Kings 2:4 and II Chronicles 6:16.

This unconditional promise, known as the Davidic covenant, has never been abrogated and is the basis of the premillennial position that Jesus Christ will someday rule from the throne of David in the millennium.

If the promise is unconditional, why does II Chronicles 7:17 seem to indicate the promise is based on Solomon's obedience? The answer seems to be along these lines: the promise is unconditional, but the enjoyment of it by Solomon or any succeeding king would be based on his obedience to the Lord.

## THE CONSEQUENCES OF NOT SEEKING GOD'S FACE

**19 But if ye turn away, and forsake my statutes and my commandments, which I have set before you, and shall go and serve other gods, and worship them;**

**20 Then will I pluck them up by the roots out of my land which I have given them; and this house, which I have sanctified for my name, will I cast out of my sight, and will make it to be a proverb and a byword among all nations.**

**21 And this house, which is high, shall be an astonishment to every one that passeth by it; so that he shall say, Why hath the Lord done thus unto this land, and unto this house?**

**22 And it shall be answered, Because they forsook the Lord God of their fathers, which brought them forth out of the land of Egypt, and laid hold on other gods, and worshipped them, and served them: therefore hath he brought all this evil upon them.**

**Falling away (II Chron. 7:19).** In keeping with the structure of ancient Near Eastern treaties, the Lord next delineated the consequences of disobedience. The specific disobedience here was going after other gods and not seeking the Lord's face. Sadly, that was exactly what Solomon and most of the succeeding kings did. They forsook the Lord and followed the false gods of the nations around them.

Solomon himself went after many false gods. In I Kings 11:5, 7-8 we read, "For Solomon went after Ashtoreth the goddess of the Zidonians, and after Milcom the abomination of the Ammonites . . . Then did Solomon build an high place for Chemosh, the abomination of Moab, in the hill that is before Jerusalem, and for Molech, the abomination of the children of Ammon. And likewise did he for all his strange wives, which burnt incense and sacrificed unto their gods."

God told Solomon that if he followed other gods, he would suffer dire consequences.

**Removal from the land (II Chron. 7:20a).** Employing an agrarian term the Israelites would understand, God said that just as a plant is pulled out of the ground, so He would "pluck them up by the roots" and remove them from the land He had given them. This also was exactly what happened to the Israelites when they were exiled from the land to Assyria and Babylon (II Kings 17:5-23; II Chron. 36:15-21).

**Destruction of the temple (II Chron. 7:20b-22).** Not only would the people be exiled to foreign lands, but the beautiful temple Solomon had just made and dedicated would be destroyed as well. The Lord said He would reject it and "make it to be a proverb and a byword among all nations." To say the temple would be a proverb or a byword means it would become an object of contempt. People everywhere would point to it as a sorry example or illustration of what sin had done.

The later history of Israel shows that such destruction did take place. We find in II Kings 25:9-10 that Nebuchadnezzar "burnt the house of the Lord, and the king's house, and all the houses of Jerusalem, and every great man's house burnt he with fire. And all the army of the Chaldees, that were with the captain of the guard, brake down the walls of Jerusalem round about."

The destruction of the temple would be so complete that people who walked past its ruins would be astonished and say, "Why hath the Lord done thus unto this land, and unto this house?" (II Chron. 7:21). God told Solomon that those people would find a ready answer to their question. They would know that the destruction was because the people "laid hold on other gods, and worshipped them, and served them" (vs. 22).

Solomon and his people started well. Solomon made and dedicated a dwelling place for the Lord. The people obeyed by offering sacrifices and keeping the prescribed feasts. They had sufficient instruction to seek the Lord's face and warning of what would happen if they did not do so.

Sadly, however, Solomon did not remain faithful to the Lord as had his father, David. He lapsed into disobedience, and his influence on the people led them into sin. After generations of disobedience, the people eventually lost their land and their temple—all because they did not seek the face of the Lord.

Earlier in this study, we said the Hebrew word for "face" can be translated "presence" because seeing someone's face means being in that person's presence. We concluded that seeking the Lord's face is to be equated with seeking His presence.

So what is involved in seeking the face, or the presence, of the Lord? In one sense we are always in the Lord's presence by virtue of His omnipresence and His indwelling, but seeking His presence is something more.

Seeking the face of God requires that we act intentionally. We have to make an effort to *seek* His presence. Where do we find God's presence, and how do we enter it? Hebrews 4:16 invites us to "come boldly unto the throne of grace, that we may obtain mercy, and find grace to help in time of need." This passage indicates that we can come to the place where the Lord dwells, the place where He is present. How do we come to that place? By prayer. Our times of prayer usher us into the very throne room of God.

Without being mystical, perhaps we should think consciously about how our prayer times bring us into the place where God Himself dwells. Before we ask, maybe we should spend time in reflection and meditation, just as if we were sitting in His presence. Once we are in His presence, we can ask Him what He wants us to do and what His plan is for our lives.

Let us recommit to making our prayer times more than reciting a list or hurrying through our prayers to get to the next part of our busy life. Let us enter into the presence of God and seek His face to guide our lives.

—Don Anderson.

# QUESTIONS

1. What were the Israelites to do when they faced difficulty?
2. Why does II Chronicles 7:14 not apply directly to Christians today?
3. What anthropomorphic expression do we find in this verse, and what does it mean?
4. What is conveyed by the mention of God's eyes, ears, and name (vss. 15-16)?
5. What promise did God make to Solomon?
6. What false gods did Solomon end up following?
7. What would happen to the people if they turned from God?
8. What would happen to the temple if the people turned from God?
9. In what way would the temple become "a proverb and a byword" (vs. 20)?
10. How do we seek the Lord's face in our lives today?

—Don Anderson.

# Preparing to Teach the Lesson

As we begin to study this passage, including the wonderful II Chronicles 7:14, which is so often quoted in connection with the promise of God's answer to our prayers, it is well to remember the title of the lesson, "Seeking His Face." There is a scriptural concept of God turning away His face from those who displease Him. The idea is that He no longer listens to their prayers and no longer blesses them with health, prosperity, and safety from enemies and disasters. It may also indicate that He might not be actively bringing them under His correction and discipline. This is not as bad as God forsaking someone, but that action on God's part is a very serious call to repent of sin and cry out to God for forgiveness and mercy.

There are consequences to ignoring God or misusing our relationship with Him. Our task as teachers is to inform and alert our students to the dangers of such behavior without causing fear or undue distress.

## TODAY'S AIM

**Facts:** to understand God's statement about seeking His face.

**Principle:** to seek God's face as we should, so we will be blessed.

**Application:** to make it a daily practice to seek God's face.

## INTRODUCING THE LESSON

The concept of seeking God's face is basic to our relationship to Him. Once we have trusted in Christ and His salvation, we are made children of God. Just as a human mother or father may be displeased and so look away from us and stop talking to us, making clear his or her displeasure with our actions, so God may also turn away His face from us (II Chron. 30:9). We are still His children, but we might lose daily blessings that come from His favor to us. We will lose the fellowship we can have with Him.

This concept may prove difficult to teach. We must teach as a process, moving from the known and the familiar to the unknown and unfamiliar. It may be that some of our students have never had a personal experience of drawing near to God and having Him draw near to them. However, we must teach as though they have had such an experience and trust that as we teach, the truth will become apparent to them and they will seek the Lord's face at whatever point in their spiritual lives they find themselves.

The most wonderful thing about the Christian life is that we have an intimate relationship with our Saviour, the Lord Jesus Christ, and with our Father in heaven. To belong to Him is to be in the most secure and blessed position we can be.

## DEVELOPING THE LESSON

**1. God's declaration to Solomon (II Chron. 7:12-16).** One of the basic building blocks of Christian doctrine is the omnipresence of God; that is, He is always present everywhere. It is also true that He chooses to make His presence known to people in certain places and at certain times. In these verses the Lord told Solomon that He was going to make the temple His special place to accept their sacrifices and, by implication, their prayers for forgiveness. His eyes, His ears, and His heart were to be there continually.

However, if they sinned against Him, He would send disasters, natural and miraculous, to discipline His people. However, if they would turn from their sin and seek His face, He would once again hear from heaven (not from the temple) and forgive their sin and heal their land. This is a wonderful promise of God's continual love for His people.

While we do not keep the Mosaic Law or the temple worship and sacrifices, we do have a similar relationship to God in that He has given us the indwelling Holy Spirit who makes intercession for us, conveying our prayers perfectly to our Father in heaven. If we sin and come under the discipline of our Heavenly Father, we can repent of our sins and seek His face and be restored to fellowship with Him.

**2. God's conditional promise to Solomon (II Chron. 7:17-18).** This is a special promise to Solomon. It involved Solomon's descendants and their ruling as kings of Israel. If they were faithful to God, He would continue to bless them and keep them on the throne. This did not continue for long because of human weakness.

**3. The consequences of failing to keep God's conditions (II Chron. 7:19-22).** Just as God promised to hear and answer the prayers of the faithful, so He also promised to discipline those who went after other gods and served them. Others would look at the calamities that befell the Israelites and make fun of them. Everyone would know that they had enjoyed the blessing of being God's chosen people for whom He worked many miracles but that they had left Him for other gods, and so God now had brought all this evil upon them.

There are consequences for the child of God who does that which displeases the Lord. We may not always see or understand how this applies today or in every circumstance, but we know that it does. God loves us too much to leave us without the discipline necessary to draw us back to Himself. He will even go so far as to take us out of this life to make the best of the situation (cf. I Cor. 11:28-32).

## ILLUSTRATING THE LESSON

God promises to hear and answer prayer made in His way.

**GOD HEARS AND ANSWERS PRAYER**

God's Way

**MADE HIS WAY**

## CONCLUDING THE LESSON

In the United States, our constitutional law guarantees that everyone is free to worship God after the dictates of his or her conscience. However, the spiritual truth is that we are really only free to worship God after *His* dictates and directives, and our conscience must be informed by the Word of God and the leading of the Holy Spirit as to what is right and heartfelt worship.

Substituting ceremonialism and ritual for the right way to worship does not put us under the right conditions as laid out for Solomon and Israel in our lesson text for today. We have a right relationship with God through faith in the finished work of Christ on the cross and a continuing relationship with Him through the work of the Holy Spirit in our hearts, leading us to confess and forsake our sins.

## ANTICIPATING THE NEXT LESSON

Next week we begin a unit on the glory and honor that are the Lord's and our place in giving Him glory and honor.
—Brian D. Doud.

# PRACTICAL POINTS

1. We should pray that God dwells in our congregation (II Chron. 7:12).
2. God's response to sin and disobedience is inevitable destruction (vs. 13).
3. God responds to earnest prayer and repentance with forgiveness and healing (vs. 14).
4. God will abide in people who are dedicated to Him (vs. 15).
5. God's people are a source of refuge and peace (vs. 16).
6. We bring blessings or destruction upon ourselves, based on whether we obey God or not (vss. 17-22).
—*Valante M. Grant.*

# RESEARCH AND DISCUSSION

1. What does God require of His people? What can we expect when we meet the requirement (II Chron. 7:14)?
2. What is the primary purpose of joining a congregation to worship?
3. What can we learn from biblical history about how to worship God?
4. How do we conduct ourselves among people who are sanctified by God for His glory?
5. How do we seek the Lord? How does He reveal Himself to us?
6. What are modern-day examples of other gods being placed before the true and living God?
7. How does God's response to sin and disobedience affect the fate of a congregation (vss. 20-22)?
—*Valante M. Grant.*

# ILLUSTRATED HIGH POINTS

**If I shut up heaven**

When disasters occur or trouble prevails, people have a tendency to ask "Why?" Perhaps we would do better to ask "Why not?" Not every problem is a direct result of sin, but there is enough sin in the world for the need to seek God's face in humble prayer and repentance.

Sadly, in the face of recent terrorist activity and mass shootings in America, the official national reaction is one of outrage, along with a declaration of strength and determination to seek out the perpetrators and bring them to justice. Instead of revenge, God desires repentance.

**And seek my face**

Most of us go to God with our hands out looking for some kind of material or medical help. It is appropriate, for Jesus said, "Ask, and ye shall receive" (John 16:24), and James said, "Ye have not, because ye ask not" (Jas. 4:2).

God also desires that we seek His face, which is another way of saying that we simply desire to be with Him. It is somewhat like an invitation I saw to a fiftieth wedding anniversary celebration, which said, "No gifts, please. Your presence will be a blessed gift to us."

God delights to give His children good gifts, but He also is pleased when we delight in Him for who He is as well as what He gives.

**As David . . . walked**

Sometimes a tiny word in a verse provides the key to the whole point. The biblical record does not mention any great moral scandal associated with the reign of Solomon, but he did not attain to the high spiritual character of his father, David. He did not walk before God *as* David did.
—*David A. Hamburg.*

# Golden Text Illuminated

**"If my people, which are called by my name, shall humble themselves, and pray, and seek my face, and turn from their wicked ways; then will I hear from heaven, and will forgive their sin, and will heal their land" (II Chronicles 7:14).**

In lesson 2, we looked at Solomon's prayer in dedicating the newly built temple to the Lord, a prayer that contained many requests for forgiveness and restoration from anticipated future lapses into sin. This week we look at God's reply to Solomon, an answer that came to him during the night.

Solomon had been concerned that his people would repeatedly stray from obedience to the Lord and sought assurance that they would not be cast aside or destroyed. God's reply in II Chronicles 7:14 contains an assurance of restoration and the way to obtain that restoration. It is both a promise and an invitation.

The first element of reassurance is that no matter what lapses or transgressions may lie in Israel's future, God still considers them "my people," the people who "are called by my name." Israel indeed committed the most atrocious breaches of faithfulness over their history, but God never abandoned them in favor of a different people. He would severely discipline them, but He never wrote them off. They remained His even when they walked far from Him.

When people realize they have fallen out of divine fellowship, they often think in terms of elaborate works or rituals they might perform to regain it. Israel was no exception, often assuming that an impressive display of sacrifices was the key to winning God's favor (cf. Mic. 6:6-7). In direct contrast, God looked for a genuine change of heart.

This change of heart was seen in four basic actions. Far from carrying out extravagant rituals, the people were simply to "humble themselves, and pray, and seek my face, and turn from their wicked ways." Humility is the first step in returning to God's favor, for without it there can be no true recognition of having done wrong. Prayer and seeking God's face describe turning to Him and reestablishing the broken relationship. Turning from wickedness is the essential mark of true repentance and the desire to please Him again.

What God wanted from His wayward people was far simpler than an extensive program of sacrifice and ritual but at the same time much more difficult. Israel often preferred the complicated sacrificial route, for the simple reason that they did not want to change their hearts. True heart change is inconvenient, disruptive, and hard. In fact, it is impossible without God's work within, and we often would rather substitute an external action that leaves our inward captivation with sin alone.

Yet God will accept nothing less than a transformed heart and a desire to be genuinely pleasing to Him. When we recognize that this is truly what we need, He pours out His blessing. He hears our prayers, forgives our sin, and brings healing into our lives. For Israel, this meant healing the land so that it bore fruit in rich harvests. For us, the end of spiritual famine and drought may be more in line with what we can expect.

Whatever form the restoration takes, it starts with a recognition of where we have gone off the rails and a sincere desire to turn back.

—*Kenneth A. Sponsler.*

# Heart of the Lesson

When I was a young teenager, my mother wanted me to establish a habit of personal devotions. She told me the story of Leland Wang, a Chinese Christian, whose motto was "No Bible, no breakfast." Wang so desired to seek the Lord's face each morning that he would forfeit breakfast, the most important meal of the day, rather than skip his time in Scripture.

**1. Answer to prayer (II Chron. 7:12).** The Lord appeared to Solomon one night after the temple dedication to assure Solomon that He had heard his prayer and had chosen the temple as the place for Israel's sacrifices.

**2. Promise to forgive and heal (II Chron. 7:13-14).** God reviewed with Solomon the negative things He would bring upon Israel if the people strayed from Him: lack of rain, locusts devouring crops, and plagues on the people. These disastrous conditions were reversible if the people did four things:

- Humble themselves. They needed to let go of their pride and realize their wrongdoing and need for God.
- Pray. They needed to confess their sins and beg God for mercy.
- Seek God's face. They needed to long for a relationship with God. Their prayers should be heartfelt.
- Turn from their wicked ways. God desired to see change in their lives. A humble attitude, prayer, and seeking God were a start. But for full restoration to occur, the people needed to abandon their sinful lifestyles and obey God.

God said if His people, the Israelite nation that called itself by His name, did these four things, He would hear their prayers, He would forgive their sins, and He would heal their land. Believers today also can restore their relationship with God through being humble, praying, seeking God's face, and changing their lifestyles to obey God.

**3. Commitment to the temple (II Chron. 7:15-16).** God reassured Solomon that He would be attentive to the prayers Israel made from the temple. God had chosen this building and set it apart to be the place of His special presence forever. God's desire was that the nation always would follow Him and that His glory would remain in Solomon's temple forever.

**4. Promises to Solomon (II Chron. 7:17-22).** God promised Solomon that if he followed the Lord as his father, David, had done, Solomon always would have a descendent on the throne to rule Israel.

But if Solomon forsook God's statutes and commandments and worshipped other gods, God said He would uproot the people from His land.

Additionally, God would reject the temple, a wonder of architecture and the home of His glorious presence. Nations would scoff and ask why God would permit such terrible things to happen to His land and temple.

The answer? God's people had forsaken their God—they gave up something they formerly had held dear. They left the God of their fathers and worshipped false gods. Therefore, the Lord had brought this evil upon them.

God gave this message to Solomon because he was to be a godly example to his people. The nation would tend to follow its king. If he followed God, the country would thrive, and he would have a dynasty. If Solomon strayed from God, he and his nation would suffer judgment. Obedience leads to blessing. Disobedience leads to disaster.

—*Ann Staatz.*

# World Missions

England was considered a spiritual cesspool at the beginning of the eighteenth century. Sir William Blackstone "did not hear a single discourse which had more Christianity in it than the writings of Cicero," and this he said after attending the church of every major clergyman in London.

Sin was rampant. Bishop Berkeley said it was "to a degree that was never known in any Christian country."

One man, George Whitefield, was converted and began preaching in the open air to the masses, and a great revival started. Another clergyman who was led to the Lord was John Wesley, who took the message to the poor in the workhouses, prisons, hospitals, and mines.

The revival spread like wildfire, and England was transformed. People became Christians, and Christians caused change. They started antislavery societies, agencies to help the poor, and prison reform groups. Many missionary groups were formed, along with the British Foreign Bible Society and the Religious Tract Society. England became the missionary-sending capital of the world.

What happened? Over time the people of England turned away from God, began to see the Bible as a book of myths, and blurred the definitions of right and wrong.

Today, England is no longer the top-sending country for missionaries or even among the top ten. Things have regressed so far that less than 3 percent of its people even go to church on a regular basis.

Will the nation of America follow a similar pattern? Today, the United States ranks number one in sending missionaries around the world, but the nation is in rapid moral decline. With prayer being abolished in schools, abortions flourishing, gender confusion expanding, and violence increasing, America is far from what the world once considered a Christian nation.

Many people around the world still think of Americans as Christians. Facts that may not be well-known include the following: Americans have the highest STD rate and teen pregnancy rate of any industrialized nation; produce an estimated 89 percent of all the pornography in the world; have the highest divorce rate in the world; have the highest rate of illegal drug use in the world; and have aborted over 50 million babies (www.thetruthwins.com/archives/100-facts).

Will America regress to the point that it no longer has missionaries to send? Our nation, once widely regarded as "under God," must go through the formula given by God for healing any land. It is the same pattern that brings an individual to salvation. We must humble ourselves and pray, seek God's face, and turn from our wicked ways (II Chron. 7:14).

So much is at stake. We need revival. Believers need to pray for God to send laborers to the harvest, not just around the world but here among us. We ourselves need to be lights in the darkness, to not waver, and especially to not be apathetic. History and missions around the world will be affected by what our generation of believers does within the culture where we have been placed. Let us pray for our nation and do what God requires for our land to be healed and made righteous before it is too late, before our influence is gone. As the psalmist said, "Blessed is the nation whose God is the Lord" (Ps. 33:12). He is our only hope.

—Kimberly Rae.

# The Jewish Aspect

The belief in the arrival of the Messiah occupies an important place in Jewish thought. This belief holds such importance for the Jew that it is included as one of the "Thirteen Principles" of the Jewish faith. "I believe in the arrival of the Messiah and the Messianic Era" is customarily recited with the other principles every day after morning prayers in the synagogue (chabad.org).

In this week's lesson, we see God as He spoke to Solomon reminding him of the covenant that He made with his father, David. David cultivated a relationship with God, and God promised him that his throne would be established forever (II Sam. 7:12-13). Jews believe according to this promise that the long-awaited Messiah will come from David's lineage.

The Hebrew word *meshiach* is the one from which we get our word "messiah." The term, however, actually means "anointed." In Jewish thought, this person, the Messiah, or God's Anointed One, will usher in the messianic age.

Today, religious Jews are awaiting a *Meshiach* (Messiah) *ben* (son of) *David,* who will bring about political and spiritual redemption in the manner that David did during his kingship. Three times per day, devout Jews pray the *Shemoneh Esrei,* or *Amidah.* The Shemoneh Esrei stands as a central prayer of Judaism. The prayer, whose name means "eighteen," consists of nineteen (originally there were eighteen) blessings—three blessings of praise, thirteen blessings of petition, and three blessings of thanks.

Blessing number fifteen of the Shemoneh Esrei, called the *Malkhut Beit David,* or Kingdom of David, petitions God to bring forth the offspring of King David, who will be the Messiah of Israel. Blessing fifteen follows the blessing that asks God to return mercy to Jerusalem and quickly set up in Jerusalem the throne of David (jewishencyclopedia.com).

The Jewish belief concerning the Messiah has changed some over the centuries. Today Jews await the appearance of Messiah ben David, the military leader who will bring peace, not only to Israel, but to all mankind. However, ancient rabbis taught that there would be four important figures during the end times.

Zechariah 1:20 mentions four carpenters or craftsmen. Rabbis believed that the four craftsmen would be Meshiach ben David, Meshiach ben Yosep (Joseph), Elijah, and a righteous priest. They also believed that each would play a pivotal part during the end times (judaismsanswer.com).

Although Messiah ben David is the long-awaited messiah, in the ancient mind, Messiah ben Joseph also plays a major role in eschatology. Rabbis believed that Messiah ben Joseph would come before Messiah ben David. He would be a suffering messiah and die fighting Israel's enemies (judaismsanswer.com). In ancient thought, two messiahs would come, each with a different purpose, but both for the ultimate redemption of Israel.

Many Jews today believe that their long-awaited Messiah will come on or before the Hebrew year of 6000. They begin the count from the creation of the world. In Jewish thought, the world will exist for six thousand years and then the seventh millennium will come. The seventh millennium will usher in the Sabbath (Davidson, "What is the significance of the year 6000 in the Jewish calendar?" chabad.org).

—*Robin Fitzgerald.*

# Guiding the Superintendent

Actions have consequences. Just about anyone can tell a story or two about how he learned this lesson the hard way.

Our text for this week tells about how God laid out blessing for those who seek His face and consequences for those who turn away.

## DEVOTIONAL OUTLINE

**1. Blessings for Israel (II Chron. 7:12-16).** The completion of Solomon's temple and its dedication (chaps. 5—6) elicited a response from God. God told Solomon his prayer was heard, and the building would now become the "house of sacrifice" (7:12) to God.

God began with a warning about the future. There would be a direct relationship between Israel's obedience and their prosperity. Solomon and the nation were reminded that future disobedience would bring discipline in the form of natural disasters like drought, locusts, and plagues.

When times of calamity came, the nation was to seek God in prayer, humility, and repentance. A very vivid picture of repentance is drawn in II Chronicles 7:14 where Israel is encouraged to "seek [God's] face."

God promised to hear and forgive their sin. Like all good discipline, God would take these actions not because He hated Israel but because He loved the nation and wanted to bless her. As a result of Israel's repentance, God would heal the land: "Mine eyes and mine heart shall be there perpetually" (II Chron. 7:16). As stated previously, actions have consequences.

**2. Blessings for Solomon's family (II Chron. 7:17-18).** God also included some encouraging personal words for Solomon. God's promise to David was repeated to Solomon. If Solomon and his descendants would walk before God, God promised that the blessings of the future throne would be theirs.

**3. Warnings for Israel (II Chron. 7:19-22).** To get His people's attention, many times God turns up the heat. If Israel refused to heed His warnings through natural disasters, God would get their attention with more severe measures—destroying the temple and sending the nation into exile. All this would result in the nation becoming a source of ridicule.

People should never believe that access to God is obtained through cathedrals or some special status but as a result of a repentant heart. When people would ask why God had allowed this to happen to His temple and His nation, the question would be answered, simply, "Because they forsook the Lord God of their fathers" (II Chron. 7:22).

## AGE-GROUP EMPHASES

**Children:** The chronicler records that the Lord used a very unusual expression to describe repentance: "Seek my face" (II Chron. 7:14). Use this expression to help your children understand what it means to repent.

**Youths:** Many teens have a very active interest in the affairs of their nation. Ask them this discussion question: What do you think God might say to our nation if He were to appear today?

**Adults:** God has promises to bless those people who obey Him (Ps. 1; Matt. 6:33; Gal. 6:7-8). The promises of national restoration made in II Chronicles 7 have generated much discussion in recent years. How closely or extensively do the promises made to Israel apply to our country today?

—*Martin R. Dahlquist.*

# Scripture Lesson Text

**LUKE 24:1** Now upon the first *day* of the week, very early in the morning, they came unto the sepulchre, bringing the spices which they had prepared, and certain *others* with them.

**2 And they found the stone rolled away from the sepulchre.**

3 And they entered in, and found not the body of the Lord Je'sus.

**4 And it came to pass, as they were much perplexed thereabout, behold, two men stood by them in shining garments:**

5 And as they were afraid, and bowed down *their* faces to the earth, they said unto them, Why seek ye the living among the dead?

**6 He is not here, but is risen: remember how he spake unto you when he was yet in Gal'i-lee,**

7 Saying, The Son of man must be delivered into the hands of sinful men, and be crucified, and the third day rise again.

**8 And they remembered his words,**

9 And returned from the sepulchre, and told all these things unto the eleven, and to all the rest.

**10 It was Ma'ry Mag-da-le'ne, and Jo-an'na, and Ma'ry *the mother* of James, and other *women that* *were* with them, which told these things unto the apostles.**

11 And their words seemed to them as idle tales, and they believed them not.

**12 Then arose Pe'ter, and ran unto the sepulchre; and stooping down, he beheld the linen clothes laid by themselves, and departed, wondering in himself at that which was come to pass.**

30 And it came to pass, as he sat at meat with them, he took bread, and blessed *it*, and brake, and gave to them.

**31 And their eyes were opened, and they knew him; and he vanished out of their sight.**

32 And they said one to another, Did not our heart burn within us, while he talked with us by the way, and while he opened to us the scriptures?

**33 And they rose up the same hour, and returned to Je-ru'salem, and found the eleven gathered together, and them that were with them,**

34 Saying, The Lord is risen indeed, and hath appeared to Si'mon.

**35 And they told what things *were done* in the way, and how he was known of them in breaking of bread.**

---

**NOTES**

# He Has Risen

## (Easter)

### Lesson: Luke 24:1-12, 30-35

Read: Luke 24:1-35

TIME: A.D. 30                    PLACES: near Jerusalem; Jerusalem

---

**GOLDEN TEXT**—"The Lord is risen indeed, and hath appeared to Simon" (Luke 24:34).

---

## *Introduction*

In the December 13, 1993, issue of *Christianity Today,* Rodney Clapp wrote an article titled "Let the Pagans Have the Holiday" with a subtitle "First, let's take back Easter." In the article, the author outlined and lamented the commercialization of Christmas, which has only accelerated since he wrote the article.

His purpose, however, was not simply to lament the commercialization of Christmas. It was to show that Easter is really our most important holiday (or better, celebration). We rejoice in the incarnation of our Saviour, which we celebrate at Christmas. But without the resurrection, which we celebrate at Easter, we have no Saviour; we are yet in our sins.

With this lesson we begin a unit of study that focuses on the resurrection of Christ and the glory and honor He deserves because of it. While we still want to maintain a proper spiritual focus at Christmas, we need to give our greater attention to Easter. We cannot concede this holiday to commercialization.

## LESSON OUTLINE

I. THE WOMEN: VISITING THE TOMB—Luke 24:1-11

II. PETER: INVESTIGATING THE TOMB—Luke 24:12

III. THE DISCIPLES: MEETING THE RISEN SAVIOUR— Luke 24:30-35

## *Exposition: Verse by Verse*

**THE WOMEN: VISITING THE TOMB**

**LUKE 24:1** Now upon the first day of the week, very early in the morning, they came unto the sepulchre, bringing the spices which they had prepared, and certain others with them.

2 And they found the stone rolled away from the sepulchre.

3 And they entered in, and found not the body of the Lord Jesus.

4 And it came to pass, as they were much perplexed thereabout,

behold, two men stood by them in shining garments:

5 And as they were afraid, and bowed down their faces to the earth, they said unto them, Why seek ye the living among the dead?

6 He is not here, but is risen: remember how he spake unto you when he was yet in Galilee,

7 Saying, The Son of man must be delivered into the hands of sinful men, and be crucified, and the third day rise again.

8 And they remembered his words,

9 And returned from the sepulchre, and told all these things unto the eleven, and to all the rest.

10 It was Mary Magdalene, and Joanna, and Mary the mother of James, and other women that were with them, which told these things unto the apostles.

11 And their words seemed to them as idle tales, and they believed them not.

### Coming to the tomb (Luke 24:1-2).

Jesus had died, and Joseph of Arimathea, along with Nicodemus, had lovingly wrapped His body and put it in a tomb that Joseph owned (John 19:38-42). Some women who had come with Jesus from Galilee followed the two, making note of the sepulchre and observing how Jesus' body was laid in it (Luke 23:55). Women were some of the more devoted followers of Christ with some even coming to Christ's crucifixion (vs. 49).

These women then engaged in what they probably thought was their final act of devotion. They returned home to prepare spices and ointments to finish preparing the lifeless body of Jesus for burial. In keeping with their devotion to the Lord and His commandments, they rested on the Sabbath Day.

After the Sabbath, having prepared the spices and ointments beforehand, the women and others with them came to the tomb early the next morning (the first day of the week) with the intent of anointing Jesus' body. (Luke 24:1 is the first reference to the "first day of the week," which begins to show that the worship day for New Testament believers changed [cf. John 20:19, 26; I Cor. 16:2].)

Mark 16:3 adds that on the way to the tomb the women wondered who would roll the stone away from the entrance so that they could anoint the body of Jesus. They asked that question because of two things they knew: the stone was large, and they would not be able to move it. When the women reached the tomb, they found to their surprise that the stone had already been moved away from the tomb entrance.

### Entering the tomb (Luke 24:3-4).

Still intending to anoint Jesus' body, the women entered the tomb. To their greater surprise, they did not see the body of the Lord Jesus! Earlier the women had seen the tomb and observed the place where Joseph had laid the body. So they knew they were looking in the right place. However, because they did not see the body of Jesus, they were "much perplexed" about what had happened.

They did not find the body of Jesus, their Saviour, but they saw two other men who are described as being clothed in dazzling robes. Matthew and Mark mention only one angel, but this is not a contradiction. Perhaps Matthew and Mark chose to write only of the one who spoke to the women. Mark 16:5 says the man had a long white robe and was at the right side of the tomb.

### Meeting the angels (Luke 24:5). The

women quickly recognized that these two men were angels. The sight of them moved the women from perplexity and surprise to fear and prostration. The angels spoke to the women with the first reference to Christ's resurrection: "Why seek ye the living among the dead?"

The women may not at that point have known exactly what happened, but they now knew that Jesus was alive. They had no use, then, for the spices and ointments they had brought to anoint His body.

**Hearing the message (Luke 24:6-7).** The angels spoke to the women with words that are etched into our memory: "He is not here, but is risen." Then the angels gently chided them with the reminder that Jesus had told them He "must be delivered into the hands of sinful men, and be crucified, and the third day rise again." The women should have remembered what Jesus had said and not have been surprised or afraid of what they found at the empty tomb.

**Remembering Christ's words (Luke 24:8).** Once the angels reminded them of Jesus' words, the women remembered what He had said. They had heard Him tell of His death and resurrection, but apparently in their grief and fear, they had forgotten His words until the angels spoke to them.

Jesus had also told the same thing to the disciples on more than one occasion, but "they understood none of these things: and this saying was hid from them, neither knew they the things which were spoken" (Luke 18:34). In fact, on one occasion Peter took Jesus aside "and began to rebuke him, saying, Be it far from thee, Lord: this shall not be unto thee" (Matt. 16:22). So the women were not alone in their forgetfulness.

After hearing the message from the angels and being reminded of Christ's words, the women went to the eleven disciples and other followers with the good news.

**Reporting to the disciples (Luke 24:9-11).** When the women found the disciples, they described what they had experienced. Verse 10 specifically names Mary Magdalene, Joanna, and Mary the mother of James. Mark 16:1 has Salome in place of Joanna. The several women, who were more than enough in number for a valid testimony (cf. Deut. 17:6), brought a firsthand account, but the apostles still refused to believe Jesus was alive. Luke 24:11 records that the women's words were like "idle tales," or nonsense, to the men.

## PETER: INVESTIGATING THE TOMB

**12 Then arose Peter, and ran unto the sepulchre; and stooping down, he beheld the linen clothes laid by themselves, and departed, wondering in himself at that which was come to pass.**

While the apostles generally did not believe the report of the women, Peter had enough interest that he decided to investigate the matter further. He ran to the tomb, stooped down, and looked inside. John 20:3-6 adds that John also ran to the tomb, with John arriving first but not entering. Peter arrived second and went inside. What he saw there eventually helped to convince him that Jesus was indeed alive.

Peter "beheld the linen clothes laid by themselves" (Luke 24:12). John 20:7 adds that he saw "the napkin, that was about his head, not lying with the linen clothes, but wrapped together in a place by itself." The picture that this description gives us is that even though the body of Jesus was gone, the linen clothes retained the shape of the body while the napkin over His face was laid aside. If someone had stolen the body of the Lord, the clothes would have either been missing entirely or hurriedly piled in a heap. Tomb robbers would not have taken the time to lay the clothes neatly in place.

Did Peter realize that Jesus had come back to life and had literally passed through the graveclothes? Whatever he thought right then, the experience led to unshakable faith.

## THE DISCIPLES: MEETING THE RISEN SAVIOUR

**30** And it came to pass, as he sat at meat with them, he took bread, and blessed it, and brake, and gave to them.

**31** And their eyes were opened, and they knew him; and he vanished out of their sight.

**32** And they said one to another, Did not our heart burn within us, while he talked with us by the way, and while he opened to us the scriptures?

**33** And they rose up the same hour, and returned to Jerusalem, and found the eleven gathered together, and them that were with them,

**34** Saying, The Lord is risen indeed, and hath appeared to Simon.

**35** And they told what things were done in the way, and how he was known of them in breaking of bread.

**Eating with Jesus (Luke 24:30-31).** In Luke 24:13-29, we find the record of two of Jesus' disciples (one named Cleopas and the other unnamed) walking from Jerusalem to Emmaus, a trip of about seven miles. As they walked along, the risen Christ met them, but the two disciples did not recognize Him. As they came near Emmaus, they invited Him to stay with them for a meal. At the meal Jesus "took bread, and blessed it, and brake, and gave to them" (vs. 30).

This action was similar to what Jesus had done in feeding the five thousand (Luke 9:10-17) and the four thousand (Mark 8:1-9) and in His institution of the Lord's Supper (Luke 22:14-23). We see in Luke 24:35 that this action played a role in both disciples' recognition of Jesus, for as soon as He gave them the bread, they understood who He was. Bringing about this recognition apparently completed Jesus' purpose with those disciples, so He vanished from their sight.

We should note that in His glorified body, Jesus could pass through grave-clothes, appear and disappear (as He did in this text), and even pass through solid objects (cf. John 20:19, 26). We are not told that Jesus ate food with the disciples in Emmaus, but He later did so in the presence of the Eleven (Luke 24:42-43), showing that He had a real body and was not a phantom or ghost.

**Returning to Jerusalem (Luke 24:32-33).** After the Lord Jesus disappeared from their sight, the Emmaus disciples recounted their experience on the road with Him. "Did not our heart burn within us, while he talked with us by the way, and while he opened to us the scriptures?" they asked. Looking back, they now understood why Jesus' message made such a powerful impact on them. They knew that Jesus had risen from the dead.

**Announcing the risen Saviour (Luke 24:34-35).** The Emmaus disciples immediately left for Jerusalem to meet with the eleven apostles and the other believers assembled there. When they arrived, they were greeted with the exclamation "The Lord is risen indeed." The two then related their experience in Emmaus and joyfully added their testimony to the resurrection of Jesus.

The Emmaus disciples were informed that Jesus had already appeared to Simon Peter (cf. I Cor. 15:5). This sequence of events seems to show that in His glorified body Jesus could travel immediately from place to place, for in this situation Jesus went back to Jerusalem ahead of the Emmaus disciples and met with Peter even before the disciples arrived from Emmaus. By the time they reached Jerusalem, the apostles were already aware of the resurrection and invited the two to share in the wonder of it all.

Luke 24:35 confirms the statement that Jesus' breaking of bread with the two disciples in Emmaus played a role in their recognition of Him.

We have found several indications in

our study of Luke 24 that Jesus rose bodily from the dead. The two angels told the women He was living (vss. 5-6), the linen graveclothes were still intact (vs. 12), Jesus appeared to two disciples (vss. 30-32), and Jesus had appeared to Simon Peter (vs. 34). These eyewitness accounts provide clear evidence of Christ's resurrection.

Luke 24 validates the truth of the bodily resurrection of Christ. It is also important in this Easter lesson to see the resurrection in its theological context.

• The resurrection of Christ was prophesied and foreshadowed in the Old Testament (Ps. 16:10; Isa. 53:10; Jonah 1:17—2:10; Matt. 12:40).

• Christ foretold His resurrection (Mark 8:31; Luke 9:22; John 2:18-22).

• The resurrection of Christ was the subject of the apostolic preaching (Acts 2:22-36).

• New Testament writers attested to Christ's resurrection (Rom. 1:4; 6:9; Phil. 3:10-11; I Pet. 1:3; 3:21).

• The resurrection of Christ is an indispensable part of God's salvation plan (Rom. 4:25; I Cor. 15:1-4).

• Belief in Christ's resurrection is essential for salvation (Rom. 10:9-10).

• Without Christ's resurrection, we have no salvation and no hope (I Cor. 15:17-18).

• Jesus' resurrection is the basis of our future hope (I Thess. 4:13-14).

• The resurrection is the motive for steadfast service for Him (I Cor. 15:58).

• The resurrection of Christ is the source for Christian morality (I Cor. 15:32-34).

• The resurrection of Christ is the basis for our Christian experience (Phil. 3:10).

• The resurrection of Christ is the measure of His power at work in our lives (Eph. 1:19-20).

During this Easter season, we need to take time to reflect on the importance of Christ's resurrection. It is the distinguishing mark of the Christian faith. No other religion has a founder who died and came back to life.

Let us meditate on the significance of Christ's resurrection by remembering these words from the chorus of Robert Lowry's well-known Easter hymn "Christ Arose":

Up from the grave He arose;
With a mighty triumph o'er his foes;
He arose a Victor from the dark domain,
And He lives forever with His saints to reign.
He arose! He arose! Hallelujah! Christ arose!
—Don Anderson.

# QUESTIONS

1. Why did the women come to the tomb?

2. Why were the women perplexed when they came to the tomb?

3. How did the angels initially make known the resurrection of Christ?

4. What did the angels remind the women about?

5. How did the apostles at first react to the report of the women?

6. What was significant about the arrangement of the graveclothes in the tomb?

7. What did Jesus do that brought recognition to the disciples in Emmaus?

8. What do we learn about the resurrected body of Christ from this passage?

9. How did the apostles react to the arrival of the disciples from Emmaus?

10. What part does the resurrection play in our salvation and Christian life?

—Don Anderson.

# Preparing to Teach the Lesson

Today we begin a new unit on "All Glory and Honor," which centers on the Lord Jesus and His postresurrection ministry. The unit includes two lessons on future events in which the Lord Jesus plays the leading role. Be sure to teach your students that these prophesied future events will take place as surely as have the past events of the Lord Jesus' earthly ministry. What He did in the past assures us that He is God come in the flesh. He will just as surely return to earth and complete the plan of God.

The best preparation for this lesson is to read the lesson text several times. Be sure you understand the story completely. You might also read it aloud to someone else. Memorizing portions of it would be splendid. The Word of God memorized is a great tool to be used by the Holy Spirit in helping you defeat Satan and endure difficult situations you may encounter.

## TODAY'S AIM

**Facts:** to understand the reality of the postresurrection events of biblical history.

**Principle:** to understand that the resurrection of Christ is crucial to the transformation of people.

**Application:** to give assurance that Jesus Christ physically rose from the dead and to make this truth central in our message to unbelievers.

## INTRODUCING THE LESSON

Most people, even non-Christians, have heard the story of the resurrection of the Lord Jesus. Many of them are exposed to the story every year at this season. However, many of them also think the story is not true, is only a myth told to make a spiritual point, or is a fanciful story added to the Bible later

to try to support the authority of the message of Christianity. The best way to combat these erroneous ideas is simply to present the truth of Scripture and let the Holy Spirit bring conviction and faith to people's hearts.

## DEVELOPING THE LESSON

**1. The women report the resurrection (Luke 24:1-10).** It is obvious but necessary to observe that the women went to the tomb of the Lord Jesus prepared to anoint His dead body with spices. They had no idea that He had risen from the dead, even though He had predicted it openly. They did not see what they expected to see, as some of the detractors of Scripture claim. Our text does not say how they expected to roll away the stone in order to get to Jesus' body, but when they arrived they found the stone already moved away from the entrance to the tomb.

The women entered the tomb. They did not find Jesus' body but did see two men in shining garments. Luke does not tell us here these men were angels, but later in the passage they are so identified (24:23). Matthew 28:2-7 also makes it clear they were angels. The women were naturally frightened by their appearance.

The two angels reminded the women of what the Lord Jesus had said as proof of their claim that He was not there but had risen. When the women soon after told the apostles about their experience, the apostles did not believe them. The apostles, like everyone else, knew the Lord Jesus had been crucified. They knew the facts of the Lord Jesus' burial by Joseph of Arimathea.

It is true that the majority of the world's population does not believe that the Lord Jesus rose from the dead.

However, there is no other plausible explanation for the boldness of faith of His followers from that day forward.

**2. Peter verifies their report (Luke 24:11-12).** Peter may not have really believed the women, either. Scripture says he was "wondering in himself at that which was come to pass." Even after Peter saw the empty tomb and the cloth in which the Lord Jesus' body had been wrapped, he still could not quite take it all in. We know that later Peter totally believed in the resurrection and preached it openly and boldly.

It is probably true that some of the staunchest believers were the hardest to convince of the truths of God's Word in the first place. If you are in this category, please do not waste a lot of time and effort in holding on to your non-belief. God tells the truth and never lies. You can safely trust that the Lord Jesus rose from the dead. God's entire plan for the redemption of humanity rests upon this fact.

**3. The Lord Jesus appears (Luke 24:30-35).** Paul wrote, "After that, he was seen of above five hundred brethren at once; of whom the greater part remain unto this present, but some are fallen asleep" (I Cor. 15:6). There were enough postresurrection appearances of the Lord Jesus to make it very plain to an unbiased person that Jesus did in fact rise from the dead. The two disciples who saw Him on the road to Emmaus recognized the Lord Jesus as He broke the bread at their table.

We can often recognize people, even at a distance, by their body movements, their habits of action, or their speech patterns. What a wonderful thing it is to be so familiar with the Lord Jesus as to thus recognize Him! The challenge of our lives is to be so familiar with the Lord and His Word that we recognize Him at work in our lives. We can then also recognize that which is false, should it appear.

## ILLUSTRATING THE LESSON

The empty tomb is a powerful proof of the resurrection.

PRAISE GOD

CHRIST IS RISEN
THE TOMB IS EMPTY

## CONCLUDING THE LESSON

We will never have the same experience all these people had at the time of the resurrection. We did not see the Lord Jesus in His earthly ministry, His death, or His resurrection. We can only see these through the eyes of faith by believing the record of those who did see Him physically.

Over the years since that wonderful event, millions of people have trusted in Him. The record of the transformations of the lives of those who came to faith in the resurrected Lord would fill many books. God personally knows each one of them and treasures them as His own children. The power of the resurrection is seen in changed lives, healing of broken hearts, and the restoration of love in families and individuals worldwide.

## ANTICIPATING THE NEXT LESSON

Our next lesson comes from the first fourteen verses in John 21 and recounts a very significant postresurrection appearance of the Lord Jesus to His disciples.

—*Brian D. Doud.*

# PRACTICAL POINTS

1. When Jesus is our priority, we will not procrastinate or be slothful (Luke 24:1).
2. When things do not go as planned, trust God's plan (vss. 2-3).
3. Jesus brings clarity to replace confusion (vss. 4-6).
4. When we believe in Jesus, we can be confident that He will do what He promised (vss. 7-8).
5. We must have the confidence to share the good news about Jesus, even when others do not believe (vss. 9-12).
6. Time spent with Jesus is a blessing (vss. 30-35).

*—Valante M. Grant.*

# RESEARCH AND DISCUSSION

1. How does listening to Jesus prepare you for unexpected situations in life?
2. What should your response be when you realize that you are dealing with a message from the Lord?
3. What kind of fear is appropriate in Jesus' presence?
4. If you trust in Jesus, how will you respond to things that seem impossible?
5. Why is it important to still trust in Jesus, even when you do not understand what is going on?
6. What is the significance of Christ's resurrection to the Christian lifestyle?
7. What is the responsibility of the believer when it comes to spreading the gospel of Christ?

*—Valante M. Grant.*

# ILLUSTRATED HIGH POINTS

### He is not here

The following words appear on a tombstone in Nantucket, Massachusetts:

> Under the sod and under the trees
> Lies the body of Jonathan Pease:
> He is not here, there's only the pod
> Pease shelled out and went to God.

We are amused and can say two things regarding Pease's theology of the resurrection. First, it does not apply to Jesus since His resurrection from the tomb involved His body. Second, because of Christ's resurrection, Pease and all others who have trusted Christ as Saviour will be raised in the future, and even the "pods" will ultimately spend eternity in glory.

### And they remembered his words

Flavius Josephus was a Jewish priest who lived in the first century. He wrote *The Wars of the Jews,* a history of the Jewish revolt of A.D. 66 and a history titled *The Antiquities of the Jews.* In the latter, he mentioned Christ, called Him the Messiah, and referred to His crucifixion and resurrection (18.3.3).

This reference to Jesus is extremely controversial and has been studied and debated by many scholars. Some accept it as authentic; others call it a fraud.

In the end it matters not. We accept the resurrection of Christ, not because of Josephus, but simply because the Bible says so.

### And their eyes were opened

As soon as they recognized Jesus during the breaking of the bread, He vanished. And He kept doing that for the next forty days to teach the early believers that they needed to walk by faith and not by sight since He would no longer be physically present (cf. II Cor. 5:7).

*—David A. Hamburg.*

# Golden Text Illuminated

**"The Lord is risen indeed, and hath appeared to Simon" (Luke 24:34).**

Our golden text this week is a ringing summary statement, part of which has become a common Easter response among Christians worldwide. Although almost no one speaks the "hath appeared to Simon" portion these days, the words "the Lord is risen indeed" are heard from many lips. The challenge is retaining our sense of wonder and excitement.

The leadup to this joyful proclamation started earlier in the day when two downcast disciples, only one of whom is named, unknowingly met the resurrected Jesus, who joined them on their walk to the village of Emmaus (Luke 24:13-18). They unburdened themselves of their disappointment and sorrow and then were amazed at the inspired exposition of Scripture they heard on their way. But it was not until the enigmatic stranger broke bread at their destination and then abruptly vanished that they recognized who had stirred their hearts so profoundly (vss. 30-32).

Not wanting to keep this revelation to themselves for even one day, the two disciples rushed back to Jerusalem to inform the Eleven, who were gathered along with other followers of Jesus. As fast as they might have traveled, however, they did not come with breaking news, for it was those in the room who responded without hesitation, "The Lord is risen indeed." For the Emmaus disciples, it was confirmation, not the heralding of unheard tidings.

Those gathered in the room added in the same breath the detail "and hath appeared to Simon." This was important to them, for as yet the risen Lord had not yet been seen by any of the other apostles. They had heard the reports of the women and had been inclined to discount these (as had the two from Emmaus). But they could not so easily dismiss Simon Peter's testimony; the Lord's early appearance to Peter was foundational in overcoming their doubts and in proclaiming the risen Christ to the world (cf. I Cor. 15:5).

It is interesting that aside from the statement in our golden text, this initial appearance to Peter is not described in any of the Gospels. Many things that Jesus said and did are not recorded for us (cf. John 21:25), but what we are told is sufficient and reliable to build our faith on. The fact that Jesus would appear first to the disciple who had denied Him demonstrates His forgiving and loving approach to His own.

The Emmaus disciples were not denied the opportunity to relate their own experience with the risen Lord, and they did so with what must have been the greatest eagerness and alacrity (Luke 24:35). It was as they were finishing their report that the Lord Himself suddenly appeared among them all, greeting them with a word of peace (vs. 36).

We may wonder why He did not show Himself to all the disciples immediately after leaving the tomb, thus putting away all doubt at the outset. But the experience of hearing and relaying testimony must have been important. And even the personal appearance among them did not erase all doubts at first.

The appearance of the risen Christ is foundational to our faith, but He wants us to rely on the sure word of testimony that He has given us.

—*Kenneth A. Sponsler.*

# Heart of the Lesson

Moments after I learned that my boyfriend had died unexpectedly, I called my mom. When I told her the news, she said, "Oh, Ann, not Tony!" and began to cry. That started my tears. Romances were not supposed to end this way. Whatever happened to "happily ever after" and our plans?

Jesus' followers felt deep grief at His death.

**1. The women find the empty tomb (Luke 24:1-8).** The women who followed Jesus knew where to find His body. They had followed Joseph of Arimathea when he took Jesus' body to the tomb (23:55). Now the Sabbath was over, and they returned to the tomb early Sunday morning, bringing spices to mask the odor of the body's decay. Likely their main concern, other than their grief, was how they were going to roll away the huge stone that sealed the tomb (cf. Mark 16:3).

But the stone was already gone. So they peeked inside the tomb. There was no body. It was missing. What? While they were puzzling over the situation, two men in shining white garments (angels; cf. Luke 24:23) appeared. Terrified, the women bowed low. The men asked them a strange question: Why were they looking for the living among the dead? The living? They had just seen Jesus die and His body buried.

The men clarified their question. Jesus, the One the women were seeking, was not here. He was risen. Did they not remember Jesus saying He would be crucified and then rise again on the third day? Slowly, His words came back to them.

**2. The women report the empty tomb (Luke 24:9-12).** The women abandoned their project and rushed back to the place where Jesus' followers were gathered in Jerusalem. The women excitedly poured out their story, but no one believed them.

Jesus' disciple Peter, however, slipped out to go see for himself. He found the stone rolled away as the women had said, looked inside the tomb, and saw the linen graveclothes lying in place. But there was no body. Peter returned home, wondering what had taken place.

**3. Two disciples encounter the risen Jesus (Luke 24:30-32).** Later that day, as two followers of Jesus were walking the seven miles from Jerusalem to Emmaus, a stranger joined them. They discussed what was on everyone's mind in Jerusalem: Jesus' death. Evening was drawing near; so the two invited the stranger to stay for the night.

As they dined together, the stranger picked up a loaf of bread and asked a blessing over it. Then He broke the bread and gave pieces to those with Him. The act was reminiscent of Jesus breaking bread at the Last Supper with His disciples. Suddenly, their eyes were opened. They knew who this stranger was—Jesus! Immediately, Jesus vanished.

The two reflected on how their hearts had burned within them as they listened to the stranger talk during their walk. They had felt something supernatural. Now they knew why. Jesus had been their Teacher.

**4. The disciples trade resurrection stories (Luke 24:33-35).** The two could not wait to tell the other disciples whom they had seen. They walked back to Jerusalem that night. But before they could tell their story, the other disciples were already sharing *their* good news. Jesus had appeared to the disciple Peter.

—Ann Staatz.

# World Missions

One common principle in marketing is that a potential customer needs to see or hear about a product seven times before he will buy.

Interestingly, that is the same number of times the average Muslim needs to encounter the gospel message before accepting Christ.

Seven is the number of completion in the Bible, and the principle of seven can help us when evangelizing the lost.

Let us consider the principle in light of the message of the resurrection. Jesus had told His disciples before His death that He would rise again. For the women, a reminder of that from angels, plus an empty tomb, was all they needed to believe. These are the success stories in missions—those who receive the message with joy and cannot wait to go tell others.

Jesus' other followers, however, were skeptical, and some were even resistant. How many times did it take for them to fully believe?

1. Jesus prophesied His resurrection before death (Luke 18:31-34).

2. The angels told the women, and they believed (24:4-6).

3. The women told the disciples, who thought it sounded like "idle tales" (vs. 11).

4. Peter left the empty tomb and wondered (vs. 12).

5. Jesus met two of His followers on the road to Emmaus and explained the Scriptures (vss. 13-27). Their eyes were opened, and they believed.

6. They told the others (vss. 33-35).

7. Jesus Himself appeared. They still had trouble believing until He ate with them (vss. 37-43).

8. Thomas, not there at the time, did not believe until Jesus appeared personally to him (John 20:19-29).

As much as we would like to see people believe the very first time they encounter the gospel message, we should expect most to need to hear it more than once, and some will need seven times or more.

This should not discourage us—quite the opposite! If we share and are resisted or our message rejected, we can consider that we may be the second or fourth out of their seven. They are one step closer to receiving salvation! Proclaiming the gospel is never wasted. God promises that His Word does not go forth void (Isa. 55:11). No matter the initial response, the Holy Spirit can nurture the truth in a person's heart over time.

Contemplate another thing. The message that resonated most was when the disciples were able to say, "We have seen the Lord" (John 20:25). God reveals Himself through creation (Rom. 1:20) and individually in people's lives. When we see God work, let us broadcast it to those around us. When we see Him in nature around us, let us show others. One example would be the Fibonacci spiral. I had never heard of it until months ago, but now that I have studied it, I see it everywhere—in plants, human anatomy, weather patterns, flowers, music, thumbprints, and more. I am in awe of the God who made such creativity within such precise order. When I see something that fits the Fibonacci spiral, I can point it out. When people ask what it is, I can use it to lead to a discussion of its Creator.

We can all mention when we "see" the Lord, and perhaps that small reference will be one of the seven times a person needs to accept Christ.

He is risen. We have seen Him. Now let us go and tell the others!

—*Kimberly Rae.*

# The Jewish Aspect

On April 14, 2014, a headline on Foxnews.com read, "Israel Prepares for Passover in the Shadow of Peace Talks." Passover remains one of the most important of the Jewish holidays. Immediately following Passover, the "counting of the omer" begins with the firstfruits offering, marking fifty days until Pentecost (Lev. 23:15-22).

When the temple was in existence, Israel was primarily an agricultural society. During this period, on the morning after the Sabbath following Passover, the first crop of the land's barley harvest was brought to the temple as an offering.

The high priest would go to the Mount of Olives. There the firstfruits of the land would be harvested and then carried to the temple. At the temple, the barley would be roasted over an open flame and winnowed to remove the unwanted chaff. Next, it would go through a conversion process of thirteen sieves to change the barley into fine flour (Oakley, *Messiah and the Feasts of the Lord,* Colorado Theological Seminary).

Today Jews begin to count the omer on the second day of Passover. They begin on this date because the rabbis believe that the first festival day of Passover is a Sabbath regardless of the day of the week on which it falls.

However, a controversy existed between the rabbis and various Jewish sects over the interpretation of "the day after the Sabbath." Some sects, including the first-century Sadducees interpreted this phrase to mean the first actual Sabbath after the beginning of Passover. In this interpretation, the omer celebration would have taken place on a Sunday (Strassfeld, *The Jewish Holidays,* William Morrow).

This holiday is also known as the Festival of Firstfruits. This week's lesson tells the story of Jesus' resurrection. Many believe that His resurrection took place on the day that the firstfruit offering was brought to the temple.

The counting of the omer connects two important holidays, Passover and Pentecost. Jews "count the omer" in anticipation and preparation for the holiday of *Shavuot,* or Pentecost.

Pentecost is a very important holiday for the Jewish people. It is known as a *second* firstfruits. While the omer offering marked the harvesting of the barley harvest, Pentecost marked the harvest of the wheat crop. Two loaves of the new meal from the wheat crop were baked. The two loaves were then waved by the priests at the temple during a special ceremony. This celebration commemorated the second harvest.

Tradition holds that after the children of Israel arrived at Mount Sinai and met God, the Torah (law) was given on Pentecost. Thus, Pentecost celebrates the giving of the law, as well as the sealing of the covenant and the experience of meeting the Divine as the voice of God was heard (Strassfeld).

Jesus was crucified during Passover. When He rose from the dead on Sunday, it is quite possible that this was the day the firstfruits offering was presented to the Lord.

We know that Jesus, the first firstfruits conquered death, hell, and the grave with His death and resurrection. His victory ushered in the beginning of a harvest of believers. Seven weeks after Jesus' resurrection, on Pentecost, the second firstfruits occurred as the Holy Spirit fell on believers (Acts 2).

—*Robin Fitzgerald.*

# Guiding the Superintendent

Biblical Christianity is based squarely on history. The Apostle Paul believed that the resurrection of Jesus Christ was so important to his faith that he taught that if the resurrection did not happen, Christian faith is little more than a cruel joke (I Cor. 15:12-19).

The Easter lesson for this year explores several key facts that indicate that Jesus Christ has risen indeed.

## DEVOTIONAL OUTLINE

**1. Empty tomb—missing body (Luke 24:1-3).** Early on Sunday morning, following the crucifixion and burial of Jesus, several women from the group came to Jesus' tomb with the purpose of anointing His body. To their complete surprise, they found that the stone was rolled away and the tomb was empty.

Over the centuries, skeptics have labored to explain why no body was found in the tomb. However, there can only be one explanation—Jesus Christ rose bodily from the grave.

**2. Perplexity of the women (Luke 24:4).** The women could not entertain the thought that Jesus had risen from the grave. Their first reaction was shock. They obviously were not expecting a resurrection.

**3. Proclamation of the angels (Luke 24:5-8).** Instead of finding a lifeless body, the women were greeted by two angels who said, "He is not here, but is risen." The strangers reminded the women of Jesus' prophecy about His resurrection.

**4. Disbelief of the disciples (Luke 24:9-12).** The skeptical disciples were the last to believe. Even after hearing the testimony of the women, the disciples did not believe. The women's words seemed like nonsense to them. Peter ran to the tomb but left wondering at what he saw. Truly, the disciples were not expecting to see Jesus alive again.

**5. Appearance of Jesus Christ (Luke 24:30-35).** It was not until Christ physically appeared to the disciples that they were finally convinced of the fact of His resurrection. Only after Jesus took the role of table host with two disciples as they travelled with Him to Emmaus that these followers realized that He had risen from the grave.

These new witnesses hurried to tell the Eleven, who reported that "the Lord [had] risen indeed" (Luke 24:34). The final proof seems to be that Jesus Christ appeared to the one person who had denied Him so strongly—Peter.

The facts are irrefutable. Christian faith is based on real history. Jesus Christ actually rose from the grave and is alive today. The empty tomb proves it. Those who were present on the day of his resurrection were very reluctant to accept that He had risen perhaps because, as Luke states, it seemed too good to be true. The facts gradually convinced them. Jesus was risen indeed!

## AGE-GROUP EMPHASES

**Children:** During Easter services around the world, many worship leaders will shout, "Christ is risen!" To which the people are to respond, "He is risen indeed!" This lesson would be a good time to introduce the children to this great proclamation of their faith.

**Youths:** By their nature, teens tend to be skeptical. The facts are clear; they point to the truth that Jesus did physically rise from the grave.

**Adults:** Use this lesson to help reassure your adults about the historical basis for their faith.

—*Martin R. Dahlquist.*

# Scripture Lesson Text

**JOHN 21:1** After these things Je'sus shewed himself again to the disciples at the sea of Ti-be'ri-as; and on this wise shewed he *himself*.

**2 There were together Si'mon Pe'ter, and Thom'as called Did'y-mus, and Na-than'a-el of Ca'na in Gal'i-lee, and the *sons* of Zeb'e-dee, and two other of his disciples.**

3 Si'mon Pe'ter saith unto them, I go a fishing. They say unto him, We also go with thee. They went forth, and entered into a ship immediately; and that night they caught nothing.

**4 But when the morning was now come, Je'sus stood on the shore: but the disciples knew not that it was Je'sus.**

5 Then Je'sus saith unto them, Children, have ye any meat? They answered him, No.

**6 And he said unto them, Cast the net on the right side of the ship, and ye shall find. They cast therefore, and now they were not able to draw it for the multitude of fishes.**

7 Therefore that disciple whom Je'sus loved saith unto Pe'ter, It is the Lord. Now when Si'mon Pe'ter heard that it was the Lord, he girt *his* fisher's coat *unto him*, (for he was naked,) and did cast himself into the sea.

**8 And the other disciples came in a little ship; (for they were not far from land, but as it were two hundred cubits,) dragging the net with fishes.**

9 As soon then as they were come to land, they saw a fire of coals there, and fish laid thereon, and bread.

**10 Je'sus saith unto them, Bring of the fish which ye have now caught.**

11 Si'mon Pe'ter went up, and drew the net to land full of great fishes, an hundred and fifty and three: and for all there were so many, yet was not the net broken.

**12 Je'sus saith unto them, Come *and* dine. And none of the disciples durst ask him, Who art thou? knowing that it was the Lord.**

13 Je'sus then cometh, and taketh bread, and giveth them, and fish likewise.

**14 This is now the third time that Je'sus shewed himself to his disciples, after that he was risen from the dead.**

## NOTES

74

# Appearance of the Risen Lord

## Lesson: John 21:1-14

### Read: John 21:1-14

TIME: A.D. 30                    PLACE: Sea of Tiberias

---

**GOLDEN TEXT**—"Jesus saith unto them, Come and dine. And none of the disciples durst ask him, Who art thou? knowing that it was the Lord" (John 21:12).

---

# *Introduction*

All of us have had the experience of receiving encouragement and reassurance from the Lord when we have faced discouragement and difficulty. Perhaps He used a Bible verse, a song, or a friend to bring that reassurance to us.

John 21 is a chapter of reassurance. The Lord Jesus had been crucified, dashing the hopes of His followers that He would bring in His kingdom immediately. He had risen from the dead, and the disciples had seen Him, but they still had trouble comprehending everything that had happened.

In this tumultuous time, we find the account of Jesus' appearance to several of His disciples as they returned to fishing. Why did the Lord appear at this time and in this setting? One of the reasons was to reassure His followers. He wanted them to know that He was surely alive, that He had a purpose for them, and that they could carry out His commission to them only in His power. He was preparing them for what He knew was ahead for them.

## LESSON OUTLINE

I. **GATHERING AFTER CHRIST'S RESURRECTION**—John 21:1-3*a*

II. **FISHING ON THE SEA**— John 21:3*b*-8

III. **MEETING JESUS ON THE SHORE**—John 21:9-14

# *Exposition: Verse by Verse*

### GATHERING AFTER CHRIST'S RESURRECTION

**JOHN 21:1** After these things Jesus shewed himself again to the disciples at the sea of Tiberias; and on this wise shewed he himself.

**2** There were together Simon Peter, and Thomas called Didymus, and Nathanael of Cana in Galilee, and the sons of Zebedee, and two other of his disciples.

**3***a* Simon Peter saith unto them, I go a fishing. They say unto him, We also go with thee.

**The disciples present (John 21:1-2).** John's Gospel records two prior instances in which the Lord had appeared to His disciples after the resurrection (to ten disciples in 20:19-23 and to the eleven disciples in verses 26-29). Now He appeared to seven of them on the shore of the Sea of Tiberias, which was another name for the Sea of Galilee (6:1). This alternate name came into use because of the town of Tiberias on the west shore of the lake.

Seven disciples were present at that time—Simon Peter, Thomas called Didymus, Nathanael of Cana in Galilee, the two sons of Zebedee (James and John), and two other unnamed disciples. This subset of the disciples poses some interesting questions and observations.

First, why were the other four not present? We are not told the reason for their absence, but it is natural to surmise that in a fishing setting, these seven were the fishermen of the group. (We know from Luke 5:1-11 that Peter, James, and John, at least, were fishermen.)

Second, why is Peter named first? Most likely, his name heads the list because he was the acknowledged leader of the group. The Lord seemed to give special attention to Peter in view of his denial of Christ and the important role he would play in the church.

Third, we note the presence of Thomas, who earlier had refused to believe Jesus was alive (John 20:24-29). This appearance of the risen Christ must have been another confirmation for him. (The words "Thomas" and "Didymus" mean "twin," apparently indicating he had a twin sibling.)

**The disciples' decision (John 21:3a).** As the seven men talked among themselves, Peter said, "I go a fishing." Why did Peter want to return to his life as a fisherman? He may have thought that the plan of Christ as he saw it had ended, so he should move on in life.

Furthermore, he may have felt such remorse over his denial of Christ that he could not see how the Lord would ever use him again. So he did the only thing he knew how to do—fishing.

On a practical level, Peter had a family, so he needed a way to support them. The other six men must have felt the same way and followed Peter's lead in returning to their previous occupation.

## FISHING ON THE SEA

**3b** They went forth, and entered into a ship immediately; and that night they caught nothing.

**4** But when the morning was now come, Jesus stood on the shore: but the disciples knew not that it was Jesus.

**5** Then Jesus saith unto them, Children, have ye any meat? They answered him, No.

**6** And he said unto them, Cast the net on the right side of the ship, and ye shall find. They cast therefore, and now they were not able to draw it for the multitude of fishes.

**7** Therefore that disciple whom Jesus loved saith unto Peter, It is the Lord. Now when Simon Peter heard that it was the Lord, he girt his fisher's coat unto him, (for he was naked,) and did cast himself into the sea.

**8** And the other disciples came in a little ship; (for they were not far from land, but as it were two hundred cubits,) dragging the net with fishes.

**A fruitless night (John 21:3b).** The men did not waste any time, for they immediately got into a boat and started fishing. What is intriguing is that veteran fishermen spent the whole night fishing and caught nothing! Interestingly, Peter, James, and John had experienced the same situation earlier when the Lord called them to follow Him (Luke 5:1-11). Did they remember that earlier occasion?

**Jesus' question (John 21:4-5).** When the morning began to dawn over the sea, Jesus came and stood on the shore. Apparently, the disciples could see a figure standing on the shore, but they could not identify him. This is not surprising considering their distance from the shore and the dim morning light. But it could also be that the Lord kept His disciples from recognizing Him, as He had done before (Luke 24:15-16; John 20:14).

Jesus called to the men with a question: "Children, have ye any meat?" (John 21:5). In other words, had they caught any fish? They had to admit, perhaps in embarrassment, that they had caught nothing. (This may been especially difficult to concede since nighttime appears to have been a prime time for fishing [cf. Luke 5:5].)

The Lord knew they had not caught any fish; it seems He posed this question to point out their inability to accomplish anything on their own. He showed them that, even though they had years of experience in fishing, their own abilities were still not enough. Christ may have especially wanted to help Peter trust Him for the work He planned for him.

**Jesus' instruction (John 21:6).** Jesus then instructed them to cast their net on the other side (the right side) of the boat. (Apparently, they had been fishing only on the left side.) The seven men obeyed the Lord's instruction. Perhaps they remembered the Lord's directive in Luke 5:4 and now began to recognize that this man was Jesus.

When they cast their net on the other side of the boat, they caught so many fish that the net was too heavy to draw in. This large catch of fish would have been another indication that this man was the risen Christ.

Could the distance of a few feet have made such a difference? Were there no fish on one side of the boat while a huge number clustered on the other side? Obviously, the Lord planned this scene to bring the men back to reliance on Him.

**Return to shore (John 21:7-8).** When the men witnessed the miraculous catch of fish, John, the disciple "whom Jesus loved" (13:23), recognized that this man had to be the Lord Jesus Christ. John was also the first to recognize the reality of Jesus' resurrection (20:8).

Peter, who was dressed for work, quickly (and seemingly impulsively) put on his outer garment and jumped into the sea to swim toward the shore. This event brings to mind the time when Peter stepped out of the boat and started walking on the water to Jesus (Matt. 14:28-31).

As Peter swam to shore, the other six disciples pulled up in the little boat, dragging the net full of fish to the shore. The Scripture records that they had been two hundred cubits (about three hundred feet) out.

## MEETING JESUS ON THE SHORE

**9** As soon then as they were come to land, they saw a fire of coals there, and fish laid thereon, and bread.

**10** Jesus saith unto them, Bring of the fish which ye have now caught.

**11** Simon Peter went up, and drew the net to land full of great fishes, an hundred and fifty and three: and for all there were so many, yet was not the net broken.

**12** Jesus saith unto them, Come and dine. And none of the disciples durst ask him, Who art thou? knowing that it was the Lord.

**13** Jesus then cometh, and taketh bread, and giveth them, and fish likewise.

**14** This is now the third time that Jesus shewed himself to his disciples, after that he was risen from the dead.

**Jesus' request (John 21:9-10).** When the disciples reached the shore, they found that Jesus had prepared a breakfast of fish and bread. Did the Lord Jesus create this food as He had done when He fed the five thousand (6:1-14)? Jesus also asked the men to bring some of the fish they had caught.

**Peter's response (John 21:11).** Upon hearing Jesus' request, Peter dragged the net full of fish to the shore. Here we find an interesting historical detail. John recorded that they caught 153 large fish. We should not see anything allegorical or symbolic in that number. Fisherman probably always counted their fish so that they could divide the catch among themselves. The only point John was making was that after a night of fruitless fishing, obedience to the Lord had resulted in a huge catch of large fish.

Another interesting historical note is that the net was not broken. We see throughout this incident the Lord's power and His provision for His disciples, all of which would reassure them for the days ahead.

We should also note that the Lord never chided the disciples for going back to fishing. This was another way He encouraged them and prepared them for the events ahead.

**Jesus' invitation (John 21:12).** When the disciples reached shore with all their fish, Jesus invited them to "come and dine." We can imagine the men were hungry after working all night.

By this time they all recognized that this man was Jesus. (Perhaps their recollection of the times when Jesus multiplied the loaves and fish helped confirm their identification here.) Even if any of them had lingering doubts, none dared to ask Him who He was, perhaps out of embarrassment. They may not have wanted to let Jesus know they had any questions about His identity.

Interestingly, in this instance the disciples apparently recognized Jesus in His resurrection body. Why did Mary and the Emmaus disciples not recognize Him earlier (John 20:14; Luke 24:35)? It seems likely that by now the disciples were accustomed to Jesus' resurrection body, both from their own experience and (perhaps) the reports of others.

**A simple meal (John 21:13-14).** In an action strikingly similar to the miraculous feedings of the five thousand and the four thousand, Jesus distributed the bread and fish to the men. His familiar actions reassured the disciples that He was the same one they had followed and that He could continue to meet their needs.

We are not told in this text that Jesus ate with the men, though that most likely was the case. We do know, however, that He had eaten with the disciples right after the resurrection (Luke 24:36-43). Eating with His followers was an added indication that He was not a phantom.

John stated that this appearance of Christ was the third time Jesus had shown Himself alive to His disciples (John 21:14). While Jesus showed Himself alive on more than three occasions (see below), this appearance was the third time John recorded His appearances to His disciples. The other two times are recorded in John 20:19, 26.

Jesus showed Himself alive after His resurrection several times, including appearances to:

• Mary Magdalene (Mark 16:9-11; John 20:11-18) and the other women at the tomb (Matt. 28:8-10)

• The two travelers on the road to Emmaus (Mark 16:12-13; Luke 24:13-34)

• Peter (Luke 24:34; I Cor. 15:5)

• Ten disciples behind closed doors (Mark 16:14; Luke 24:35-43; John 20:19-25)

- Eleven disciples behind closed doors (John 20:26-31)
- Seven disciples while fishing (John 21:1-14)
- Eleven disciples on the mountain (Matt. 28:16-20)
- A crowd of more than five hundred people, most of whom were still living at the time of Paul's writing (I Cor. 15:6)
- James and all the apostles (I Cor. 15:7)
- The disciples in Jerusalem (Luke 24:44-49)
- Those who watched Him ascend into heaven (Mark 16:19-20; Luke 24:50-53; Acts 1:3-8)
- Paul at his conversion (Acts 9:1-22; I Cor. 15:8)

We believe in the resurrection of Christ by faith in what the Bible records. His resurrection would be true even if there were no eyewitnesses. These accounts, however, give credible and irrefutable evidence that Christ indeed rose from the dead and appeared in a real, glorified body.

The Apostle Paul, one of the eyewitnesses of the risen Lord, put the resurrection of Christ in its theological perspective by describing things that would be true if Christ had not resurrected.

First, our preaching and teaching would be useless: "If Christ be not risen, then is our preaching vain" (I Cor. 15:14). Second, our faith would be useless: "If Christ be not raised, your faith is vain" (vs. 17). Third, we would still be under the penalty of our sin: "If Christ be not raised, . . . ye are yet in your sins." Fourth, we would be hopeless and miserable: "If in this life only we have hope in Christ, we are of all men most miserable" (vs. 19). Finally, believers who have died are lost forever: "And if Christ be not raised, . . . then they also which are fallen asleep in Christ are perished" (vss. 17-18). This would be true because our resurrection is based on Christ's resurrection (I Thess. 4:14).

Paul concluded, however, that "now is Christ risen from the dead, and become the firstfruits of them that slept" (I Cor. 15:20). So our preaching has purpose, our faith is solid, our sins are forgiven, we experience true joy, and we have the confidence that we shall see our loved ones again. All this is true because of the resurrection of Christ.

Let us reflect not only on the verifiable facts of Christ's resurrection but also on the immense theological implications. Praise to the resurrected Christ!

—Don Anderson.

# QUESTIONS

1. Who were the seven disciples in this account?
2. Why is Peter named first among these men?
3. What might Peter have meant when he said, "I go a fishing" (John 21:3)?
4. Why did Jesus ask the disciples if they had caught any fish?
5. Why would the men obey a stranger's instruction in fishing technique?
6. What did the large catch of fish reveal to the disciples?
7. What kept the disciples from asking Jesus who He was?
8. In what way did Jesus' actions reassure His disciples?
9. Who were some of the other people Jesus appeared to after His resurrection?
10. What are some of the theological implications of Christ's resurrection?

—Don Anderson.

# Preparing to Teach the Lesson

There are many spiritual lessons in Scripture, and they are all recorded for our benefit. We cannot take in all spiritual truth; because of our spiritual weakness and capacity as human beings, we are limited in our understanding. If it were not for our new nature implanted in us when we were saved, and the resident Holy Spirit sent by the Lord Jesus, we could not even take in a small amount of spiritual truth. It is better to teach well small amounts of spiritual truth and answer questions about it than to try to pass on huge amounts of truth and overload the capacity of our students. Then, too, we want to instill in all our students the truth and trustworthiness of Scripture.

## TODAY'S AIM

**Facts:** to see how the Lord Jesus helps the faith of His disciples.

**Principle:** to see how the Lord Jesus is fully capable of meeting all our needs.

**Application:** to put ourselves in the way of blessing by being available to God.

## INTRODUCING THE LESSON

Today we study another and very important postresurrection appearance of the Lord Jesus to His disciples. Seven out of the remaining eleven of Jesus' disciples were together. This reminds us of the importance of being together as the Lord's followers. Simon Peter was their de facto leader in the absence of the Lord Jesus. It is true that Peter had also denied his Master three times during Jesus' trials, but even with his failure, Peter was a changed man, especially after the resurrection. We need to be constantly thankful for the fact that when the Lord Jesus saves us, He changes us from what we would be and used to be.

This Scripture, shows us that the Lord can deal with our basic fallen human nature and instill in us the desire to follow Him and do His will. Only as the Lord Jesus saves us and directs our lives can we do anything that will honor Him.

## DEVELOPING THE LESSON

**1. The futility (John 21:1-3).** Peter, along with and James and John, the sons of Zebedee, had been fishermen before the Lord Jesus came and called them to follow Him. Now as the disciples waited in Galilee for Jesus, Peter suggested that they go fishing. The other disciples immediately said they would go with him, and they did.

This probably seemed like the obvious thing to do. They were waiting on Jesus to meet them. It did not seem at this point there was any more preaching to be done. They could not help Him, as they did by distributing food to the crowd or picking up the leftovers. They probably had answered some questions about the Lord Jesus and His teachings from people who had followed Him, but otherwise they were just waiting; so, they went off to do something useful. It did not work.

Sometimes we prosper when we do our own thing. Sometimes we prosper when we do the wrong thing. We cannot necessarily tell whether something is the Lord's will by the success or failure of it. It is very dangerous spiritually to assume that the success of your current enterprise is the Lord's blessing or approval on what you are doing. However, in the case of our text, John seems to make a point of their catching nothing. Taking charge of the direction of their lives was not going to work.

**2. The difference (John 21:4-8).** The disciples were tired from working all night and were most certainly hungry. They may have wondered why the Lord had not blessed them with a catch of fish. After all, Peter, their leader, was a professional fishermen. It is almost a surprise that when the Carpenter told the fisherman how to catch fish, they did not say, "Yeah, right!" and refuse to do it. Their compliance with His suggestion got them a net so full of fish that they could not pull it into the boat. That is very interesting, because if you knew your net would catch so many fish, you probably would have used a smaller net.

This unusual instruction and the resultant catch of fish told John (that disciple whom Jesus loved) that it was the Lord who had instructed them. The catch was miraculous; therefore this must be the Miracle Worker. John had heard and seen enough to know it was the Lord. Maybe if we loved the Lord enough and were familiar enough with Him and His personality and ways, we would know more easily and quickly whether what we want to do is from the Lord. As soon as Peter realized who the one on shore was, he wanted to get to Him as soon as possible, so he swam to shore.

**3. The needs (John 21:9-14).** Jesus had already made a fire and started cooking. He knew what the disciples' needs were and had made provision to meet those needs. It is of note that the Lord Jesus met their physical need first. This may sometimes be the first order of work in our evangelistic endeavors. People may not be able to listen to the gospel when they are physically and mentally exhausted.

Jesus told the disciples to bring some more fish, and we may be called upon to bring what we can (as provided by the Lord) to the table. Jesus invited them to come and eat. Again, miraculously, the net had not broken, and the fish had not escaped. When we obey Him, the Lord takes care of our needs and preserves the result of our efforts.

## ILLUSTRATING THE LESSON

Is the voice we hear the Lord or our own ideas?

LISTEN

FOLLOW GOD'S WAY

## CONCLUDING THE LESSON

It is easy to see why these events were recorded for us. The lessons are obvious. It is true that the text records historical facts. However, it is also inescapable that this type of interaction between the Lord and His followers is the sort of thing we would expect from Him. We do not need, nor should we desire, to take direction of our own lives. We cannot possibly achieve the success or the fulfillment in life that Christ promises. Also, we are assured by these events that He rose from the dead and is the same marvelous Lord of miracles and of the ordinary events of life that He was so long ago.

## ANTICIPATING THE NEXT LESSON

Next week we continue in John 21 with the personal call of God upon the life of Peter.

—*Brian D. Doud.*

# PRACTICAL POINTS

1. Jesus' presence is with those who follow Him (John 21:1-3).
2. Do not become discouraged when it seems that your efforts are futile (vs. 4).
3. When you follow Jesus' directions, you will find what you need (vs. 5).
4. A good follower recognizes and appreciates the wisdom of his leader (vss. 6-7).
5. Jesus brings abundance where there was lack (vss. 8-9).
6. Jesus makes preparation for His children and provides for them (vss. 10-14).

*—Valante M. Grant.*

# RESEARCH AND DISCUSSION

1. How is Jesus present with Christians today?
2. When Jesus comes to you, how do you recognize Him?
3. How do situations turn around because Jesus is present in the midst of them (John 21:5-6)?
4. How can we remain productive in times of uncertainty?
5. How does teamwork and cooperation impact Christian relationships?
6. What example of leadership did Jesus set by the way He fellowshipped with His disciples?
7. What is the similarity between this appearance by Jesus to the disciples and the day that Jesus called Peter to be a disciple (cf. Matt. 4:18)?

*—Valante M. Grant.*

# ILLUSTRATED HIGH POINTS

**Cast the net**

Some kinds of fish are taken by spear, some by line, and some by net. The wise fisherman knows which to use with each particular type of fish. He never angles for a whale or tries to harpoon a trout!

Some are called to be evangelists, privileged to proclaim the gospel to large crowds.

**On the right side**

Today the serious fisherman can purchase an electronic fish finder, which gives him an underwater view in a lake or at sea. In John 21, the fish finder is the resurrected Christ.

In the world of evangelism, fishers of men (cf. Matt. 4:19) do not need a fish finder to locate people who need salvation. They are as near as one of our family, a coworker, or our next-door neighbor. But one does need the guidance and help of the Holy Spirit to enable him to be wise and winsome in the sharing of the gospel.

**An hundred and fifty and three**

Fisherman have been known to exaggerate the number and size of their catches. Oliver Herford, the American writer, said, "There are more fish taken out of a stream than ever were in it." Perhaps you have heard about the man who caught a fine specimen. A friend asked, "Are you going to have it mounted?" "No," he replied. "If I do that, it won't grow anymore."

The Apostle John wrote his Gospel some fifty to sixty years after his experience on the Sea of Tiberias. The catch of fish was so large that he remembered the specific number, 153. We can trust the fisherman of the fourth Gospel because "all scripture is given by inspiration of God" (II Tim. 3:16).

*—David A. Hamburg.*

# Golden Text Illuminated

**"Jesus saith unto them, Come and dine. And none of the disciples durst ask him, Who art thou? knowing that it was the Lord" (John 21:12).**

Several years ago, the mayor of Philadelphia made headlines when he served breakfast to a group of veterans. Many people were impressed that a high-ranking official would perform such a humble task. Almost two thousand years ago, the risen Lord of the universe served breakfast to seven men (John 21:2) in a quiet place by the Sea of Galilee, garnering no attention from the world but leaving an indelible impression on these disciples.

It was several days or perhaps weeks after the momentous events of Easter, and Jesus' disciples had made their way back to Galilee. One evening, Peter and six others decided to go out on the lake fishing. They spent all night at it but caught nothing. At daybreak an unrecognized figure on shore called to them, inquiring about their success. When they answered, the person told them to throw in their nets on the other side of the boat. They did, with immediate results—an enormous haul of fish that strained the nets. Suddenly the stranger's identity was clear; it was unmistakably Jesus.

When the men came ashore, they found that the Lord already had a small fire going with some fish frying over it (where those fish had come from is not explained), along with bread. Jesus invited the men to bring some of the fish they had just caught, which they did with some difficulty owing to their great number.

It was at this point that the risen Lord of all creation invited His men to sit down and have breakfast. It was not the first time He had humbly served them. His whole ministry had illustrated the truth,

"The Son of man came not to be ministered unto, but to minister" (Mark 10:45).

We might think that, having risen from the dead and accomplished His primary mission, Jesus' time for serving would be over. Our text, however, sheds light on the character of our Lord, and it is a precious truth that we see. Serving others was not something He did out of expediency or for show; it expressed His loving heart for His people.

The disciples' reaction is interesting. None "durst ask him, Who art thou? knowing that it was the Lord." It would appear that at least some of them inwardly desired to ask for a final confirmation of Jesus' identity, but none dared to voice the question. They knew all too well who was speaking to them.

The question arises: If they knew it was Jesus, why would they want to ask who it was? We must remember that Jesus' physical appearance after the resurrection was different in some ways. Mary Magdalene had failed to recognize Him at first (John 20:14) as had the two on the road to Emmaus (Luke 24:13-16). Just moments before, the seven disciples had not recognized the Lord until the miraculous catch of fish opened their eyes. Yet now they could not deny whose presence they were in.

There are times when we know something with utter certainty even though we may not have access to ordinary ways of ascertaining facts. When God makes something clear—especially truth regarding His Son—let us not doubt or insult Him with demands for further verification.

—*Kenneth A. Sponsler.*

# Heart of the Lesson

A friend introduced me to fly fishing, and for a year I fished a number of rivers in the Northwest. I loved standing in a cool mountain stream, wearing my waders and casting on a hot day. Once I saw an eagle swoop down and fly away with a fish. But I never caught anything.

Peter and several other of Jesus' disciples were commercial fishermen. In today's lesson, they too, experienced fruitless fishing until they took instruction from the risen Christ.

**1. Fishing failure (John 21:1-5).** After Jesus had appeared to a number of people following His resurrection, the disciples headed north to Galilee to meet Him. At one point, Peter and six other disciples decided to go fishing. Nighttime was best for fishing on the Sea of Galilee. But after an entire night of fishing, the disciples had caught nothing.

Morning came. On the shore stood a lone figure—Jesus. But the disciples did not recognize Him yet, perhaps because of the distance or because of the dim light. Jesus called to them, asking if they had caught any fish. They were close enough to shore to hear His voice, and the water probably helped carry it.

**2. Copious catch (John 21:6-8).** The disciples admitted they had been unsuccessful. Jesus suggested they lower the net on the right side of the boat, and they would catch plenty of fish. They followed Jesus' instructions and caught so many fish that even seven burly men could not haul the net back into the boat.

John, known as the disciple Jesus loved and the author of the Gospel of John, seemed to have a special spiritual sensitivity regarding Jesus. He was first to recognize that the figure on the shore was Jesus. When John mentioned this to Peter, impetuous Peter threw on his coat, jumped into the lake, and swam to shore. He wanted to be first to greet Jesus.

Jewish law required a person to be clothed for all religious acts. Because the law considered offering a greeting to be a religious act, the loincloth Peter wore for fishing was inadequate apparel for a greeting (Barclay, *The Gospel of John,* Westminster).

**3. Bountiful breakfast (John 21:9-14).** The other six disciples stayed with the boat and their catch. They were about three hundred feet away from Jesus and soon landed the boat. On the shore they saw a fire, fish cooking over the coals, and bread. Jesus knew their needs: a hot breakfast for seven tired men.

Jesus asked them to bring some of the fish they had caught. Peter dragged the net onto shore. Inside the net were 153 fish, but the net was unbroken. Jesus invited the seven to eat with Him. No one dared ask who He was; they now knew this was Jesus, their Lord. Jesus served them just as He had done before—washing their dusty feet at the Last Supper. Even though Jesus was in His glorified body, about to return to heaven and take His seat at God's right hand, Jesus still was an example of humility and servanthood. He still cared about His followers' needs.

This was Jesus' third appearance to the disciples as a group after His resurrection. In His appearances, Jesus was assuring them of His bodily resurrection and building their faith. He was no vision or apparition. He could be touched. He could cook. He could eat. The disciples carefully recorded these appearances, providing evidence of Christ's bodily resurrection for future believers—for us.

—*Ann Staatz.*

# World Missions

Jeremiah 29:13 promises that those who seek God with their whole hearts will find Him. Sometimes, however, He appears even to those who are not seeking. He comes and offers hope and provision where there had been none. In those times, people see that supernatural help has come. They do not need to ask whether that person had help from above. They only need to ask who this God is and how they can know Him too.

A man in a difficult situation was invited by a national missionary and his family to come live in their home with them. This man, Idhant, was loved as one of their own, and their daily kindness and goodness led him to want what they had. Idhant became a follower of Jesus and began to travel with the pastor telling others. Even so, his financial struggles remained, and when a gift of a rickshaw was given through Gospel for Asia (www.gfa.org), the pastor requested that it be given to Idhant.

Idhant dedicated his new rickshaw to the Lord. Every day he took gospel tracts with him to share with his passengers and others around town.

One set of passengers was on their way to the hospital. Doctors had been unable to help the wife's illness, but Idhant told them Jesus had the power to heal. He gave them literature and encouraged them to read about the God who loved them. The next week he saw them again. They asked for more information about Jesus. "Can your Jesus heal my wife's sickness?"

Idhant said yes, Jesus could. He invited them to church. They came, God healed the wife, and both put their faith in Christ.

Over time word spread about the man who gave away literature from his rickshaw. One young woman, who had run away from a terrible family situation and hopeless life, heard of the rickshaw man. *Could his God help me?* she wondered.

Yet how was she to find one rickshaw in a city of over 100,000? It seemed impossible, but while she searched for shelter, she saw a rickshaw driver passing out papers to people.

"Rickshaw driver! Please stop!" she yelled and ran toward him. She asked whether he was a Christian. When he said yes, she said, "I have seen you on the way while you were distributing literature and heard that your God loves, and you Christian people are good and help the poor people. So would you please help me?"

Idhant took her to his pastor, who showed her the same compassion he had shown Idhant years before. Like Idhant, the pastor invited this new woman to live with his family, and in time the woman also put her faith in Christ. Soon she was traveling to other villages and teaching of Christ.

After two years, the woman married another national pastor, and they now serve in a church together. Idhant continues to drive his rickshaw, using it to share Christ with his city.

It is obvious that God is with them. Are our lives a similar witness? If someone was seeking hope and truth, would they know we had it? Would they know we belong to the Lord by looking at our lives and our actions? How can we use the resources God has given us—our cars, our homes, our jobs and our activities—to share His love with others?

—Kimberly Rae.

# The Jewish Aspect

In this week's lesson, we see Jesus as He prepared food for His disciples. As one of His last acts on earth, He broke bread and fellowshipped with His followers.

Food and fellowship play an important part in Jewish culture. Both are prominent in most of the Jewish holidays.

The Jewish festivals are an important part of Jewish life. The festival calendar is cyclical. The holidays begin at sundown on what Americans would consider the eve of the holiday. This occurs because the Jewish day is different from the American day. A Jewish day runs from sundown of one day until sundown of the next day.

The Jewish calendar also differs from the calendar with which we are familiar. The Jewish calendar is based on the cycles of the moon; in other words, it is a lunar calendar.

The Jewish calendar celebrates both major and minor holidays. Three very important holidays—Sukkot, also called the Festival of Tabernacles; Pesach, also called Passover; and Shavuot, also called Pentecost—make up the three pilgrimage holidays. When the temple was in existence, Jewish males were supposed to celebrate these holidays in Jerusalem.

Each of the three pilgrimage holidays builds in some way on the narratives surrounding the Exodus from Egypt. Passover tells the story of the Exodus. Receiving the Ten Commandments at Mount Sinai is celebrated on Pentecost. The Festival of Tabernacles gives remembrance to the wandering of the Israelites in the wilderness and how God sheltered them with His presence.

The Jewish calendar has both a civil and a sacred new year, so it can be difficult to pin down a starting place for the cycle of festivals. However, the festivals always occur in the same progression—Hanukkah, Purim, Passover, Festival of Trumpets, Yom Kippur, and the Festival of Tabernacles.

In addition, one time per week Shabbat, or Sabbath, takes place. Sabbath begins on Friday at sundown and continues until Saturday at sundown. The Jewish Sabbath, as with most of the holidays, is filled with food and fellowship.

The Sabbath begins with the lighting of the Sabbath candles. Traditionally, the woman of the house lights them. A minimum of two candles are lighted. As the woman lights the candles, she shields her eyes and says a blessing over them.

After the candles are lit, the father customarily blesses each child with a special blessing and then recites Proverbs 31, expressing admiration for his wife.

At the completion of a Sabbath song, a prayer is recited over the wine. Next, the participants perform a special handwashing ceremony. Then the challah, the special braided bread, is blessed and eaten. It is tradition to have two challot on the dining room table covered by a special cloth.

The challah is cut or torn and distributed. Later during the meal, another special song might be sung. The meal ends with grace, thanking God for the food that He has provided.

Families and friends come together to celebrate Sabbath. Worries and cares are forgotten; love and joy are experienced instead. The Jewish people look forward to the Sabbath.

It would benefit Christians to familiarize themselves with the Jewish holidays. Each paints a picture of Jesus and His work.

—Robin Fitzgerald.

# Guiding the Superintendent

Anyone who has ever gone fishing knows how the disciples felt. After a long night of unrewarding labor, the fishermen had nothing to show for all their labor. It was probably best to just call it a night. Then, out of the early morning mist, a stranger appeared on the shore to encourage them to try one more time. The clearing mist became symbolic of the fishermen's realization of the stranger's true identity.

## DEVOTION OUTLINE

**1. Life without Jesus (John 21:1-3).** Despite the fact that the resurrected Jesus Christ had made several appearances to His followers, the disciples still had not fully come to grips with who Jesus really was and their special calling. It had been three years since they had first met and agreed to follow Jesus of Nazareth. It was time to move on. They had to do something with their lives.

Without Jesus, life seemed so empty. Several of the disciples had found their way to the shore of the Sea of Galilee, their old fishing grounds.

Peter had an idea that seemed to make sense—to go fishing! The men were soon out on the lake, but their efforts were in vain. They were starting to realize that life without Jesus was futile.

**2. Jesus seen but not recognized (John 21:4-6).** Out of the mist the stranger called out to the struggling fishermen, inquiring whether they had caught anything. To their negative answer the stranger made a suggestion, to throw their nets on the other side of boat. With nothing to lose, they complied. To their surprise, they made one of the biggest catches of their lives.

**3. Jesus recognized as the Lord (John 21:7-8).** Following the suggestion of the disciple "whom Jesus loved" (John), Peter recognized the stranger for who He was.

As the morning mist cleared, Peter, having suddenly recognized that the stranger was the Lord, jumped into the water and swam to shore. The rest quickly pulled their boat and the catch to the shore, as Peter assisted with the net.

**4. Fellowship with Jesus (John 21:9-14).** This was no chance meeting. It was all planned by Jesus. Suddenly, it was the good old days again—sitting and talking and eating with Jesus. Eating a meal together is a universal symbol of friendship and fellowship.

The events of that night and early morning became very symbolic of life, both with and without Jesus. Life without Jesus is much like that empty evening of fishing. There was a lot of work and effort and nothing to show for it. Then Jesus appeared but was not recognized. In faith the men heeded Jesus' instructions and were rewarded with a great miracle.

Life with Jesus is so different from a futile life without Him. Now the men were sitting, talking, and fellowshipping with Him. Slowly, the dark days of life after the death of Christ melted away into joy.

## AGE-GROUP EMPHASES

**Children:** Have your children imagine what it would be like to go camping and to have breakfast with Jesus.

**Youths:** Discuss what would it take for your young people to see Jesus in their everyday experiences.

**Adults:** Have the adults describe their "aha moment" when they realized that Jesus is Lord.

—Martin R. Dahlquist

# Scripture Lesson Text

**JOHN 21:15** So when they had dined, Je'sus saith to Si'mon Pe'ter, Si'mon, *son* of Jo'nas, lovest thou me more than these? He saith unto him, Yea, Lord; thou knowest that I love thee. He saith unto him, Feed my lambs.

**16 He saith to him again the second time, Si'mon, *son* of Jo'nas, lovest thou me? He saith unto him, Yea, Lord; thou knowest that I love thee. He saith unto him, Feed my sheep.**

17 He saith unto him the third time, Si'mon, *son* of Jo'nas, lovest thou me? Pe'ter was grieved because he said unto him the third time, Lovest thou me? And he said unto him, Lord, thou knowest all things; thou knowest that I love thee. Je'sus saith unto him, Feed my sheep.

**18 Verily, verily, I say unto thee, When thou wast young, thou girdedst thyself, and walkedst whither thou wouldest: but when thou shalt be old, thou shalt stretch forth thy hands, and another shall gird thee, and carry *thee* whither thou wouldest not.**

19 This spake he, signifying by what death he should glorify God.

And when he had spoken this, he saith unto him, Follow me.

**20 Then Pe'ter, turning about, seeth the disciple whom Je'sus loved following; which also leaned on his breast at supper and said, Lord, which is he that betrayeth thee?**

21 Pe'ter seeing him saith to Je'sus, Lord, and what *shall* this man *do?*

**22 Je'sus saith unto him, If I will that he tarry till I come, what *is that* to thee? follow thou me.**

23 Then went this saying abroad among the brethren, that that disciple should not die: yet Je'sus said not unto him, He shall not die; but, If I will that he tarry till I come, what *is that* to thee?

**24 This is the disciple which testifieth of these things, and wrote these things: and we know that his testimony is true.**

25 And there are also many other things which Je'sus did, the which, if they should be written every one, I suppose that even the world itself could not contain the books that should be written. Amen.

---

**NOTES**

# Follow Me

## Lesson: John 21:15-25

Read: John 21:15-25

TIME: A.D. 30                    PLACE: by Sea of Tiberias

---

**GOLDEN TEXT**—"Jesus saith to Simon Peter, Simon, son of Jonas, lovest thou me more than these? He saith unto him, Yea, Lord; thou knowest that I love thee. He saith unto him, Feed my lambs" (John 21:15).

---

## *Introduction*

We understand what the word "Christian" means, and we delight to use it of ourselves and fellow believers. The word calls to mind our Saviour, Jesus Christ, and what He has done for us. However, today the word "Christian" is used so broadly and generically at times that it can lose any real meaning. It seems most people we meet call themselves Christians.

We want to keep using the word "Christian," but perhaps at times we may need to use a term that better defines us. We sometimes use the term "born-again Christian," which more precisely describes what we mean by the word "Christian."

In John 21:19, Jesus exhorted Peter, "Follow me." The Lord Jesus issued that same command on several previous occasions (Matt. 4:19; 8:22; 9:9; 16:24; 19:21). So perhaps another phrase we should use more often is "follower of Christ" to clearly identify us. More important, let us give glory and honor to the Lord by truly being followers of Christ.

## LESSON OUTLINE

I. **JESUS' QUESTIONS TO PETER**—John 21:15-19

II. **PETER'S QUESTION TO JESUS**—John 21:20-23

III. **THE CONCLUSION OF JOHN'S GOSPEL**—John 21:24-25

## *Exposition: Verse by Verse*

**JESUS' QUESTIONS TO PETER**

**JOHN 21:15** So when they had dined, Jesus saith to Simon Peter, Simon, son of Jonas, lovest thou me more than these? He saith unto him, Yea, Lord; thou knowest that I love thee. He saith unto him, Feed my lambs.

16 He saith to him again the second time, Simon, son of Jonas, lovest thou me? He saith unto him, Yea, Lord; thou knowest that I love thee.

He saith unto him, Feed my sheep.

**17** He saith unto him the third time, Simon, son of Jonas, lovest thou me? Peter was grieved because he said unto him the third time, Lovest thou me? And he said unto him, Lord, thou knowest all things; thou knowest that I love thee. Jesus saith unto him, Feed my sheep.

**18** Verily, verily, I say unto thee, When thou wast young, thou girdedst thyself, and walkedst whither thou wouldest: but when thou shalt be old, thou shalt stretch forth thy hands, and another shall gird thee, and carry thee whither thou wouldest not.

**19** This spake he, signifying by what death he should glorify God. And when he had spoken this, he saith unto him, Follow me.

Jesus had just finished serving His disciples breakfast on the shore of the Sea of Tiberias (John 21:1-14). Jesus had brought reassurance to all the disciples by showing them He was alive and all-powerful. In verses 15-19, Jesus then directed His attention to Peter.

Peter had denied Jesus three times (John 18:15-27). Jesus knew he was full of sorrow and regret over this. At the same time He knew that Peter was to play a major role in the founding of the church a few weeks later (Matt. 16:18; cf. Acts 2:14-36). So now Jesus took the time to lovingly restore Peter and prepare him for his leadership role. He did this by asking a series of three questions.

**Jesus' first question (John 21:15).** Jesus addressed Peter as "Simon, son of Jonas," using the apostle's given name. Jesus' first question to Peter was, "Lovest thou me more than these?" This first question raises two interpretive issues. First, who are "these" in the phrase "more than these"?

Two explanations are possible. Jesus could have referred to the fish the disciples had just brought in and asked Peter whether he loved Him more than his occupation as a fisherman. This meaning would especially be significant since Peter had earlier said he was going back to fishing.

A second possible explanation is that Jesus referred to the other disciples gathered on the shore. And within this explanation, two interpretations are possible: Did Peter love Jesus more than he loved the other disciples, or did he love Jesus more than they did? The second is more likely for the following reason:

Peter had boasted that he would always follow the Lord even if all the other disciples abandoned Him (Matt. 26:33). Jesus now appears to be challenging Peter by asking him, in essence, "Peter, you denied Me three times; so do you really love Me more than these other disciples love Me, as you claimed you would?"

No matter which explanation we take, the basic idea is the same. Did Peter love his Lord supremely and at all costs? Jesus was testing him and restoring him to a place of effective service for Him.

The second interpretive issue concerns the words Jesus and Peter used for "love" in their recorded exchange. In John 21:15 (as well as in verse 16), Jesus used a form of the word *agapaō*, the strong word for love that carries the meaning of supreme commitment. In essence, He asked, "Peter, are you totally devoted to Me more than anything else?"

Peter responded by using a form of the word *phileō*, which could indicate fond affection but not necessarily total commitment. Some scholars see no difference in the two words, but when Jesus used the strong word and Peter responded with a different word, Peter seemed to make a distinction.

If there is a distinction, was Peter saying he was not totally committed to Christ? Not necessarily. Perhaps he was merely reluctant to make such a strong claim for himself again in view of his three previous failures.

To Peter's response, Jesus said, "Feed my lambs" (John 21:15). The Greek word for "feed" here (also used in verse 17) carries the idea of tending or feeding. Jesus used the word "lambs" perhaps to show Peter's responsibility of tending to all believers, even the younger ones.

**Jesus' second question (John 21:16).** Jesus' second question was similar to His first one. "Simon, son of Jonas, lovest thou me?" Jesus addressed Peter in the same way but did not add the phrase "more than these." As in the first question, Jesus used the stronger word for "love." Peter responded in the same manner as the first question. "Yea, Lord; thou knowest that I love thee." Peter again used the weaker word for "love," still reluctant to make a full claim of devotion to Christ.

Jesus responded with the command for Peter to feed His sheep. Here Jesus used a different word for "feed," which has the idea of shepherding or actually pastoring. This second question and Peter's response was another way the Lord restored Peter and prepared him to have a major shepherding role in the early church.

**Jesus' third question (John 21:17).** Jesus asked a third question, reminding Peter of his three denials and giving him an opportunity to affirm his love for Jesus and his commitment to Him.

Three differences appear in this question from the earlier ones. Here Jesus used a form of the word *phileō*, the same word Peter had used in his first two responses. Perhaps Jesus was tenderly and gently helping Peter by not demanding such a high commitment in view of his reluctance.

The second difference was Peter's reaction—he was grieved by this third question. Perhaps his grief came from his heightened awareness of his three denials of Christ.

The third difference was Peter's reply. Dropping all claim to love, he simply declared that the Lord knew all things. In limiting his answer this way, Peter may have meant, "Lord, You know my heart. I am struggling because of my failures, but I want to be totally devoted to You." Jesus reiterated His previous commands by using the verb for "feed" from His first command and the word for "sheep" from His second. The distinctions are subtle, but we can be assured that the inspired Greek accurately reflects the tone of the (most likely) original Aramaic conversation.

Before we leave these verses, we need to reflect on their importance in our lives. What things might take God's place in our lives? Do we love the Lord more than anyone or anything around us today? The Lord's desire is that we be totally committed and devoted to Him. Even if we have failed, we can return to obedience and usefulness in the Lord's work.

**Jesus' response (John 21:18-19).** After helping Peter recover from his three denials, Jesus then prophesied his martyrdom. The Lord knew Peter needed to be restored before he would be ready to accept the assignment He had for him. Jesus told Peter that when he was young, he put on his own clothes and walked wherever he wanted to go. He was not dependent on anyone. However, Jesus said, "When thou shalt be old, thou shalt stretch forth thy hands, and another shall gird thee, and carry thee whither thou wouldest not." The Gospel writer, John, interpreted this statement for us by commenting, "This spake he, signifying by what death he should glorify God."

Church tradition records that in old age Peter's hands were stretched out on a cross, and he was crucified. Reportedly, he was crucified upside down, because he did not want to be crucified in the same manner as his Saviour. Peter probably knew from Jesus' statement what was in store for him, but he faithfully served the Lord for many more years.

The whole purpose of this conversation between Christ and Peter is found in Jesus' command to Peter to follow Him. Jesus wanted to bring Peter to a point of supremely loving Him and being fully devoted to Him for use in the days to come. The Lord wanted Peter to commit to Him, no matter what the end might be. We believers today should adopt the same attitude of being willing to follow the Saviour, no matter what that may mean for us.

## PETER'S QUESTION TO JESUS

**20 Then Peter, turning about, seeth the disciple whom Jesus loved following; which also leaned on his breast at supper and said, Lord, which is he that betrayeth thee?**

**21 Peter seeing him saith to Jesus, Lord, and what shall this man do?**

**22 Jesus saith unto him, If I will that he tarry till I come, what is that to thee? follow thou me.**

**23 Then went this saying abroad among the brethren, that that disciple should not die: yet Jesus said not unto him, He shall not die; but, If I will that he tarry till I come, what is that to thee?**

**Peter's question (John 21:20-21).** During this conversation, the other disciples were still nearby. After being restored to fellowship and given his assignment, Peter turned around and saw John, who is described as the one "whom Jesus loved" and the disciple who at the Last Supper had inquired about who would betray Jesus. The Lord had just told Peter what would

happen to him, so he was perhaps naturally curious about what would happen to John.

**Jesus' response (John 21:22-23).** Jesus mildly rebuked Peter for his question by saying, "If I will that he tarry till I come, what is that to thee? follow thou me." The Lord was not announcing that John would remain alive until He returned. Jesus was simply trying to emphasize to Peter that what might happen to John was none of Peter's concern. Jesus wanted Peter to follow Him even if, hypothetically, John were to live until He returned. This instruction was designed to help Peter give complete obedience and supreme devotion to Christ, no matter what happened to John or to any of the other disciples.

Interestingly, Jesus' hypothetical statement about John became known to other believers and caused a little stir. The word started to spread that John would not die before the Lord's return. Perhaps the other disciples repeated the statement without knowing the context or the purpose of the statement. John then clarified for his readers that Jesus did not say he would never die but only that if that turned out to be the case, it should be of no concern to them.

Jesus' words to Peter have important meaning to us today. Sometimes when we face difficulties, we wonder why other Christians are not suffering the same things. We have to realize that God's plan is different for each one of His children.

We should not question what God is doing in our lives but rather accept the fact that He knows what is best for us. We have to be faithful to follow the Lord and "run with patience the race that is set before us" (Heb. 12:1) and not compare our situation to others. We need to keep our eyes on the Lord and, as Jesus said to Peter, follow Him.

## THE CONCLUSION OF JOHN'S GOSPEL

**24** This is the disciple which testifieth of these things, and wrote these things: and we know that his testimony is true.

**25** And there are also many other things which Jesus did, the which, if they should be written every one, I suppose that even the world itself could not contain the books that should be written. Amen.

**The authorship of the book (John 21:24).** This verse identifies the Apostle John as the writer of this Gospel. He based his writing on his eyewitness experience of the events described in the book. The verse also presents an interpretive question. Some feel it may have been written by someone other than John, for it speaks of John in the third person ("we know that his testimony is true").

Final statements from a person other than the writer are not without precedent in the Scripture (cf. Deut. 34:1-12; Josh. 24:29-33). If John 21:24 is from another writer, it may have been from believers in one of the early churches ("we know").

On the other hand, John may have used the word "we" in an editorial sense, referring to himself or to the apostles collectively (cf. John 1:14; I John 1:1-4; III John 1:12). Either way, John 21:24 is an endorsement of John ("his testimony is true") as a reliable eyewitness of what he has written in this book.

**The nature of the book (John 21:25).** This verse makes an important statement about this fourth Gospel. We learn from the first part of the verse that under the inspiration of the Holy Spirit, John chose only some of the events of Christ's earthly life for inclusion ("there are also many other things which Jesus did"). John apparently chose the events that presented Jesus as the Messiah and would have brought people to faith in Him (cf. 20:30).

Second, in the latter part of the verse, we learn that Jesus was a busy man in His earthly ministry. Using figurative language, John said that if each detail of Christ's life were recounted, the world could not contain the number of books it would take to record the events.

The Gospels record only a small sampling of what Jesus actually did. Jesus' three years of public ministry probably spanned more than one thousand days, yet the Gospels record probably no more than fifty days in the life of our Saviour. When we take into account the events in all the unrecorded days of His ministry, we can understand how the world could not contain all the books needed to record what He did.

*—Don Anderson.*

# QUESTIONS

1. What are the two possible meanings of the phrase "more than these" in John 21:15?

2. What was Jesus emphasizing in His question about Peter's love for Him?

3. What was Peter emphasizing in his reply?

4. What did Jesus tell Peter to do when he affirmed his love for Him?

5. What did Jesus' command to feed His sheep point to?

6. What might have been Jesus' reason for changing the wording in His third question?

7. What prophecy did Jesus make about Peter's death?

8. What did Jesus say to Peter's question about John?

9. What command did the Lord give twice to Peter (vss. 19, 22)?

10. What do we learn about Jesus' ministry from this passage?

*—Don Anderson.*

# Preparing to Teach the Lesson

We never know when we will teach our last lesson, either in the classroom or in the normal activities of life. As teachers of the Lord's Word to His people, we must make sure that the lesson is true, accurate, and Holy Spirit led. This passage of Scripture is especially appropriate for this task.

## TODAY'S AIM

**Facts:** to see clearly how Jesus challenged Peter.

**Principle:** to see that everything in God's Word is there for our learning.

**Application:** to govern our life's choices by the clear indications of Scripture.

## INTRODUCING THE LESSON

As students of the Word of God, we must always seek to understand what it says, be accurate as to what it does not say, and be led by the Holy Spirit in this evaluation and the resultant lessons. This passage is very simple in language. There is no hidden meaning, no prophecy that needs special interpretation, and no other Scripture that must be brought to bear in order to understand what is going on. The passage interprets itself and is a historical narrative.

Besides being inspired by the Holy Spirit and placed in the Word of God, this was written by an eyewitness, the Apostle John, who had a special love for the Lord. John not only wrote this Gospel narrative, but also wrote the three epistles that bear his name, and the book of Revelation, the only book of prophecy in the New Testament.

Following Jesus means being exclusively His—knowing that to one day be with Him is all you really need.

## DEVELOPING THE LESSON

**1. The Lord Jesus' question (John 21:15-17).** After the Lord Jesus had miraculously made breakfast for the disciples, it may have been that He and Peter went for a walk and John followed them closely enough to hear their conversation. It is interesting that the Lord asked Peter the same question three times, and that He used the name Simon, son of Jonas, when addressing Peter. It was the Lord Jesus who called Simon to follow Him as His disciple and gave him the name "Peter" (John 1:42). Scripture says the Lord Jesus looked at Simon intently when He said this, so we know it was not just an offhand remark. In fact, the name would have future significance.

Simon, the impetuous one, quick to speak and act, would become a rock (Greek, *petros,* a solid and stable one). So when the Lord Jesus kept saying, "Simon, son of Jonas," He seemed to be emphasizing Peter's humanity and willingness to take immediate action without being patient and waiting for the Lord, even if it proved to be in error or at least needless.

As to the three times Jesus asked Simon the same question, it may be that He would have asked it until He got the reaction from Simon for which He was looking. John 21:17 says Peter was grieved. (John's use of the name "Peter" here may indicate that John and the others typically used "Peter," but it was important that John report the Lord's use of "Simon, son of Jonas" here.) The Lord Jesus, having got Peter's attention, said the third time, "Feed my sheep," which obviously refers to those who follow the Lord Jesus.

**2. The Lord Jesus' commission (John 21:18-19).** The Lord here reminded Peter that he had always done his own will, but He gave Peter a prophecy indicating that the manner of his death would be something against his will. Some ancient sources relate that Peter was crucified for his testimony about the Lord Jesus and that he requested to be crucified upside down because he was not worthy to be crucified in the same manner as his Lord.

The Lord Jesus then gave to Peter the commission to follow Him. Even if the Lord Jesus did not explicitly ask Peter to follow Him at their first meeting (John 1:42), He certainly did here. To be true to Him, Peter would have to follow the Lord Jesus all the way through his life and ultimately to martyrdom.

**3. The Lord Jesus' clarification (John 21:20-23).** Again, we have no idea if this question put to the Lord by Simon was out of jealousy, curiosity, or was for some other reason, but Peter did ask what the Lord's will would be for John. Peter knew that Jesus and John had a very close and loving relationship. In essence, Jesus' answer was that whatever the Lord wanted for John should make no difference to Peter. Peter was still called upon to follow the Lord Jesus. We do not follow what others are saying but simply follow the Lord and His Word.

**4. John's epilogue (John 21:24-25).** John assured his readers that he was telling the truth about all this. He said that in his opinion, if everything the Lord Jesus did were to be written, it would be more than the world could contain. Given that the Lord Jesus, as the Second Person of the Trinity, was and is God, John may well have been right, with little exaggeration.

## ILLUSTRATING THE LESSON

No matter what life brings, we must follow Christ.

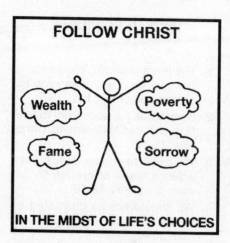

FOLLOW CHRIST

Wealth Poverty Fame Sorrow

IN THE MIDST OF LIFE'S CHOICES

## CONCLUDING THE LESSON

If you have been saved, you have already been called to Christ. Indeed, every person who has been called to trust the Lord Jesus has also been called to follow Him. But you might ask, "Where is He going, and how do I follow Him?" He is going ahead of you through all the rest of your life. Following Jesus will take you to your next job, your next friendship, and your next move in life. Following Him may lead you through health or illness, prosperity or poverty, joy or sorrow, or sometimes through combinations of these things. Following Jesus led Peter to publicly preach Him as crucified and risen. It also led Peter to dying for the sake of his Lord and Saviour.

Following Jesus involves studying His Word in order to be mentally and spiritually equipped for what lies ahead. It involves humility, confessing and forsaking sin, ignoring every potential distraction, and looking for His hand in every situation. It involves listening for His voice and rejecting the voice of others at every decision point.

## ANTICIPATING THE NEXT LESSON

Our next lesson on the Lord's glory and honor is from Revelation 4 and the glorious heavenly scene there.

—Brian D. Doud.

# PRACTICAL POINTS

1. The most powerful expression of our love for Jesus is keeping His commandments (John 21:15).
2. Sometimes it is necessary to reaffirm our commitment to Christ (vss. 16-17).
3. We have to follow Jesus even when it leads where we do not want to go (vss. 18-19).
4. We should not be distracted by God's plans for other believers (vss. 20-23).
5. We should be eager to testify to the goodness of Jesus (vs. 24).
6. The wondrous works of Jesus are unlimited (vs. 25).

—Valante M. Grant.

# RESEARCH AND DISCUSSION

1. Why did Jesus ask Peter whether he loved Him? Why did Jesus question His disciples when He knows all?
2. Why is Jesus referred to as the Shepherd? How are we His sheep?
3. What did Jesus mean by the command "Feed my sheep" (John 21:17)?
4. How do Peter's responses to Jesus' questions in John 21 compare to his responses to being questioned about being Jesus' disciple at the High Priest's palace? Why are Peter's answers in each case repeated three times?
5. What does it mean to follow Jesus? Explain and discuss.
6. Why was Peter concerned with Jesus' plans for John? Were his concerns valid? Why or why not?

—Valante M. Grant.

# ILLUSTRATED HIGH POINTS

### Feed my lambs

Jesus asked Peter three times, Do you love me? Peter assured the Lord that he did. After each affirmation, Jesus challenged Peter to feed His sheep. Peter went on to serve Christ faithfully the rest of his life.

Peter was not like the humorous fellow who texted his girlfriend, "Darling, I'd climb the highest mountain, sail the widest ocean, cross the hottest desert just to see you. P.S. I'll be over Saturday night if it doesn't rain." In fact, according to John 21:19, Peter's love eventually bought him a cross.

### Follow me

"Follow me" are welcome words. After church in a distant city, my friend Tom said he would like to take my wife and me to lunch and mentioned a place some distance away. I looked puzzled, so he simply said, "Follow me." After twenty minutes of twists and turns, we arrived. Without him, I might still be lost.

Following Jesus is the one and only way for a blessed life.

### The world itself could not contain

John closed his account of Jesus' life by declaring that there was much more that could be included, but it was simply impossible.

We are reminded of the third stanza of F. M. Lehman's gospel song, "The Love of God." The following words are probably from an eleventh-century poem written by Rabbi Meir Ben Isaac Nehorai:

Could we with ink the ocean fill,
And were the skies of parchment made,
Were every stalk on earth a quill,
And every man a scribe by trade,
To write the love of God above,
Would drain the ocean dry,
Nor could the scroll contain the whole,
Though stretched from sky to sky.

—David A. Hamburg.

# World Missions

Sometimes we may think of children's ministry as a spiritual version of babysitting while we reach or train the adults, but Jesus never saw it that way. Statistics cite that 85 percent of people who accept Christ do so before age eighteen. This alone should make reaching and then discipling children a major priority.

For starters, we need to train the young people God has placed into our own homes and churches. Current studies claim that anywhere from 50-70 percent of children growing up in our churches will not embrace the faith as their own by the time they leave for college. This is a tragedy! How can this happen?

John Trent once asked several hundred churchgoing parents the following three questions. Their answers reveal how believers have failed God's command to feed His lambs.

**1. Do you think it's important to pass down your faith to your children?** Over 90 percent said, "Yes! It's very important!"

**2. Do you think your child will have a strong faith when he or she gets out of college?** Again, 90 percent said yes.

**3. Outside of going to church, what are you doing intentionally to introduce and build a growing faith in your child?** Fewer than 30 percent were doing *anything* purposefully to grow their children's faith during the 166 hours a week their children were at home.

If we truly want to reach the world—not only in this generation but for generations to come—we need to spiritually feed our own lambs. Regular prayer time, family devotions, memorizing Scripture together, doing a discipleship program for kids, and regularly talking about life and how God's Word applies to their everyday situations are great ways to start.

Then we can move on to feeding God's lambs throughout the world.

One great way to reach and train a new generation of missionaries is through *The Greatest Journey.* This discipleship program started through *Operation Christmas Child,* the famous outreach in which people all over the world pack shoe boxes of gifts that go to over one hundred countries with love, joy, and the gospel. Over one hundred million shoe boxes have been given, and many, many children have been saved. Those children needed to be discipled; therefore, *The Greatest Journey* was born.

The program is new, but already extremely effective. Over seven million children have enrolled in the program. They learn in sixty-nine different languages by over three hundred fifty thousand trained teachers.

It costs so little, and so many children are ready to learn and grow. Just six dollars pays for a child to receive twelve lessons that will teach him how to grow in his new faith and how to share that faith with others. It also pays for a child to have a copy of the New Testament in his language, which for many is their first Bible ever.

Children graduate and get a certificate when they complete the program. Many of them go on to reach their own villages, children and adults, with the gospel of Christ. You can get involved at www.samaritanspurse.org/what-we-do/the-greatest-journey/ or even order the program in English for your own home or church at www.thegreatestjourney.org.

What a wonderful way to find and feed more lambs—from our own homes to the ends of the earth!

—*Kimberly Rae.*

# The Jewish Aspect

In this week's lesson, Jesus asked Peter three times if he loved Him. Here two different Greek words are used for love. While the two words are synonyms, most scholars see some distinct emphases in their use. Another Greek word for love is found in literature outside the New Testament.

As in the Greek, there are several Hebrew words that express the idea of love. The most common is *ahavah*. It is used to describe intimate or deep feelings between parent and child, close friends, or a man and woman.

A modern Jewish wedding blessing says, "Blessed is the one who rejoices that the love between this woman and this man is as the first love in the Garden" (themodernjewishwedding.com). Marriage, family, and love serve as important concepts in Jewish society.

"Judaism teaches that the home is a reflection of the ancient Jewish Holy Temple in Jerusalem" (Shafner, *The Everything Jewish Wedding Book*, Adams Media). The home is built around the joining of two people in love.

In Judaism, the wedding day is considered the day that seals this union. The wedding brings with it a transformation from one person into a totally new identity consisting of the two joined together.

Ancient Jewish weddings give us insight into the beautiful picture of God's loving plan for mankind. Until the Middle Ages, Jewish marriages consisted of two ceremonies—first the betrothal and later the wedding.

Before the betrothal, a young man or his father might send a servant into a village to find the young man a bride. The servant would go into the town with the best monetary offer the man could afford and then make the girl's father a proposal to enter into marriage.

If the girl's father was impressed, he would accept the offer. Then he would ask for his daughter's response. If she accepted, the servant would leave part of the agreed-upon payment and go back with the news. The bridegroom would then go to meet his bride.

This stage was called the betrothal or *erusin.* The wedding, or *nissuin,* would come later.

Under the *huppah,* or canopy, the couple would express their intention to be betrothed. The groom would give the woman a bridal gift, sign the *ketubah* (contract), and seal the agreement with wine.

Once the couple was betrothed, they were considered bound together. They would need a divorce to break the agreement. During this period the couple would prepare themselves to enter into the covenant of marriage.

During the betrothal, the groom was responsible for preparing a home for his future wife. In biblical days, he would build on to his father's house.

The father of the groom would determine when the home was ready. When asked the time of the wedding, the groom might answer, "No man knows the day or the hour, only my father knows" ("The Ancient Jewish Wedding Ceremony," laydownlife.net).

During the preparation period, the bride would wait for the groom. At the sounding of the shofar, the wedding party would proceed to the bride's home. At the home, the party would pick up the bride and take her to her new home.

—*Robin Fitzgerald.*

# Guiding the Superintendent

God never gives up on a person—no matter who that person is or what he has done. God is a God of grace and forgiveness. There is always room for repentance and restoration.

The Apostle John closed out his gospel story of Jesus with a reminder that no matter how grievous a person's actions may be, God is not only ready to forgive but also ready to use that one again in service. The last lesson in John is simple but profound—it is never too late to return to Christ.

Earlier in the Gospel of John (18:17-27), Peter had publicly denied Jesus Christ. Now Jesus restored Peter in a most public fashion.

## DEVOTIONAL OUTLINE

**1. Feed My sheep (John 21:15-17).** After a breakfast of fish was over (see lesson 6), Jesus turned to Peter and issued a call to a shepherding ministry.

Three times Peter had denied Jesus (John 18:17, 25, 27). Now Jesus gave Peter three chances to declare his love for Him. Each time Peter responded with a positive yes, the Lord commissioned him anew to feed His sheep and lambs. The focus is never on our failure but on God's forgiveness. Jesus was not trying to "rub it in." Rather, He was emphasizing Peter's need to have unconditional love for Him.

Some of the Bible's greatest heroes were failures at some point—Noah, Abraham, Moses, David, Elijah, Jonah. Now Peter joined their ranks. Peter's future would involve shepherding the sheep and fishing for men.

**2. Follow Me (John 21:18-25).** After giving Peter a commission for ministry, Jesus gave a most solemn prophecy of Peter's death. He would be crucified ("Thou shalt stretch forth thy hands"). Following Christ can be most difficult for many people.

Peter's reaction is interesting. He turned around and asked what would happen to John (the disciple who had "leaned on [Jesus'] breast at supper" [John 21:20]).

Jesus responded with a mild rebuke, telling Peter that this was not his business. "God's plans for Christians vary and His reasons are not often made known" (Walvoord and Zuck, eds., *The Bible Knowledge Commentary,* Cook). God would take care of others. Peter's focus needed to be on Jesus, not others. Peter had to learn the same lesson that all followers of Christ need to learn. Service for Christ means looking to Jesus, not others.

These last words of Jesus to Peter conveyed the same message as when Peter first met Him: "Follow thou me" (John 21:22; cf. Mark 1:17).

John closed his gospel by telling readers that there were not enough books to contain all the stories about Jesus. It is interesting, then, to see that he included just this story about Peter. The lesson is tremendous—no person is a failure. God can use any repentant sinner.

## AGE-GROUP EMPHASES

**Children:** The thrice-repeated question to Peter has fascinated people for centuries. Have the children discuss how they would have reacted if asked the same question three times.

**Youths:** Many teens struggle with comparing themselves to others. Use this lesson to help them see that their focus should be on Christ and their relationship with Him.

**Adults:** Ask your adults to discuss why John's final gospel narrative is about Peter.

—*Martin R. Dahlquist.*

# Scripture Lesson Text

**REV. 4:1** After this I looked, and, behold, a door *was* opened in heaven: and the first voice which I heard *was* as it were of a trumpet talking with me; which said, Come up hither, and I will shew thee things which must be hereafter.

**2 And immediately I was in the spirit: and, behold, a throne was set in heaven, and *one* sat on the throne.**

3 And he that sat was to look upon like a jasper and a sardine stone: and *there was* a rainbow round about the throne, in sight like unto an emerald.

**4 And round about the throne *were* four and twenty seats: and upon the seats I saw four and twenty elders sitting, clothed in white raiment; and they had on their heads crowns of gold.**

5 And out of the throne proceeded lightnings and thunderings and voices: and *there were* seven lamps of fire burning before the throne, which are the seven Spir'its of God.

**6 And before the throne *there was* a sea of glass like unto crystal: and in the midst of the throne, and round about the throne, *were* four beasts full of eyes before and behind.**

8 And the four beasts had each of them six wings about *him;* and *they were* full of eyes within: and they rest not day and night, saying, Ho'ly, holy, holy, Lord God Almighty, which was, and is, and is to come.

**9 And when those beasts give glory and honour and thanks to him that sat on the throne, who liveth for ever and ever,**

10 The four and twenty elders fall down before him that sat on the throne, and worship him that liveth for ever and ever, and cast their crowns before the throne, saying,

**11 Thou art worthy, O Lord, to receive glory and honour and power: for thou hast created all things, and for thy pleasure they are and were created.**

**NOTES**

# The Lord God Almighty

## Lesson: Revelation 4:1-6, 8-11

Read: Revelation 4:1-11

TIME: about A.D. 96            PLACE: Patmos

---

**GOLDEN TEXT**—"Thou art worthy, O Lord, to receive glory and honour and power: for thou hast created all things, and for thy pleasure they are and were created" (Revelation 4:11).

---

# Introduction

In the last three studies, we looked at the resurrection and appearances of the Lord Jesus Christ. Such studies humble us and lead us to give Him all glory and honor for His resurrection work.

No study, however, that focuses on the glory and honor of Christ would be complete without an examination of Revelation 4 and 5—two chapters that take us to the height of true worship. In this lesson, we study Revelation 4 with a focus on the Lord God Almighty who sits on His throne. Next week, we move to Revelation 5 and highlight the fact that Christ's glory and honor will continue forever.

These studies will give us a clearer picture of true worship. So often we equate worship with singing songs, praying, and listening to a sermon. All of those elements contribute to worship, but they are superficial if we do not have a heart attitude of adoration of our Lord. Revelation 4 will help us develop the proper heart attitude.

Use this lesson to help your learners raise their level of understanding what true worship is.

## LESSON OUTLINE

I. **CAUGHT UP TO GOD'S THRONE**—Rev. 4:1-2

II. **THE SCENE AROUND GOD'S THRONE**—Rev. 4:3-6, 8a

III. **WORSHIPPING AROUND GOD'S THRONE**—Rev. 4:8b-11

# Exposition: Verse by Verse

## CAUGHT UP TO GOD'S THRONE

**REV. 4:1** After this I looked, and, behold, a door was opened in heaven: and the first voice which I heard was as it were of a trumpet talking with me; which said, Come up hither, and I will shew thee things which must be hereafter.

2 And immediately I was in the spirit: and, behold, a throne was set in heaven, and one sat on the throne.

In Revelation 4, John recorded what he saw in his vision while on the island of Patmos (1:9-10). In that vision God gave him a glimpse of what was to come. Correct interpretation is important in understanding Revelation. In chapters 4 and 5 we face two interpretive issues.

First, we believe in a literal interpretation of Revelation, which means we take John's words in their literal sense (unless we see an obvious figurative sense). When he later referred to a period of one thousand years (20:2), we believe he actually meant one thousand years. When we read the events in Revelation 4, we believe they will literally happen someday in heaven. John's words were not simply a poetic way of expressing a general worship scene.

Second, we hold to a futuristic view of the events of Revelation 4 and on through the end of the book. These events have not happened yet, no matter what similarities people might see in past events. The events from Revelation 4 through 22 are what Jesus meant in 1:19 when He instructed John to write "the things which shall be hereafter." With that understanding, we begin our examination of chapter 4.

The words "after this" in Revelation 4:1 take us back to John's vision of Christ as recorded in chapter 1 and the Lord's messages to the seven churches in chapters 2 and 3. After seeing and hearing all these things, John saw in his vision a door standing open in heaven. He then heard a voice like a trumpet saying, "Come up hither, and I will shew thee things which must be hereafter." This expression, similar to the one in 1:19, shows the future nature of these events.

Upon hearing the words in Revelation 4:1 John was immediately "in the spirit" (vs. 2) and taken by a vision to the door in heaven where he saw the throne and God Himself sitting on the throne. The words "in the spirit" may refer to John's spirit or to the Holy Spirit. Perhaps we can see both ideas here in that John's spirit, through the work of the Holy Spirit, was taken to heaven while he physically remained on Patmos. (Note a similar expression in Revelation 1:10.)

The invitation to come up calls for special attention. Some see these words as a reference to the rapture of the church (the church saints will come up from earth to heaven). However, the invitation may simply refer to the fact that for John to see the heavenly throne room, he had to come up from Patmos.

Even if these words do not refer to the rapture of the church, this verse is still significant in support of the pretribulational position (the church will be raptured before the tribulation begins). Revelation 2 and 3 addressed seven local churches, but starting in Revelation 4:1, the church is not seen again until she comes back with her Lord at His return in Revelation 19. (To be fair, many of those who hold other views will say that the church is simply not a focus of concern in chapters 4 through 19.)

Still, the absence of the church from Revelation 4 through 19 may well suggest that the church is not on earth during the tribulation period (Rev. 6—18) but rather is in heaven with the Lord.

## THE SCENE AROUND GOD'S THRONE

**3 And he that sat was to look upon like a jasper and a sardine stone: and there was a rainbow round about the throne, in sight like unto an emerald.**

**4 And round about the throne were four and twenty seats: and upon the seats I saw four and twenty elders sitting, clothed in white rai-**

ment; and they had on their heads crowns of gold.

5 And out of the throne proceeded lightnings and thunderings and voices: and there were seven lamps of fire burning before the throne, which are the seven Spirits of God.

6 And before the throne there was a sea of glass like unto crystal: and in the midst of the throne, and round about the throne, were four beasts full of eyes before and behind.

8a And the four beasts had each of them six wings about him; and they were full of eyes within.

**God Himself (Rev. 4:3).** As John peered into the heavenly throne room, he first saw God Himself sitting on the throne. John compared the appearance of the Lord to the brilliance of gems like jasper and sardine (sardius). Jasper stones today are opaque, but in Revelation 21:11 John mentioned jasper and described it as "clear as crystal." So the stone may have been a diamond that reflected the glory and radiance of God. The sardius stone was ruby in color. These two stones will be part of the foundation of the New Jerusalem (vss. 19-21).

John also recorded that he saw a rainbow around the throne that glowed like an emerald. Perhaps the rainbow had its usual several colors, but a brilliant green hue was dominant. The point of the description is the beauty and magnificence of God. (Note Ezekiel 1:28 for another description of the Lord involving a rainbow.)

**The elders (Rev. 4:4).** Next, John recorded that he saw twenty-four elders sitting on twenty-four smaller thrones. These elders seem to represent redeemed saints since they are clothed in white robes, have crowns on their heads, and sing the song of the redeemed (cf. 5:8-10). The Old Testa-

ment and tribulation saints are not yet in heaven, so the elders probably represent the church saints. Why are there twenty-four elders? One possibility is that the Mosaic priesthood had twenty-four orders (I Chron. 24:7-18), so twenty-four may be the number of representation.

**The surroundings (Rev. 4:5-6a).** In this heavenly scene, John observed lightning and heard thunder and voices. (Thunder is also mentioned in 6:1, 8:5, 11:19, 14:2, 16:18, and 19:6.) These elements contributed to the awe-inspiring and powerful nature of the scene. He next noted "seven lamps of fire burning before the throne" (4:5), which he identified as the "seven Spirits of God."

These seven Spirits are not seven separate beings; rather, they identify the Holy Spirit. The phrase probably refers either to the sevenfold character of the Holy Spirit (cf. Isa. 11:2) or to the lampstand with seven lamps (Zech. 4:1-10), which pictured the Holy Spirit.

The number seven represents perfection, showing the perfection of the Holy Spirit. So in Revelation 4 we see God the Father on the throne and God the Holy Spirit also present. This scene prepares us for the appearance of God the Son in chapter 5.

The final element in the scene is a sea of glass, which looked like crystal. These words refer to the pavement under and in front of God's throne that spread out like a crystalline sea or expanse (cf. Exod. 24:10; Ezek. 1:22). Though we may not be sure exactly what some of these elements are, we know enough to visualize a resplendent, majestic worship scene in heaven.

**The living creatures (Rev. 4:6b, 8a).** Around the throne are four beasts, or living creatures, who assist in the worship of the Lord. Who are these creatures? While several ideas have been proposed, they most likely are a special order of angels who are often associated with the presence, holiness, and majesty of God. We find a similar scene in Isaiah 6:1-2, where the angels are identified as seraphim. The angels in Ezekiel 1:4-25, identified as cherubim (cf. 10:15), also seem similar.

Revelation 4 speaks of four living creatures, the same number as identified in Ezekiel 1:5. Why are there four angels around God's throne? Some suggest the number represents four attributes of God or the pictures of Christ in the four Gospels. Perhaps the number four represents the wide extent and reach these angels have to the four corners of the earth.

John described these living creatures as "full of eyes before and behind" and "full of eyes within" (Rev. 1:6, 8; cf. Ezek. 1:18). These eyes may represent the angels' awareness of all that goes on in the Lord's presence.

These living creatures also have six wings, similar to the seraphim in Isaiah 6. (The cherubim described in Ezekiel 1:6 had four wings.) Perhaps the wings represent the swiftness with which these heavenly beings can carry out their responsibilities.

The scene is set. God the Father in His glorious beauty is on His throne surrounded by lamps of fire representing the Holy Spirit. Lightning, thunder, and voices fill the area. Twenty-four elders and four angels complete the scene. Now we are ready to consider the worship of the awesome and holy God.

## WORSHIPPING AROUND GOD'S THRONE

**8b And they rest not day and night, saying, Holy, holy, holy, Lord God Almighty, which was, and is, and is to come.**

**9 And when those beasts give glory and honour and thanks to him that sat on the throne, who liveth for ever and ever,**

**10 The four and twenty elders fall down before him that sat on the throne, and worship him that liveth for ever and ever, and cast their crowns before the throne, saying,**

**11 Thou art worthy, O Lord, to receive glory and honour and power: for thou hast created all things, and for thy pleasure they are and were created.**

**Worship by the living creatures (Rev. 4:8b-9).** The four angelic beings worship the Lord continuously ("they rest not day and night") with the words "Holy, holy, holy, Lord God Almighty, which was, and is, and is to come." This worship draws attention to three attributes of our Lord. First, and most obviously, He is holy. A single mention of His holiness, however, is hardly sufficient. Like the seraphim in Isaiah 6:3, the living creatures extol His holiness in a threefold expression of praise.

Second, the angels worship the Lord for His power. He is not a creature like them. He is the Lord, the Almighty God; He is all-powerful. Third, the angels praise the Lord as the eternal God who was, who is, and who is to come. He has always existed and always will exist in His glorious splendor.

Revelation 4:9 sums up the worship by the angels by saying they "give glory and honour and thanks to him that sat on the throne, who liveth for ever and ever," a reference again to God's eternality.

**Worship by the elders (Rev. 4:10-11).** Verse 9 tells us that whenever the four beings worship the Lord, the twenty-four elders also join in. They fall before the throne of God and "worship him that liveth for ever and ever" (vs. 10). This is the third reference to God's eternality, which shows that praise for His eternality should be a major part of our worship. Verse 10 also states that these elders will "cast their crowns before the throne." The elders represent the church saints, so the crowns must be what the Lord gives to believers for their service for Him on earth.

These crowns will be given at the judgment seat of Christ, which will occur at the rapture of the church (cf. I Cor. 4:5; I John 2:28). These crowns are referred to in I Corinthians 9:25, I Thessalonians 2:19, II Timothy 4:8, James 1:12, and I Peter 5:4. The elders' act of casting their crowns before the Lord shows their awareness that anything they accomplished was only because the Lord enabled them to do so. The glory is all His, not theirs.

As the elders cast their crowns before the Lord, they acclaim His worthiness to receive their worship. "Thou art worthy, O Lord, to receive glory and honour and power" (Rev. 4:11). (We will see the worthiness of the Lord Jesus Christ in chapter 5.) The elders specifically identify God's creation work as that which makes Him worthy of worship.

While many deny His role as Creator, we extol Him as the One who created all things "that are in heaven, and that are in earth, visible and invisible, whether they be thrones, or dominions, or principalities, or powers" (Col. 1:16). Paul added the thought that "all things were created by him, and for him." This thought is expanded on in Revelation 4:11 in the statement that God performed His creation work not primarily for us but for His own pleasure.

The worship scene of Revelation 4 will take place in heaven someday, but we can learn from it how to worship our Almighty God today. First, in our worship let us try to capture in our minds the awesomeness and splendor of our Lord. No one else is like Him in the universe.

Second, when we worship, we need to get a clearer picture of the holiness of our God. His holiness does not simply mean He does not sin. Rather, holiness is His nature and the very essence of His being. We need to acclaim His holiness in our worship.

Third, in all our worship let us proclaim His eternality—the One who was and is and is to come.

Fourth, whenever we worship, let us frequently acknowledge Him as the Creator of all things. He is pleased when we do so because He created everything for His own pleasure.

Worship for us should not be a mechanical, mundane activity. Rather, we should strive to engage in meaningful, vibrant praise of our Lord God Almighty.

—*Don Anderson.*

# QUESTIONS

1. What are the possible meanings of "in the Spirit" in Revelation 4:2?

2. Why is the appearance of God compared to precious stones?

3. What is the most likely identification of the twenty-four elders?

4. Who is pictured by the seven lamps of fire?

5. What is the most likely identification of the four living creatures?

6. What do their eyes and wings represent?

7. What three attributes of God are emphasized by the angelic worship?

8. What does casting crowns before God represent?

9. What did the elders specifically identify as making God worthy of worship?

10. How can you better incorporate the attributes of God noted in our lesson into your worship?

—*Don Anderson.*

# *Preparing to Teach the Lesson*

There are several new teachings abroad today that purport to "reveal" what will be in heaven and what will be done there. These are speculative, although verses are quoted to support these misguided ideas. We must remember, in all our teaching of the Scriptures, not to add or subtract from the plain teachings of the Word of God (cf. Rev. 22:18-19). We must not "deduce" or add products of our own thinking, no matter how grand or well-intentioned.

We might not think it makes much difference if we add our speculations to the text on such a future matter as heaven. We might say, "No one will miss heaven because he thought wrongly about it," but if we change one tiny "insignificant" item here, we have opened the door to further changes elsewhere. This is extremely dangerous, as Revelation 22:19 suggests.

## TODAY'S AIM

**Facts:** to learn truths about God and our eternal home and occupation.

**Principle:** to understand that we can always learn much, even from prophecies and visions recorded in Scripture.

**Application:** to live as the Lord's people, praising Him daily.

## INTRODUCING THE LESSON

This very short chapter records a vision of heaven and describes those present there along with their activities. God did not have to tell us this. His great eternal plan will still roll on whether or not we understand what He is doing. However, He seems to delight in letting His children know of events and truths the world does not otherwise know. Our best course of action, then, is to study what has been given us and see what lessons or inspiration we might derive from it.

## DEVELOPING THE LESSON

**1. The scene in heaven (Rev. 4:1-6).** These verses do not depict the fanciful imagination of the Apostle John but rather the experience he was given and told to record for us.

Any preacher worth his salt is bound to mention that God's door is always open in heaven, where we may approach the Lord in prayer. The invitation to trust in the Lord and be saved is always open, as is the opportunity to confess our sins to Him, be cleansed, and get back on track living for Him.

John was immediately in the Holy Spirit, ready to listen and respond to the Lord. John's spirit was caught away by the Holy Spirit and shown heaven. He saw a throne and God seated upon it. The beauty he described is unearthly, yet it does not seem unreal.

He also saw twenty-four elders sitting around God's throne. He described thundering and lightning and voices and "seven lamps of fire . . . which are the seven Spirits of God" (Rev. 4:5). These seven spirits are mentioned elsewhere in Scripture (1:4; 3:1). This expression may represent the sevenfold (signifying complete and perfect) Spirit of God. John mentioned a sea of glass like crystal and four beasts, or living creatures, in the midst of and around the throne. Again, all that John saw was definitely not like anything in this world, and yet it is totally real and does not seem too far beyond our comprehension. We are assured that all these things are, in fact, in heaven.

**2. The activity of the four beasts (Rev. 4:8-9).** In verse 6, we read that the four supernatural creatures are "full of eyes before and behind." Verse 8 further indicates that they are covered with eyes everywhere. These creatures appear to be angelic beings, perhaps cherubim (cf. Ezek. 10:1-22). Their many eyes probably symbolize great knowledge.

The four living creatures never rest or stop saying the words recorded here. They are so impressed with and in awe of the holiness of God and the eternity of God that they just cannot get over it. The thought is continually new and exciting.

It may be that when God's people get to heaven, they will be so in awe of God's holiness that they cannot stop talking about it. He is infinitely holy (cf. Isa. 6:3). If we were likewise acquainted with the power and splendor of God's presence, we would surely be thinking and talking about them constantly. As A. W. Tozer used to say, "Acquaint yourself with God" (*The Knowledge of the Holy,* Harper Collins).

The words of the four beasts are equated in Revelation 4:9 with giving glory and honor and thanks to God. This triggers the worship and praise of God by the twenty-four elders.

**3. The praise of the elders (Rev. 4:10-11).** The twenty-four elders, whoever they are, are seen falling down before the Lord. This is a position of worship. They cast their crowns before His throne in an act of submission and obedience. Their contribution to what is said in heaven is to attribute to God worthiness to receive glory and honor and power. The reason for this praise is that He has created all things for His pleasure.

It is amazing how many times in Scripture the truth that God is the Creator of everything is mentioned. This is why Satan so hates the thought and seeks through any and all means to negate it, especially by teaching evolution. Satan obviously does not want humans to think that God is their Creator and that they owe Him any obedience or responsibility for their thoughts and actions.

## ILLUSTRATING THE LESSON

Heaven will be filled with worship that is too wonderful to fully describe.

## CONCLUDING THE LESSON

Our purpose in life is to praise God for all that we know at present to be true of Him. The ultimate truth is that God is our Creator and is worthy of our highest praise. He is gloriously beautiful beyond our comprehension. His virtues and attributes are more magnificent than we can possibly imagine. Saying back to Him what He has shown us to be true about Him is our highest praise. This must come, of course, from a humble and believing heart.

This chapter gives us a pattern for praise, reasons for praise, and even the way to praise God. God is not made bigger or greater by our praise, nor does He need it to be happy or fulfilled. He is complete in Himself. However, He has delighted to share these things with us. We can do no better than to joyfully enter into them.

## ANTICIPATING THE NEXT LESSON

Our next lesson continues the heavenly scene with the focus on the Lamb and the praise He is due.

—*Brian D. Doud.*

# PRACTICAL POINTS

1. We can only be guided by God's wisdom when we are filled with the Spirit of God (Rev. 4:1-3).
2. God has prepared a place for us in heaven (vs. 4).
3. God's majesty is awesome. Nothing on earth compares to His glory (vss. 5-6).
4. God's power extends far beyond the four corners of the earth into the heavens and throughout the universe (vs. 6).
5. All living things were created to worship and glorify God (vss. 8-10).
6. All creation belongs to God (vs. 11).
   —Valante M. Grant.

# RESEARCH AND DISCUSSION

1. How do visions of eternal heaven provide comfort for us in this temporary, earthly world?
2. What does the sound of the trumpet represent?
3. What do descriptions of the throne of God indicate about God's power?
4. What message do visions of jasper, emerald, and gold tell us about the value of salvation?
5. How do earthly positions of authority compare to the sovereign power of God?
6. How is John's vision of the throne of God similar to Isaiah's vision of God's throne (cf. Isa. 6:1-5)?
7. What is your vision of God? How does it impact the way that you worship Him? Discuss.
   —Valante M. Grant.

# ILLUSTRATED HIGH POINTS

**Lightnings and thunderings**

Some people delight to view a thunderstorm (from a sheltered place, of course) because they know the odds of being struck by lightning is 1/600,000. Others are terribly frightened.

When John had the vision of God on His throne, there was beauty but also the manifestation of power, judgment, and holiness.

**Rest not . . . saying, Holy, holy, holy**

We may not think about it much, but there is a constant prayer meeting going on in heaven. It is not like most of ours here on earth, which tend to major in trivial issues. The one is heaven gives constant praise, honor, and glory to the eternal Creator and Redeemer.

A. W. Pink's (1886-1952) mother taught him the following poem about prayer and the importance for sincerity as one prays:

> I often say my prayers,
> But do I ever pray?
> And do the wishes of my heart
> Go with the word I say?
> I may as well kneel down
> And worship gods of stone,
> As offer to the living God
> A prayer of words alone.

**And worship him**

Many Christians equate worship with church attendance. If they simply show up, most people assume they have fulfilled their duty in worshipping God. J. S. Bouchier penned "Why They Go to Church," which challenges us:

> Some go to church for just a walk,
> Some go to stare, laugh, and talk,
> Some go there to meet a friend,
> Some their idle time to spend,
> Some for general observation,
> Some for private speculation;
> Some to seek or find a lover,
> Some a courtship to discover; . . .
> Some to sit and doze, and nod,
> But few to kneel and worship God!
> —David A. Hamburg.

# Golden Text Illuminated

**"Thou art worthy, O Lord, to receive glory and honour and power: for thou hast created all things, and for thy pleasure they are and were created" (Revelation 4:11).**

When we stand before God, what will we say to Him? Many people contemplate this moment; some have drawn up mental lists of questions they plan to put to the Lord, as if they will be the ones interrogating the Creator for His missteps and shortcomings! Some even seem to imagine they will ask the one question that will stump God (and that they will be the first to ask it)!

When John was given a vision of a great assembly before the throne of God in heaven (Rev. 4:1-11), things were quite different. Nobody called attention to himself or presumed to bring questions that God had to answer. The elders and living creatures cast all their attention to the One who sat on the throne. Although they were impressive beings themselves in John's eyes, they counted themselves as nothing in the presence of the Almighty Majesty. Casting their crowns before the throne, they put everything into proclaiming His glory.

What the twenty-four elders and four living creatures said (or sang—the Greek for "saying" in Revelation 4:10 was frequently used in musical contexts) can provide a condensed version of what we will likely be giving voice to throughout eternity. Let us look closely at their words.

"Thou art worthy, O Lord." If we looked at ourselves, we would be compelled to declare that we are not worthy. We are certainly not worthy of any divine blessing or favor. But those before the throne were not looking at themselves; they were looking at God. And what they saw more than anything was His worth, His absolute preeminence and importance above all things.

Parents sometimes tell a demanding child who expects them to cater to his whims, "It's not all about you." The world does not revolve around us, and the sooner we learn that, the better off we will be. But the converse is completely true: It *is* all about God. *Everything* revolves around Him, and the sooner we learn that, the better off we will be in every possible way.

"To receive glory and honour and power." We might wonder, *How can God receive glory, honor, and power when He already possesses these in infinite measure?* This is entirely true, but the point here is the recognition of this reality by His subjects. People are constantly giving, or ascribing, honor and importance to any number of things in life. The only one who is worthy of our doing this, however, is God Himself.

"For thou hast created all things." Here the heavenly assembly supplied one of the most important reasons for God's unmatched worthiness—without Him, nothing else would exist. He is our Creator; we are the works of His hands. We have the privilege of joining with all the rest of creation to acknowledge our joyful dependence on our Maker.

"For thy pleasure they were and are created." This is a most important truth to grasp and remember. God did not create us because He needed us but because it pleased Him to do so. We exist to bring Him joy, and that truth gives us more significance than all the accolades or praise the world can muster.

—*Kenneth A. Sponsler.*

# Heart of the Lesson

My first real job was working as a sales clerk in a family-owned jewelry store. One of the initial things I learned was to name and identify all the birthstones. In our lesson today, John referred to precious stones to help describe what he saw in his first glimpse of heaven.

**1. God's throne room (Rev. 4:1-6a).** As John continued to experience a divine revelation of the future, he looked up and saw a door opened to heaven. Jesus' trumpet-sounding voice, which John had heard earlier, invited him to come up and see what would occur following the things he had just witnessed in his vision.

Immediately, in the Spirit, John was in heaven, viewing a throne with someone sitting on it. John described no details of the figure on the throne; God the Father is spirit and dwells in inapproachable light. Thus John described as best he could the light emanating from the throne and from the One sitting on it.

The One on the throne glowed in a mixture of colors: the red, brown, and yellow of jasper and the deep red of sardius. An emerald-green rainbow circled the throne.

Also surrounding God's throne were twenty-four elders sitting on twenty-four thrones. The elders wore white garments, signifying purity, and gold crowns. Flashes of lightning, peals of thunder, and voices proceeded from the throne. In front of the throne burned seven lamps. A glassy sea, sparkling like crystal, stretched out from before the throne. In John's time, clear glass was nearly nonexistent. To John, this sea would be of priceless materials.

**2. Worship at God's throne (Rev. 4:6b, 8-11).** The final thing John saw around the throne were four living creatures covered with eyes. Eyes even covered both sides of their six wings. Many scholars believe that these living creatures are cherubim, a special class of angels.

Without ceasing, they proclaimed God's holiness. He is the Lord God Almighty, the One set apart, morally pure, all-powerful, and sovereign over the universe. They noted God's everlastingness—He is without beginning or end. In their worship, the creatures were acknowledging who God is and His attributes. That is a good starting place for us in our worship.

Each time the living creatures gave glory, honor, and thanks to God, the elders also worshipped. They left their thrones—their places of honor—and fell before God to give Him greater honor. Then they placed their crowns before His throne.

The elders praised God, saying He was worthy to receive glory, honor, and power. They especially praised God as the Creator, who created all things for His pleasure. How humbling but how wonderful to think that the Almighty God delights in you and me.

Praise and worship continued nonstop in God's throne room. Our earthbound minds cause us to question whether the creatures and elders ever tire from their perpetual worship. But God is so awe-inspiring and fulfilling that they want nothing more than to bask in His presence.

When in love, we gaze into our beloved's eyes and long to simply be with that person. Or while on vacation, we view a sunset and wish we could linger and watch. Those are imperfect hints of the wonder the living creatures and elders felt in God's presence. Someday, all believers will see God face-to-face and experience His majesty.

—Ann Staatz.

# World Missions

Imagine you lived in unimaginable wealth, in a grand mansion with more than enough food and clothing and resources of all kinds. Next to you was a slum, where people made homes from sodden cardboard or scraps of plastic. The people in the slum never had enough to eat. They died of sickness because they could not afford doctors or medicine. They lived in anguish and had no hope.

This is not a terrible nightmare, but rather a terrible reality. In one country where I lived, a few very wealthy people live lives of ease while millions around them are dying.

We may feel a sense of righteous indignation. How can they ignore the needs around them? How can they be so uncaring, so heartless?

Were we in that situation, we would do something about it. We would help the hurting, the needy, the dying. We would share.

Or would we?

Spiritually, we live in unimaginable wealth. We have access to the riches of heaven (Eph. 1:3). Yet the world around us is dying—hungry, sick, and in despair. They try to make do with paltry materials. They fill their lives with things that can never satisfy.

Are we sharing?

Are we showing the needy, the hurting, and the dying that there is hope? That there is another way, one that can heal and save them?

Materially, we are among the richest people in the world. Just because the slums are not adjacent to our houses does not mean those who live in them are not our neighbors.

Consider the Dalits, the untouchable caste of over two hundred million in India, considered worthless and unclean. Ostracized and exploited, they have no chance of changing what is considered their destiny.

One Dalit, Rajan (name changed), had to leave school in fifth grade to work all day for a rich man who beat and mistreated him. Rajan's family was paid four dollars a month for Rajan's labor. One day the rich man's son taunted Rajan and threw rocks and dirt clods at him. One got stuck in Rajan's eye, and the blood flowed.

The rich man took his "damaged property" to the hospital, but he refused to pay to have the clod removed. Rajan's eye became infected, and he lost sight in that eye. The man fired him and sent him home, where he went completely blind. His father began drinking. His mother died in despair. He prayed to the gods, but they did not help. He truly believed himself the worthless dog he was told he was.

We know Rajan is not worthless. We know he was created by a loving Heavenly Father. We know there is hope for Rajan—he has worth and value to Jesus.

But how could that change Rajan's life if no one tells him?

One man did. One person went to Rajan's area and told him about Jesus. Rajan's life changed forever. Still blind, he now goes to neighboring villages using a walking stick and tells people about Christ. "I am precious to God and of infinite worth," he shares. "And you are too."

Every Dalit was created with purpose and love. Will we share some of our abundant resources to give that message? (See *Gospel for Asia*, www.gfa.org.)

You can change a life like Rajan's today. Will you?

—*Kimberly Rae.*

# The Jewish Aspect

A January 2016 article from World Jewish Daily, titled "The Numbers," reports that the grandchildren of concentration camp survivors are copying their grandparents' concentration-camp tattooed numbers (worldjewish daily.com). The numbers are important to them because they are a reminder of the atrocious acts of the past. But numbers in general play a significant role in Judaism.

Numbers also play a part in this week's lesson. As you look at the text, you see that it makes mention of one who sat on the throne (Rev. 4:2), twenty-four thrones and elders (vs. 4), seven lamps (vs. 5), seven spirits of God (vs. 5), four living creatures (vs. 6), and six wings on each of the four creatures (vs. 8). Each of these numbers has importance in the Jewish mind.

Some Jews even believe that numbers are one way of reaching the divine. Gematria, which is a form of Jewish mysticism, is a numerological system in which words and sections of the Torah are converted into numbers, which in turn are believed to reveal hidden truths. In fact, not only can Hebrew words be converted into numbers, but each Hebrew letter can also be converted into a numerical value.

Twenty-two letters comprise the Hebrew alphabet. There are no vowels. However, to aid in pronunciation, the medieval rabbis created a system of dots and dashes called nikkud. These dots and dashes are placed above, below, or within the letters, and today are used as vowels.

The Hebrew alphabet is written from right to left, the opposite of the way we read English. The alphabet begins with the letter aleph and ends with the letter taw.

Each letter has a numerical value.

For example, aleph through yod have values one through ten. After yod, the numbers have values of ten, until one hundred is reached. At the letter qoph, which has the value of one hundred, the letters have values of hundreds. The last letter, taw, has the value of four hundred.

Many numbers are significant or sacred to Judaism. Some numbers are valued more than others. For example, the number one signifies unity, wholeness, and divinity (Dennis, "Judaism & Numbers," myjewishlearning.com). The Shema Yisrael, or the prayer that serves as a morning and evening prayer service starts, "Hear O Israel: the Lord our God is one Lord" (Deut. 6:4).

Four, an important recurrent number in Judaism, has special worth. The seder, the special meal that takes place on Passover, contains several examples of important fours. During the seder there are four questions, four sons, and four cups of wine (Dennis). Four "denotes completeness and sufficiency" (Levias, "Numbers and Numerals," jewishencyclopedia.com).

Seven, one of the most important numbers in Judaism, represents Creation and blessings. The days of creation and the seven lamps for the lampstand in the tabernacle (Exod. 25:37) utilize the number seven. In addition, seven full weeks are counted between Passover and Pentecost.

"The number twenty-four symbolizes abundance" (Dennis). The number forty usually denotes "a time of radical transition or transformation" (Dennis) and "stands in the Bible for a generation" (Levias). The number seventy signifies the nations of the world.

—Robin Fitzgerald.

# Guiding the Superintendent

One moment the Apostle John was languishing in exile on an island, and the next he was transferred to the very center of the universe. John found himself in a place that perhaps no other person has ever seen. He saw "a door . . . opened in heaven" (Rev. 4:1) and heard a voice that bid him to go in.

With the sights, sounds, color, and glory of heaven, John was introduced to those around the throne that praises the Lord God Almighty.

## DEVOTIONAL OUTLINE

**1. Heavenly worship center (Rev. 4:1-6).** Upon entrance into heaven, John's attention was drawn to a throne and the One who sat on it. John used the shimmering quality of two types of gem stones, jasper (green) and sardine or carnelian (red), to describe this heavenly Ruler.

Around the throne was a rainbow resembling an emerald. Unlike earthly rainbows, this one was one color. Since Noah, the rainbow (Gen. 9:12-17) has been a sign of God's faithfulness.

Seated around the throne were twenty-four elders dressed in white, and wearing crowns (Rev. 4:4). This crown is the *stephanos,* or reward crown.

Lightning and thunder proceed from the throne in a laser-like light show, and seven menorahs stand before the throne, symbolizing the Holy Spirit ("the seven Spirits of God" [Rev. 4:5]). Before the throne John saw "a sea of glass like unto crystal" (vs. 6).

**2. Heavenly worship (Rev. 4:8-11).** Led by four angelic creatures, the assembly before the throne was engaged in worship of God. First, God was worshipped because He is holy. Three times God was praised for His moral perfection, or holiness. He was praised using three of His Old Testament names: Lord (or Yahweh), God (or Elohim), and Almighty (Lord of Hosts). To all this praise was joined a great cry celebrating God's eternal nature, "which was, and is, and is to come."

Second, God was worshipped because He is sovereign. Glory, honor, and thanks were heaped on the one who lives forever. The worship vocabulary is specific: "glory" (praise), "honour," and "thanks" (Rev. 4:9).

Finally, God was worshipped because He is the Creator and Sustainer of the universe. The twenty-four elders responded to all this worship by falling down before God and casting their crowns before the throne. The crowns are rewards the elders had received, and now they were giving them back to God in worship.

Two more words are added to the worship vocabulary: "worthy" (deserving) and "power" (Rev. 4:11). This is not destructive power but creative power.

God sits at the very center of the universe, and there He is worshipped by all His creation as the great Creator of the world. Today many questions swirl around in the church about what worship really is. The lesson this week emphasizes one important fact about worship. Worship is more a reaction to the Creator God than a planned agenda on our part.

## AGE-GROUP EMPHASES

**Children:** Invite your children to imagine they are John in this vision of heaven. What are they seeing and thinking?

**Youths:** Have the young people discuss how creation demonstrates God's glory and power.

**Adults:** Have your adults discuss what true worship really is.

—*Martin R. Dahlquist.*

# Scripture Lesson Text

**REV. 5:6** And I beheld, and, lo, in the midst of the throne and of the four beasts, and in the midst of the elders, stood a Lamb as it had been slain, having seven horns and seven eyes, which are the seven Spir'its of God sent forth into all the earth.

**7 And he came and took the book out of the right hand of him that sat upon the throne.**

8 And when he had taken the book, the four beasts and four *and* twenty elders fell down before the Lamb, having every one of them harps, and golden vials full of odours, which are the prayers of saints.

**9 And they sung a new song, saying, Thou art worthy to take the book, and to open the seals thereof: for thou wast slain, and hast redeemed us to God by thy blood out of every kindred, and tongue, and people, and nation;**

10 And hast made us unto our God kings and priests: and we shall reign on the earth.

**11 And I beheld, and I heard the voice of many angels round about the throne and the beasts and the elders: and the number of them was ten thousand times ten thousand, and thousands of thousands;**

12 Saying with a loud voice, Worthy is the Lamb that was slain to receive power, and riches, and wisdom, and strength, and honour, and glory, and blessing.

**13 And every creature which is in heaven, and on the earth, and under the earth, and such as are in the sea, and all that are in them, heard I saying, Blessing, and honour, and glory, and power, *be* unto him that sitteth upon the throne, and unto the Lamb for ever and ever.**

14 And the four beasts said, Amen. And the four *and* twenty elders fell down and worshipped him that liveth for ever and ever.

## NOTES

# Blessing, Glory, and Honor Forever

### Lesson: Revelation 5:6-14

#### Read: Revelation 5:1-14

TIME: about A.D. 96

PLACE: Patmos

---

**GOLDEN TEXT—"Worthy is the Lamb that was slain to receive power, and riches, and wisdom, and strength, and honour, and glory, and blessing" (Revelation 5:12).**

---

# Introduction

The word "forever" is a big part of our Christian vocabulary. We speak of the Lord who has lived and shall live forever, and we rejoice in the fact that we shall live forever in heaven.

We know that the word "forever" means "without end," or "eternal," but many of us do not take enough time to ponder the concept of the word "forever." Though we can never grasp its meaning fully, we would do well to meditate regularly on this important truth.

The Triune God has lived forever. He had no beginning. There never was a time when He did not exist. We cannot ask where God came from or how or when He began. Our finite minds cannot grasp this truth.

Looking ahead, we know that all of us who believe and trust the Lord will worship the Lord forever and ever! We will never cease to worship Him. Lead your students in this study to capture a small part of this eternal worship.

# LESSON OUTLINE

I. **THE LAMB IN THE MIDST OF THE THRONE—Rev. 5:6-7**

II. **THE WORSHIP AROUND THE THRONE—Rev. 5:8-14**

# Exposition: Verse by Verse

**THE LAMB IN THE MIDST OF THE THRONE**

**REV. 5:6  And I beheld, and, lo, in the midst of the throne and of the four beasts, and in the midst of the** elders, stood a Lamb as it had been slain, having seven horns and seven eyes, which are the seven Spirits of God sent forth into all the earth.

**7 And he came and took the book out of the right hand of him that sat upon the throne.**

**The Lamb's description (Rev. 5:6).** In Revelation 4, we were introduced to the throne room in heaven where John saw God the Father on the throne (vs. 2), surrounded by four creatures and twenty-four elders. We also saw God the Holy Spirit represented in the seven lamps of fire (vs. 5). In the first five verses of Revelation 5, we read about an event in this throne room that prepares us for the appearance of God the Son. In the Father's right hand is "a book written within and on the backside, sealed with seven seals" (vs. 1).

This book was probably in the form of a scroll. The seven seals were most likely not all on the outside of the rolled scroll. Rather, every time the scroll was rolled once, a seal was put on it to hold it. Thus, when a person unrolled the scroll, he had to break the seals one by one.

What was written in the book? We are not told, but some have thought it was the terms to a deed, similar to what is described in Jeremiah 32:7-15. If this is the case, perhaps this book is the title deed to the universe. The universal worship in the last part of Revelation 5 would certainly support that idea.

We must also connect this book with Revelation 6, 7, and 8, where we learn that the Lamb unrolled the scroll and opened each of the seven seals, which brought judgments on the earth. The fact that the book had seven seals reminds us of God's perfection, even in judgment.

John then saw a "strong angel" who asked this question: "Who is worthy to open the book, and to loose the seals thereof?" (Rev. 5:2). We are not told the identity of the "strong angel," but it may be Gabriel since his name means "God is my strength." The answer immediately came back that no one in the universe ("no man in heaven, nor in earth, neither under the earth") was able to open the book or even to look inside of it (vs. 3).

Evidently, the heavenly worshippers, especially John, were concerned that no one was able to open the seals and look in the book. That is why John wept bitterly when no one was found who could open it.

Why were John and the others so concerned that no one was able to open the book? If the book is the title deed to the universe, then perhaps they recognized that earth's history was coming to a point of culmination and that they did not know who would sovereignly control everything.

At that point one of the elders around God's throne said, "Weep not: behold, the Lion of the tribe of Juda, the Root of David, hath prevailed to open the book, and to loose the seven seals thereof" (Rev. 5:5). The elder informed John that Christ had already "prevailed to open the book, and to loose the seven seals thereof," so John did not need to continue weeping.

We know that the elder was speaking about none other than the Lord Jesus Christ (cf. Gen. 49:8-10; Isa. 11:1). Then in Revelation 5:6-14, we learn more about the Lord Jesus and what He will do.

John then saw the Lord Jesus Christ standing in the throne room in the midst of the four living creatures (beasts) and twenty-four elders. The fact that He is standing shows His victory over death and His readiness to take the book. The living creatures are probably angels, and the twenty-four elders likely represent the redeemed from the church age. (See the comments in last week's study on Revelation 4:4-6.)

Revelation 5:6 describes Jesus as

"a Lamb as it had been slain." This description brings to mind Jesus' work as the Passover Lamb who was sacrificed for us (Isa. 53:7; John 1:29). When John saw the Lord Jesus, he could tell He had been slain because He still bore the marks of His crucifixion.

Interestingly, John first described Jesus as a lion, and now he described Him as a lamb. Perhaps the analogy to a lamb refers to His first coming in meekness and His role as a lion to His second coming in power.

John wrote that the Lord Jesus had seven horns and seven eyes, which he identified as the seven Spirits of God that He had sent out into every part of the earth. Animals use their horns to exert strength and power, so the horns probably represent Jesus' authority and power. The seven eyes are described as being the seven Spirits of God. This phrase, also used in Revelation 4:5, probably points to the Holy Spirit in His sevenfold character (Isa. 11:2) or to the Holy Spirit as pictured in lampstand with seven lamps (Zech. 4:1-10). The number seven represents perfection, showing the Spirit's perfection.

Here we have the Triune God in His full display. God the Father is seated on the throne with the book in His right hand. God the Son is standing in the midst of this scene as the Lamb who was slain for our sins. God the Holy Spirit is represented through the seven eyes of the Lamb. No wonder the worshippers were overawed by the scene!

**The Lamb's triumph (Rev. 5:7).** This section concludes with Jesus' triumphal act of receiving the book from the hand of God the Father. This action shows that the Lord Jesus is indeed worthy to take the book and open its seals. He is the Creator and Owner of the universe, and He will direct the course of the events that are described in the book of Revelation.

## THE WORSHIP AROUND THE THRONE

8 And when he had taken the book, the four beasts and four and twenty elders fell down before the Lamb, having every one of them harps, and golden vials full of odours, which are the prayers of saints.

9 And they sung a new song, saying, Thou art worthy to take the book, and to open the seals thereof: for thou wast slain, and hast redeemed us to God by thy blood out of every kindred, and tongue, and people, and nation;

10 And hast made us unto our God kings and priests: and we shall reign on the earth.

11 And I beheld, and I heard the voice of many angels round about the throne and the beasts and the elders: and the number of them was ten thousand times ten thousand, and thousands of thousands;

12 Saying with a loud voice, Worthy is the Lamb that was slain to receive power, and riches, and wisdom, and strength, and honour, and glory, and blessing.

13 And every creature which is in heaven, and on the earth, and under the earth, and such as are in the sea, and all that are in them, heard I saying, Blessing, and honour, and glory, and power, be unto him that sitteth upon the throne, and unto the Lamb for ever and ever.

14 And the four beasts said, Amen. And the four and twenty elders fell down and worshipped him that liveth for ever and ever.

**The worshippers—beasts and elders (Rev. 5:8).** Revelation 5:8-14 describes three groups of worshippers and their acclamation of praise to the

Lamb. In verses 8-10, we find the first group of worshippers and their song of praise. When Jesus Christ had taken the book, showing His authority and ownership, the four living creatures (beasts) and the twenty-four elders fell down before Him. They had in their hands harps and "golden vials full of odours," meaning golden bowls full of incense.

The harp was used in the Old Testament to accompany praise to God (cf. I Chron. 25:6) and prophetic statements (cf. I Sam. 10:5). Perhaps this dual purpose is in view here as the worshippers praise God and note the fulfillment of prophecies.

The Scripture states that the bowls of incense are the prayers of the saints. These prayers, wafting up to God like incense, may be the prayers believers have prayed through the ages concerning the culmination of God's redemptive plan.

**Their worship (Rev. 5:9-10).** The elders sang a new song of worship to the Lamb. (The worship song uses the word "us," so likely the elders, not the creatures, are the ones who sing this song since the elders, not angels, are the ones who were redeemed.) Their song highlighted three aspects of Christ's life and work.

The first aspect is His worthiness. "Thou art worthy to take the book, and to open the seals thereof" (Rev. 5:9). The second is His worldwide redemption. "For thou wast slain, and hast redeemed us to God by thy blood out of every kindred, and tongue, and people, and nation." The third is His elevation of believers. "And hast made us unto our God kings and priests: and we shall reign on the earth" (vs. 10).

**The worshippers—angels (Rev. 5:11).** Accompanying the creatures and elders is a second group of worshippers—an innumerable host of an-

gels. The phrase "ten thousand times ten thousand, and thousands of thousands" (literally, "myriads of myriads") is not meant to be a mathematical equation; rather, it is meant to convey a number beyond calculation (cf. Heb. 12:22).

**Their worship (Rev. 5:12).** The combined voices of the elders, creatures, and angels then offer their praise to the Lord. They speak "with a loud voice" because of the majesty of the Lamb. Like the worshippers in verses 9 and 10, they highlight the Lamb's worthiness and crucifixion and exclaim what He is worthy of receiving: power, riches, wisdom, strength, honor, glory, and blessing. This sevenfold ascription of praise is a good model for us to follow as we worship the Lord.

**The worshippers—every creature (Rev. 5:13).** The worship scene reaches a crescendo as "every creature which is in heaven, and on the earth, and under the earth, and such as are in the sea, and all that are in them" join the throng around the throne. In essence, this description says that everyone and everything in the universe will join in praising the Lamb. Apparently, even the land and sea animals will participate in this worship time.

**Their worship (Rev. 5:14).** In this grand finale of praise, all living beings, which includes all of us, offer to the Lamb blessing, honor, glory, and power. This group adds a new thought in their worship—the eternal nature of the worship of Christ. Our worship of the Saviour will not be an occasional experience, but we will gather around His throne through all eternity to worship the Lamb who redeemed us.

The worship scene comes to a conclusion as the four living creatures bow and say "amen" and the elders fall down to worship the Lamb. John closed this section with a clear expression of the eternality of Christ. He is the one who lives forever and ever. Our worship of Christ will go on for all eternity because Jesus Christ will live forever.

We have looked at the different parts of this great chapter, but let us step back now to see some of the lessons about worship.

First, true worship is about the Lord Himself, not about us. Some worship today tries to bring in human elements and focuses in part on what we do or what benefits we may gain. Revelation 5 shows that Jesus Christ is the sole object and end of worship. All we can do is fall before Him.

Second, true worship is about giving, not getting. Sometimes we hear people say, "I did not get much out of the service this morning." Getting is not the point of worship. Rather, we come to give something—we give the Lord our heartfelt worship.

Third, true worship places a great emphasis on Christ's death. Look back through the words of Revelation 5 to see how many times John referred to Christ's death: "A Lamb as it had been slain" (vs. 6), "For thou wast slain, and hast redeemed us to God by thy blood" (vs. 9), and "Worthy is the Lamb that was slain" (vs. 12). In our singing, praying, and preaching, let us exalt the crucified Christ.

Fourth, true worship ascribes to the Lamb what He deserves—power, riches, wisdom, strength, honor, glory, and blessing. In our prayers, our singing, and even in personal conversations, let us tell the Lord that He is indeed worthy of all these ascriptions of praise. He never tires to hear these words from our lips.

Speaking of music, this chapter also gives us insight into music used in worship. True worship music extols the death of Christ, His marvelous attrib-utes, and expressions of His great worth. Music based on the expressions of worship in this chapter and other chapters of the Bible leads us to the throne room of God.

Fifth, true worship will be our eternal activity. We do not know all that we will do in heaven someday, but we do know that our time will be filled with regular and unending worship and praise for the Lamb. Such heavenly worship is possible because Jesus Christ, the Lamb, lives forever and ever.

The truths of Revelation 5 should lead us to more meaningful private worship times and more expressive corporate worship with our church family.

—Don Anderson.

# QUESTIONS

1. What might have been contained in the book with the seven seals?

2. Why did John see Jesus Christ in the form of a lamb?

3. How do we see the three Persons of the Triune God in this chapter?

4. Why is Jesus worthy to take the book and open its seals?

5. What is the significance of the harps and the bowls?

6. What three aspects of Christ's work are highlighted in the elders' song?

7. How many angels are involved in worshipping the Lamb?

8. How extensive or widespread is the worship of the Lamb?

9. How does Christ's eternal nature impact our worship?

10. What lessons can we learn about true worship?

—Don Anderson.

# *Preparing to Teach the Lesson*

This lesson completes our unit on "All Glory and Honor" with a most appropriate text glorifying and honoring God and the Lamb of God. We are to be praising God and honoring Him every day of our lives, and we will continue to do so throughout all eternity. God does not need our praise, since He is perfect and complete and has no needs, but we certainly have a deep-seated need within our souls to praise Him.

The most wonderful thing we can have in our lives is a right relationship with God. It is not possible for a human being to be fulfilled without this, for we would always have a "God-shaped void" in our inner being. Without the new birth through Jesus Christ, we are dead spiritually and incapable of knowing or responding to God, or of being rightly related to Him or to our fellow human beings. To be a born-again person, to have all our sins confessed to Him and forsaken, and to be yielded to His Holy Spirit puts us in the right place spiritually, mentally, and emotionally to be well-adjusted, happy people.

## TODAY'S AIM

**Facts:** to understand the implications of the heavenly worship of the Lamb.

**Principle:** to better see how we can be living in and for Christ.

**Application:** to make it a daily practice to honor and praise God and the Lamb of God above all else.

## INTRODUCING THE LESSON

In our previous lesson, we saw that God is worthy to receive glory and honor and power because He created everything for His own pleasure. When we see all that mankind has done with what God has given us, we could wonder if God is not completely displeased and saddened by the way His creation is turning out!

We are thankful for all those who honor Him and are walking with Him, but there are many people in this world who seem bent on being as wicked and sinful as possible. So in this passage, we are doubly heartened to see that it will all be resolved to the point where God is given all praise and honor, and everything is made right. The plans and purposes of God will be carried out to His complete satisfaction, and it will be to our great blessing.

## DEVELOPING THE LESSON

**1. The Lamb is worthy (Rev. 5:6-7).** From our background Scripture, in the first five verses of this chapter, we see this highly important book, or scroll, in the hand of God on His throne. The question comes from an anonymous "strong angel" (vs. 2) asking who is worthy to open this very important document. No man is found worthy.

In our society, we are used to practically worshipping education. We give degrees to those who accomplish much in our schools of higher education. We praise and honor those who contribute to humanity through medicine, inventions, art, and science. We applaud the selfless dedication of missionaries and servants of humanity in difficult places. While it is all well and good that we do this, no human being is really capable or worthy to initiate the things that are in the hand of God alone. The great mysteries of life, death and the future, sin, righteousness, and judgment to come cannot be completely understood by any of us. Much less can we do anything about them.

**2. The Lamb is worshipped (Rev. 5:8-10).** When the Lamb in John's vision proves worthy and takes the book, this triggers worship of the Lamb by the four beasts and the twenty-four elders. The Lamb was slain and has redeemed the elders and a countless host from all humanity by His blood. He has elevated them to be kings and priests who will reign on the earth.

Worthy of note are the golden vials full of the prayers of the saints. Our "unanswered" prayers have not been forgotten. They will yet be presented before the throne of God and answered.

**3. The great multitude (Rev. 5:11-14).** The great multitude includes the representatives of every redeemed person (the elders), many angels, the four beasts, and many thousands of beings who speak our golden text: "Worthy is the Lamb that was slain to receive power, and riches, and wisdom, and strength, and honour, and glory, and blessing." This sevenfold blessing, denoting fullness and completeness, is in response to the Lamb's perfections—seven horns (all power) and seven eyes (all vision or knowledge, vs. 6), and the scroll's perfection with seven seals (vs. 1). We learn later that the scroll contains prophecies of God's judgment on sin. Right up to the end, we see God's justice, mercy, and forgiveness for all who trust Him.

We then see every creature in heaven and earth echoing this same praise and honor "for ever and ever" (Rev. 5:13). The four beasts say, "Amen" (vs. 14), which means "so be it." All those who thus bless God are being and will be blessed themselves. The appropriate answer of our hearts to this revelation is praise and worship. Much of worship is saying back to God, from our hearts, what we know to be true of Him. We thank Him for all that He is and does. We acknowledge Him in all His perfections and the glorious things we know to be true about Him. We will have all eternity to revel in and bask in all His perfections. It will be fulfilling and exciting and rewarding beyond our highest expectations.

## ILLUSTRATING THE LESSON

The Lamb of God, Jesus Christ, is worthy of our praise forever.

**WORTHY IS THE LAMB**

**AMEN**

## CONCLUDING THE LESSON

We have read the verses and tried to see what has been so carefully written for us, but we must admit—it is still beyond us and our experience. However, if we continue to walk in the light of this revelation and continue to praise God and the Lamb, we can come into a fuller understanding of it. We know that for the child of God through faith in Christ, all will come out well—very well. Our prayers are presented at God's throne, and He will answer them.

Nothing is a surprise to God. He has made arrangements for everything from your salvation to your ultimate blessing. Bless and honor Him now while you have opportunity. We sow what we reap. We reap it later, and we reap it multiplied.

## ANTICIPATING THE NEXT LESSON

Our next lesson starts a new unit on "Give Praise to God."

—*Brian D. Doud.*

# PRACTICAL POINTS

1. Jesus died on earth so that we can live in heaven with Him (Rev. 5:6).
2. Jesus is the only person with the power to redeem mankind (vss. 7-8).
3. The blood of Jesus has the power to save people of every nation (vs. 9).
4. As believers, we become royalty through the grace of God and reign with Him (vs. 10).
5. All living creatures in heaven and earth must worship Jesus (vss. 11-13).
6. Jesus is worthy of eternal praise (vs. 14).

—Valante M. Grant.

# RESEARCH AND DISCUSSION

1. How can Jesus be both the Good Shepherd and the Lamb of God? Discuss.
2. What does the number seven signify throughout the Bible? How does it relate to the description of the Lamb?
3. How does Jesus' death, burial, and resurrection affect eternity for believers?
4. Compare and contrast the humble beginning of Jesus' life on earth with the glory and majesty of His return.
5. What can we learn from Jesus' example of sacrifice and humility, even though He is the Lord God Almighty?
6. As believers, how can we honor the Lord with the praise that He is worthy of while we are still on earth?

—Valante M. Grant.

# ILLUSTRATED HIGH POINTS

**Out of every . . . nation**

In his book *Be Victorious* (Cook), Warren W. Wiersbe repeated the story of a man who happened to come to a missions conference. During the offering, he told the usher, "'I don't believe in missions!' 'Then take something out,' said the usher, 'It's for the heathen.'"

Thankfully, others have faithfully gone out to reach the lost, and many will have their place in the Lamb's kingdom.

**Shall reign on the earth**

From time to time, the world's leading scientists review what they call the Doomsday Clock and try to calculate how close the world is to total destruction due to climate change, the proliferation of nuclear weapon arsenals, and other issues. Recently, they calculated that it was still resting on "three minutes to midnight."

Yes, there is doom in the future due to God's judgment, but Christians look forward to a future of blessings with Christ as He returns and sets up His kingdom. Believers are confident that God is in control of the world.

**Ten thousand times ten thousand**

Some seventy years ago, we thought one thousand was a big number. Then it was one million, which later became one billion. Now our government talks about spending one trillion dollars. Will our grandchildren be facing government spending of one quadrillion (one thousand trillion)?

In Bible times, the greatest number was the "myriad"; but even when that number was multiplied by itself, it did not exhaust the number of heavenly angels. There were still thousands more. John saw an infinite number praising the Lamb.

—David A. Hamburg.

# Golden Text Illuminated

**"Worthy is the Lamb that was slain to receive power, and riches, and wisdom, and strength, and honour, and glory, and blessing" (Revelation 5:12).**

At first glance the golden text for this week is very similar to last week's text. It might be wondered what more could be added to what was already said there. But there are some key differences.

Anyone who has heard these words in a majestic performance of Handel's oratorio *Messiah* has gained perhaps a faint glimmer of what this scene will be like in its awesome reality. It is the pinnacle of worship and what our hearts long for as we offer imperfect and halting praise here on earth.

There has been a definite progression since the utterance of praise in last week's text. There we saw twenty-four elders and four living creatures offering praise to the One who was seated on the heavenly throne. As the scene continued to unfold before John (chap. 5), he saw a Lamb standing in the midest of these figures (vs. 6). The Lamb had the appearance of having been slain but now was very much alive. The identity of this Lamb was so perfectly obvious that John needed no identification, especially after an elder had spoken of "the Lion of the tribe of Juda, the Root of David" (vs. 5).

After taking a mysterious but clearly important scroll, the Lamb became the object of a cascade of praise. Now the elders and living creatures were joined by a vast company of angels: "ten thousand times ten thousand, and thousands of thousands" (vs. 11). Even before their words were uttered, it was plain that all attention was focused on a Person of unparalleled importance and preeminence.

The vast host began to proclaim or sing a chorus of praise: "Worthy is the Lamb that was slain." The same "worthy" that was directed to the Lord God on the throne (4:11) was now applied to the Lamb—Jesus. It is an equation that might seem blasphemous if the Lamb were anything less than divine Himself.

Just as God was earlier said to be worthy to "receive" things that He already possessed in infinite measure, so now the Lamb is proclaimed worthy to receive these same things and even more. It is perhaps instructive to see in the carefully chosen words of our text the final vindication of Jesus over the unbelief, scorn, and contempt that He endured from the world. The fact that He was slain was seen by many as proof of unworthiness; in fact, it was the basis for His victory.

As He walked this earth, Jesus was subject to the power of ungodly men and institutions. Yet He will be acknowledged as worthy of all power. In terms of material goods, Jesus was poor on earth; by contrast, He is eternally worthy of all riches. Many contemporaries dismissed Jesus' teachings as the words of a madman; in reality, He has all wisdom.

Jesus lived in the weakness of human flesh and allowed His enemies to abuse Him. Yet He has all strength. He was dishonored but will receive all honor. He bore the shame of the cross but will wear the robe of everlasting glory. He endured the curses of many and accepted the ultimate curse of being hanged on a tree, but His eternal existence is one of pure blessing. And thankfully, it is a blessing He shares with all of us! Worthy is He indeed!

—*Kenneth A. Sponsler.*

# Heart of the Lesson

I joined the oratorio society my freshman year of college. Twice a year, this massive choir, comprising all music majors and other musical students, performed a major oratorio such as Handel's *Messiah*. Singing with several hundred voices was exhilarating. But our lesson describes a choir too big to number as it praised Jesus, the Lamb.

**1. The Lamb receives the scroll (Rev. 5:6-7).** John had entered God's throne room as part of his vision and saw an angel searching for someone worthy to open a scroll that revealed the world's destiny. Finally, John saw the only One in all the universe who was found worthy to open the scroll: Jesus the Lamb, who was still bearing the marks of having been slain. He had seven horns, representing His majestic power, and seven eyes, showing He was all-seeing and all-knowing.

The Lamb took the scroll from the right hand of God the Father as He sat on His throne. The Lamb was worthy; God relinquished the scroll.

**2. Worshippers sing a new song (Rev. 5:8-10).** Immediately, the twenty-four elders and four living creatures surrounding God's throne fell down before the Lamb to worship Him. The elders had harps and golden bowls of incense. The incense signified the prayers of the saints. God views His people's prayers as a fragrant offering to Him—a pleasing expression of trust.

The elders and living creatures began to sing a new song, a new composition especially for this occasion. Did they break out in glorious harmony as they praised the Lamb? Perhaps. But what mattered most were their words. They proclaimed Jesus as worthy to take the scroll and to open its seals because of His death on the cross.

But He was worthy not just because of His death but because of what His death accomplished. The singers praised Him for redeeming people from every kindred, language, people, and nation on earth. His death united this diverse group into God's kingdom of priests, ones who could now approach God personally and also bring the good news of Jesus to everyone on earth. These redeemed persons had a glorious future of reigning on the earth.

**3. Angels join the praise (Rev. 5:11-12).** Suddenly John heard the voices of angels around the throne praising the Lamb. He was at a loss to describe the number of angels he heard: "ten thousand times ten thousand, and thousands of thousands." Thousands—perhaps millions—of angels proclaimed, "Worthy is the Lamb" along with the elders and living creatures.

They sang that the Lamb was worthy to receive power, riches, wisdom, strength, honor, glory, and blessing.

**4. The universe worships the Lamb (Rev. 5:13-14).** Then the biggest round of praise ever heard began. Every creature in heaven, every creature on the earth, and every creature under the earth praised God and the Lamb. All living creatures ascribed to God the Father and Jesus blessing, honor, glory, and power forever and ever. All of nature and all created beings joined in worship.

The worship ended with the four living creatures saying, "Amen." Then the elders fell down in worship before God the Father and the Lamb.

We, the redeemed, can embrace the words of heaven to praise God and the Lamb. Sing your praise, write it, say it, pray it, think it. The Lamb is worthy of our praise.

—*Ann Staatz.*

# World Missions

"If God is good and loves people, why doesn't He come down and stop this evil?" The question came from a woman at an event on fighting human trafficking. Others have asked similar questions throughout the ages.

If God has all power, why does He let bad things happen?

Why does God not put an end to world poverty and suffering?

If God has all power and wisdom and strength and honor, why are there still people who have never heard?

Sometimes when Jesus was asked a question, He replied with another question that led deeper into the heart of the matter. Let us consider this from a heavenly perspective.

What if God made a perfect plan where every person on the planet would get to hear the gospel? Suppose He gave specific instructions to certain people and resourced those people with everything they needed to succeed. What would happen if those people, who had been given such a significant task, refused to obey?

Over one billion people in the world claim to be Christians. If each believer did what it took to get the gospel to ten people, we could reach the world in just one generation. Not everyone would respond in faith, but the world would be reached and be radically changed.

The problem of twenty to thirty million slaves worldwide could be eradicated. If only one-tenth of the people who claim to be followers of Christ did what it took to rescue just one person, the world would run out of slaves before even half of that one-tenth could succeed.

If God's people truly obeyed the instructions in Scripture, imagine how the statistics would change regarding world poverty, despair, orphans on the street, crime, exploitation, and the other evils in our world today.

Jesus Himself said God sent Him to "heal the brokenhearted, to preach deliverance to the captives" (Luke 4:18). If we truly long to follow Him and to be like Him, we will care about what He cares about. We will do what He did.

The problem is not that God does not have power. The problem is not even that He does not have a plan. He does have a plan, and He gave specific instructions to His children on how to carry out that plan, which means the reason there are still millions who have not heard can be narrowed down to one thing: Many of God's people are not obeying. Why?

We love ourselves more than we love our neighbor.

Do we love ourselves more than we love God?

If He says go, give, and pray, do we come up with reasons why it is impossible or unreasonable or too much to ask?

William Wilberforce, the well-known British member of parliament who spent most of his adult life fighting slavery, said, "If there is no passionate love for Christ at the center of everything, we will only jingle and jangle our way across the world, merely making a noise as we go."

John Stott said, "We must be global Christians with a global vision because our God is a global God."

Instead of asking God why He does not do something, perhaps we should instead ask what *we* are to do in His name.

As John Piper concluded, "Go, send, or disobey."

—Kimberly Rae.

# The Jewish Aspect

On October 6, 1973, during the holiday of Yom Kippur, Egypt and Syria invaded Israel's territories. Because it was Yom Kippur, many of the Israeli soldiers had been given leave. The size of the attacking armies was large, and Israel's army was small, so initially the foreign armies made rapid advances. However, within a week, Israel had driven back the enemy forces. It was a Yom Kippur miracle.

This week's lesson deals with the throne of God. On the holiday of Yom Kippur, the Jews believe that God moves from His throne of justice—where He is believed to be seated on Rosh Hashanah—to the throne of compassion (Heschel, "Holiday Resources—Yom Kippur," www.heschel .org). The Jewish person believes that on this day God hears his prayers and accepts his repentance.

Yom Kippur, also known as the Day of Atonement, falls on the tenth of Tishri, the seventh month in the Jewish calendar. Usually this holiday occurs in September. Jews consider Yom Kippur the most important and holiest day of the year.

Yom Kippur brings to a close the ten days of repentance that begin with Rosh Hashanah, the Festival of Trumpets. Rosh Hashanah, Yom Kippur, and the days in between are called the Days of Awe. The holiday of Rosh Hashanah begins the Days of Awe and lasts two days. Yom Kippur, ends the Days of Awe, and lasts one day.

Jews believe that on Yom Kippur, the gates of heaven are closed. If a person is to have his name sealed in the book of life for the year, it must be written in the book by this day.

Yom Kippur rituals take place primarily in the synagogue. Jews observe a twenty-five-hour fast and follow certain traditions. Prayer is an important element in the holiday.

When the temple stood, there were elaborate ceremonies and sacrifices on Yom Kippur based on Leviticus 16. One of the most interesting parts of the ancient ceremony involved two sacrificial goats.

At the prescribed time, two goats would be made ready for the ceremony. The high priest would place two golden tablets in an urn. On one tablet were the words, "For YHWH" (the Lord). On the other, were the words, "For Azazel" (the scapegoat). The high priest would shuffle the tablets and withdraw them one at a time. He would put "For YHWH" on one goat and "For Azazel" on the other. If "For YHWH" came out in the high priest's right hand, it was considered a good omen. If "For YHWH" came out in his left hand, it was considered a bad omen.

After slaughtering a bull, the high priest would gather its blood in a basin. Then, he would fill the Holy of Holies with smoke from incense and sprinkle the bull's blood on the mercy seat.

Next, he would move to the eastern side of the courtyard and slaughter the "For YHWH" goat. He would then enter the Holy of Holies and sprinkle this blood.

After finishing all the requirements, the high priest would begin the symbolic process of transferring the sins of the people to the Azazel goat. This goat, known as the scapegoat, would be led to a high cliff and pushed over the edge—an expansion on the original command in Leviticus 16:21-22. This act signified the evil inclinations and sins of the people being carried off forever.

—Robin Fitzgerald.

# Guiding the Superintendent

The Apostle John's great heavenly experience continues from Revelation 4 (see lesson 8) into chapter 5. In a moment of time, John was transported from his island exile to the very throne room of heaven. John's attention was quickly drawn to the Person sitting on the throne.

The reader soon learns this is God Himself. With deep reverence, color, and sound, He was worshipped as the Creator by the heavenly beings assembled around the throne. In chapter 5, the attention is drawn to Jesus Christ.

## DEVOTIONAL OUTLINE

**1. The Lamb described (Rev. 5:6).** Using symbolic language, Jesus Christ is described. He is like a lamb that was slain. The Lamb had seven horns and seven eyes. Encircled by the four living creatures and twenty-four elders, the Lamb stood near the throne.

The threefold description identifies this special Lamb as none other than Jesus Christ. First, the Lamb was seen "as it had been slain" (Rev. 5:6). Slaughtered lambs were often seen in the markets of the day, but this one was alive. This could be none other than Jesus Christ.

Second, the Lamb had seven horns, not two as a normal lamb would. Horns in Revelation are usually a picture of strength (cf. Rev. 12:3; 13:1).

Third, the Lamb had seven eyes. This is a picture of the all-seeing, all-watching God.

**2. The Lamb worshipped by all heaven (Rev. 5:7-14).** With the same passion that they worshipped God as seen in chapter 4, so the living creatures and elders worshipped the Lamb here, with instrumental music (harps) and incense, which is the prayers of the saints (Ps. 141:2).

They sang a new song that extolled the worthiness of the Lamb to take the book from the One who sat on the throne, because He was slain and has redeemed people from all ethnic groups. They completed their new song by exclaiming the future reign of this great multitude of people.

Next, John saw and heard such a large assembly of angels that they could not be numbered. To the worship vocabulary found in Revelation 4:11, four new words are added (5:12). It was customary to bring a valuable gift, "riches," when visiting an ancient sovereign. "Wisdom" focuses on knowledge and judgment. "Strength" emphasizes the personal nature of Christ's power. "Blessing," meaning praise, ascends from those worshiping the Lamb.

Almost like a zoom lens, the view pulls back so that the reader sees and hears all creation in praise to the Lamb (Rev. 5:13-14). They cannot stop their worship. John heard them saying, "Blessing, and honour, and glory, and power, be unto him that sitteth upon the throne, and unto the Lamb." The four creatures joined this choir with shouts of "Amen."

Revelation 5 ends with the entire universe voicing praise to the Father and the Son. A great anthem of praise resounded throughout heaven. The Lamb is indeed worthy of all our worship.

## AGE-GROUP EMPHASES

**Children:** This is a great lesson to teach children about how one should worship Jesus Christ.

**Youths:** Revelation 5 contains one of the most unique descriptions of Jesus Christ. What can your teens learn about Jesus from this chapter?

**Adults:** To aid your adults in worship, help them distinguish the meanings of the seven worship words found in Revelation 5.

*—Martin R. Dahlquist.*

# Scripture Lesson Text

**EXOD. 35:20** And all the congregation of the children of Is'ra-el departed from the presence of Mo'ses.

**21 And they came, every one whose heart stirred him up, and every one whom his spirit made willing, *and* they brought the** LORD**'s offering to the work of the tabernacle of the congregation, and for all his service, and for the holy garments.**

22 And they came, both men and women, as many as were willing hearted, *and* brought bracelets, and earrings, and rings, and tablets, all jewels of gold: and every man that offered *offered* an offering of gold unto the LORD.

**23 And every man, with whom was found blue, and purple, and scarlet, and fine linen, and goats' hair, and red skins of rams, and badgers' skins, brought *them*.**

24 Every one that did offer an offering of silver and brass brought the LORD's offering: and every man, with whom was found shittim wood for any work of the service, brought *it*.

**25 And all the women that were wise hearted did spin with their hands, and brought that which they had spun, *both* of blue, and of** purple, *and* of scarlet, and of fine linen.

26 And all the women whose heart stirred them up in wisdom spun goats' *hair*.

**27 And the rulers brought onyx stones, and stones to be set, for the ephod, and for the breastplate;**

28 And spice, and oil for the light, and for the anointing oil, and for the sweet incense.

**29 The children of Is'ra-el brought a willing offering unto the** LORD**, every man and woman, whose heart made them willing to bring for all manner of work, which the** LORD **had commanded to be made by the hand of Mo'ses.**

**II COR. 9:6** But this *I say*, He which soweth sparingly shall reap also sparingly; and he which soweth bountifully shall reap also bountifully.

**7 Every man according as he purposeth in his heart, *so let him give;* not grudgingly, or of necessity: for God loveth a cheerful giver.**

8 And God *is* able to make all grace abound toward you; that ye always having all sufficiency in all *things*, may abound to every good work.

## NOTES

# Giving from a Generous Heart

## Lesson: Exodus 35:20-29; II Corinthians 9:6-8

Read: Exodus 25:1-7; 35:4-29; Leviticus 27:30-33; II Corinthians 9:6-8

TIMES: 1445 B.C.; probably A.D. 56          PLACES: Mount Sinai; Macedonia

---

**GOLDEN TEXT**—"Every man according as he purposeth in his heart, so let him give; not grudgingly, or of necessity: for God loveth a cheerful giver" (II Corinthians 9:7).

---

# Introduction

Though we do not live under the Old Testament sacrificial system, we still are instructed to bring sacrifices to the Lord. Prominent among these is "the sacrifice of praise to God . . . the fruit of our lips giving thanks to his name" (Heb. 13:15). Just as the Lord was pleased with the offering of animals in the Old Testament, He is pleased today by the different ways we bring praise to Him.

In this final unit of our study, we focus on the important topic of giving praise to God. This first lesson explores passages from the Old Testament and the New Testament to illustrate generosity, explain what generosity involves, and show how our generosity gives praise to the Lord.

Generosity should be a hallmark of the Christian. We should be generous because God Himself was generous in offering His Son as the sacrifice for our sins. The first few words of John 3:16 are "For God so loved the world, that he gave."

## LESSON OUTLINE

I. GENEROUS HEARTS—
   Exod. 35:20-21

II. GENEROUS OFFERINGS—
    Exod. 35:22-29

III. GENEROUS GIFTS—
     II Cor. 9:6-8

# Exposition: Verse by Verse

## GENEROUS HEARTS

**EXOD. 35:20 And all the congregation of the children of Israel departed from the presence of Moses.**

**21 And they came, every one whose heart stirred him up, and every one whom his spirit made willing, and they brought the Lord's offering to the work of the tabernacle of the congregation, and for all his service, and for the holy garments.**

As recorded in Exodus 25 through 28, God met with Moses on Mount Sinai and gave him the directions for building the tabernacle, the place where God would dwell among His people. In Exodus 34:29-35, we find Moses descending from the mountain and conveying to the Israelites what God had told him.

In Exodus 35:4-9, Moses asked the Israelites to bring gifts and offerings for the structure and furniture of the tabernacle. Moses also asked for skilled workmen to construct the tabernacle, its furnishings, and the priest's garments (vss. 10-19). Verse 20 then states that the people left the presence of Moses and began to gather the gifts and offerings needed for the construction of the tabernacle.

Many people responded to Moses' call for gifts and offerings. Exodus 35:21 describes these people as "every one whose heart stirred him up, and every one whom his spirit made willing." The phrase "whose heart stirred him up" means that something deep down in their hearts stirred them, or prompted them, to respond to Moses' call to bring gifts. The phrase "whom his spirit made willing" shows that when they were stirred to make a response, they did it willingly. They did not need to be coerced. This was exactly the kind of response the Lord had asked for earlier (25:2).

Exodus 35:21 emphasizes that the people brought "the Lord's offering." They had a deep sense that what they brought was for the Lord and not just to build their place of worship.

## GENEROUS OFFERINGS

**22 And they came, both men and women, as many as were willing hearted, and brought bracelets, and earrings, and rings, and tablets, all jewels of gold: and every man that offered offered an offering of gold unto the Lord.**

**23 And every man, with whom was found blue, and purple, and scarlet, and fine linen, and goats'** hair, and red skins of rams, and badgers' skins, brought them.

**24 Every one that did offer an offering of silver and brass brought the Lord's offering: and every man, with whom was found shittim wood for any work of the service, brought it.**

**25 And all the women that were wise hearted did spin with their hands, and brought that which they had spun, both of blue, and of purple, and of scarlet, and of fine linen.**

**26 And all the women whose heart stirred them up in wisdom spun goats' hair.**

**27 And the rulers brought onyx stones, and stones to be set, for the ephod, and for the breastplate;**

**28 And spice, and oil for the light, and for the anointing oil, and for the sweet incense.**

**29 The children of Israel brought a willing offering unto the Lord, every man and woman, whose heart made them willing to bring for all manner of work, which the Lord had commanded to be made by the hand of Moses.**

**Offerings of gold (Exod. 35:22).** Verse 22 records that both men and women who had willing hearts brought offerings of gold for the tabernacle and its furnishings. They specifically brought "bracelets, and earrings, and rings, and tablets, all jewels of gold." The Hebrew word translated "tablets" is used only here and in Numbers 31:50. The exact meaning is not clear, though some think the objects were armlets or necklaces. What we do know is that they and all the other pieces of jewelry were made of gold and thus were quite valuable.

The Israelites used the gold to make the mercy seat and the cherubim (Exod. 25:17-21), the lampstand (vss. 31-39), and the items for the table of shewbread (vs. 29). They used the gold to overlay the ark of the testimony (vss.

10-16), the table of shewbread (vss. 23-28), the altar of incense (30:1-5), and the poles that carried the furniture (25:13, 28; 30:5).

Where did the Israelites get this amount of gold as well as the silver and brass mentioned later (Exod. 35:24)? Probably most of these items came from the Egyptians as the Israelites left Egypt (12:35-36). Moses had instructed the people to ask for these items before they left Egypt (11:2-3), and the Egyptians willingly complied. The Israelites took so much gold and silver that they plundered the Egyptians. It was a small payment for their years of slavery.

**Offerings of linen and animal skins (Exod. 35:23).** The Israelites also brought a large amount of linen and animal skins for the tabernacle. They brought fine linen, again no doubt from Egypt since the Egyptians were known for its production. The "blue, and purple, and scarlet" probably refers to the colored thread or yarn to be used in making the coverings for the tabernacle and for the priests' garments (vss. 25-26; cf. 39:1). The Israelites used this cloth to make the curtains for the court (27:9-15), the curtains for the covering of the tabernacle (26:1-6), and the veil (26:31).

The people also brought "goats' hair, and red skins of rams, and badgers' skins" (Exod. 35:23). Uncertainty exists about the meaning of "badgers' skins"; interpretations run the gamut from fine goatskin leather to porpoise or seal skins. The Israelites used the skins as coverings for the tabernacle structure itself (26:14).

**Offerings of silver, brass, and wood (Exod. 35:24).** The silver and brass (bronze) probably came from Egypt, and the "shittim wood," or acacia wood, was abundant in the desert. This wood was used to make the ark of the testimony, the table of shewbread,

the boards for the tabernacle, the altar of burnt offering, the altar of incense, the poles for carrying the articles of furniture, and the pillars (26:32). The bronze was used to make the laver (30:17-21) and to overlay the altar of burnt offering (27:1-8). The silver was used for the sockets on the boards (26:19-25).

We know the people offered these gifts willingly, but Exodus 36:3-5 tells us that the people were so generous that they brought more than enough. Finally, Moses had to tell the people not to bring any more! "So the people were restrained from bringing. For the stuff they had was sufficient for all the work to make it, and too much" (vss. 6-7). This kind of response shows the extreme generosity of the people and their willing sacrifice. (See also I Chronicles 29:1-9 for another instance of generosity.)

**Skilled workmanship from the women (Exod. 35:25-26).** The women who were "wise hearted," or skilled in sewing, contributed to the preparation for the tabernacle by spinning blue, purple, and scarlet yarn or thread into cloth and fine linen. This cloth was used for the coverings of the tabernacle and for the veil that separated the holy place from the most holy place.

Exodus 26:1 tells us that the coverings and the veil were made with cherubim figures skillfully woven into them. Apparently, these women embroidered the design of the cherubim right into the fabrics. These women also spun goats' hair into coverings for the tabernacle (vs. 7).

**Offerings from the leaders (Exod. 35:27-28).** The leaders of Israel did their part by bringing onyx stones to be used in the ephod and breastplate for the priests (28:9, 20). The two onyx stones in the ephod were engraved with the names of the tribes of Israel. The leaders also brought spices and oil for the lampstand, for the oil used to anoint the priests, and for the incense used on the altar of incense.

**Willing offerings (Exod. 35:29).** This section of Scripture concludes with the reaffirmation that the Israelites brought all these gifts as "a willing offering unto the Lord." They gave freely and generously for the construction of the tabernacle. They were not stingy. Their generous giving was their way of giving praise to the Lord for His deliverance from Egypt and for His provision for their needs.

## GENEROUS GIFTS

**II COR. 9:6 But this I say, He which soweth sparingly shall reap also sparingly; and he which soweth bountifully shall reap also bountifully.**

**7 Every man according as he purposeth in his heart, so let him give; not grudgingly, or of necessity: for God loveth a cheerful giver.**

**8 And God is able to make all grace abound toward you; that ye, always having all sufficiency in all things, may abound to every good work.**

We have seen from Exodus 35 an example of generous giving that brought praise to the Lord. We now turn our attention to a New Testament instruction related to generous giving in II Corinthians 9. Paul wrote these instructions to the Corinthians to encourage them to complete their promised contribution to the needy saints in Jerusalem (cf. Gal. 2:10; Rom. 15:25-28).

Apparently, about a year before, the Corinthians had begun collecting money for the Jerusalem believers (II Cor. 8:10), but they had lagged in completing their gift. Paul now used the example of the Macedonian churches (vs. 1) to prompt them to complete their gift. In his encouragement, he cited three principles for freewill giving.

**Give generously (II Cor. 9:6).** Paul urged the Corinthians to give bountifully, or generously, and used a principle of agriculture to reinforce his statement. A person who sows seed sparingly should expect to have a small harvest. However, the one who sows his seed generously can expect to have a large harvest. Paul used this illustration to urge the Corinthians to give generously to the needy saints. In doing so they would have a rich reward.

**Give cheerfully (II Cor. 9:7).** Paul knew that a person could give generously but begrudgingly, so he went one step further and urged the Corinthians to give cheerfully as well. Giving cheerfully involves four components that provide a model for us to follow. First, we should give purposely. We should have a regular plan for giving and not give randomly here and there. In I Corinthians 16:2, Paul urged the believers to set aside some money on the first day of every week. That kind of purposeful, intentional giving pleases the Lord.

Second, we should not give grudgingly. Our attitude should not be "I really don't want to part with this money, but I guess I will anyway." Rather, we should give with a willing and glad spirit.

Third, we should not give out of necessity, that is, under pressure. Our attitude should not be "I guess I had better give, or I'll be in trouble." Rather, we should give freely and gladly out of response to the Spirit's work in our hearts.

Fourth, we should remember that God is most pleased with a cheerful giver. The Greek word for "cheerful" is the word from which we get our English word "hilarious." God wants us to give happily from our hearts.

**Reap abundantly (II Cor. 9:8).** Paul had already told the Corinthians that if they gave generously, God would reward them generously (vs. 6). In verse

8, he elaborated on that principle by naming three blessings God gives to generous, cheerful givers.

First, if we give generously, God will provide us with all blessings in abundance. If we are generous with Him, He will be generous with us. He will make all grace, or all His provisions, abound to us. God will not simply give us His grace and provisions in small measure, but He will make them abound to us. God will give us an overflowing measure of His grace.

Second, if we give generously, we will have everything we possibly need. We will not lack when God gives. He will provide for us in all areas of our lives.

Third, if we give generously, we will have an abundance left over for every good deed. A heart of generous giving leads to more good works in fulfillment of God's plan and purpose for us (cf. Eph. 2:10).

Notice the repetition of the words "all" and "every" in II Corinthians 9:8: "And God is able to make *all* grace abound toward you; that ye, always having *all* sufficiency in *all* things, may abound to *every* good work" (emphasis added). Generous giving brings the fullness of God's blessings on us in every area of our lives.

This lesson has looked at the subject of generosity in giving. The Israelites were generous in giving to construct the tabernacle, and the New Testament saints were generous in helping needy believers.

So how much giving is generous giving? The amount is not really the issue. To a person with limited means, giving $25 would be generous. To someone with greater means, giving $2,500 would be a generous gift.

The real issue in generous giving is a willing heart. The Scripture passage uses such phrases as "every one whom his spirit made willing" (Exod. 35:21), "as many as were willing heart-ed" (vs. 22), "a willing offering unto the Lord" (vs. 29), and "not grudgingly, or of necessity: for God loveth a cheerful giver" (II Cor. 9:7). Generosity is measured not by the amount but by the heart.

A generous heart starts with the realization that Christ displayed the greatest act of generosity. "For ye know the grace of our Lord Jesus Christ, that, though he was rich, yet for your sakes he became poor, that ye through his poverty might be rich" (II Cor. 8:9). Then, in gratitude to Him, we need to give our "own selves to the Lord" (vs. 5). When we follow our Lord's example and commit everything we have to Him, generous giving will be part of our lives.

—Don Anderson.

# QUESTIONS

1. What words describe the Israelites' spirit in giving?
2. What gifts did they bring for the construction of the tabernacle?
3. What fact reveals the extent of their generosity?
4. What agricultural analogy did Paul use to encourage giving?
5. What does it mean to give grudgingly?
6. How do we avoid giving under pressure?
7. What kind of giver pleases the Lord the most?
8. What is promised to those who give generously?
9. What words did Paul use to underscore the greatness of God's blessings?
10. What is the real issue in generous giving?

—Don Anderson.

# Preparing to Teach the Lesson

We have been studying about worshipping God, about His glory and honor and praise, and we now continue with giving as an act of worship. We are all familiar with the saying, "Put your money where your mouth is." This does not refer to the physical location of your coins and dollar bills but rather to doing something that demonstrates the practical reality of what you have been saying. Most of us have to work and exchange our time and effort for money, so our money has value to us. We need it to buy food and shelter and the many other things for which we are responsible. When we give to the Lord in whatever form that takes, we are giving value from our lives. We are showing Him, in a proportionate way, what He means to us.

## TODAY'S AIM

**Facts:** to make an effort to see what God is telling us about giving to Him as we worship.

**Principle:** to give thought to giving the right amount for the right reason to fit in with God's plan and His best for us.

**Application:** to structure our giving so as to honor the Lord.

## INTRODUCING THE LESSON

Whenever we discuss worship, the subject of giving to God or to the church or to charity comes up. Why should we give if God owns everything anyway? Can He not proportion it around to whomever and wherever He wants? How much and of what substance should we give?

We may have heard of a legalistic approach that says we must give a certain amount in a certain way for God to accept us or bless us, sort of a "give-to-get" idea. Scripture refutes this idea and supplies us with better answers.

## DEVELOPING THE LESSON

**1. Giving from a willing heart (Exod. 35:20-29).** God gave Moses instructions for how the children of Israel were to honor Him through giving materials for the construction and furnishing of the tabernacle. Over and over we read that the Lord stirred their hearts, made their spirits willing, and even made them wise-hearted to bring valuable objects and materials for the tabernacle, the priests' garments and all the objects needed for sacrifices. The key to it all seems to have been a willing heart to give of what they already had at hand at the time. It all seemed good and natural and even exciting for them to "pitch in" and help with the project.

This should be our spirit: giving with a willing heart from what we have. The people of Israel seemed delighted to be in on the project of building the tabernacle in which to worship God. We also need to get excited about being in on what God is doing in our neighborhood and abroad. Getting excited about it is usually a simple matter of looking at the value of what we are doing as we give to further God's work.

**2. Giving generously and cheerfully (II Cor. 9:6-7).** How much to give is often the main question raised. Israel was supposed to give a tithe, or one tenth, of their income. There were also offerings beyond that they were to give. The principle taught here is that of sowing and reaping. We reap what we sow, we reap it later, and we reap it multiplied. So we are encouraged to give bountifully.

We are also to give with purpose; that is, we are to think it through under the Lord's guidance and give as we think He wants us to. Since God gives to us generously, we can and should give generously to His church, His servants, and His projects.

I knew a Christian brother, who has now gone to be with the Lord, who had not thought about how much he was giving. When challenged to figure it out, he found that he was giving 17 percent of his income. God blessed him with protection and wisdom through a nasty strike and union dispute at the factory where he was the supervisor. No one but God and I knew what he was giving, and I never told anyone while he was alive.

God loves a cheerful giver! Did you notice giving was to be "not grudgingly, or of necessity" (II Cor. 9:7)? Do not give if you are thinking, *Well, I suppose I have to.* Get your heart right with God first. Get your priorities straight first, get cheerful about it first, and then give.

**3. Giving from sufficiency and grace (II Cor. 9:8).** When we think of how much God has given us in forgiving our sins and making us His children, any material thing we can give is very small indeed. It certainly does not even come close to the praise and thanks we should be giving Him daily. Even our thanks throughout all eternity will be inadequate.

We also must remember that God gives us the ability to earn income and blesses and prospers us materially way beyond anything we deserve. Everything we have is a gracious gift from His hand, and it would be unthinkingly selfish to grasp it to ourselves and refuse to give generously.

## ILLUSTRATING THE LESSON

We are to give as God enables us to give.

**GIVE WILLINGLY**

Give Here

**GIVE GENEROUSLY**

## CONCLUDING THE LESSON

There is an item that we have not thought of yet: giving generously is the right thing to do. Often in life it is hard to know what to do. This is not one of those cases! Your church probably has dozens of things that need your attention. If not, there are people all around you who do. There are probably widows, shut-ins, and others in need who would be blessed and maybe drawn to the Lord by your gifts and kindness.

Remember that it is more blessed to give than to receive. If you give, it is because you have been given and have enough left after your necessities that you can give. If you receive, you probably do not have enough in the first place. It can be humbling to receive a gift, but in so doing you are allowing the giver to be blessed by God.

Remember to give simply. The Lord Jesus said, "Let not thy left hand know what thy right hand doeth" (Matt. 6:3). That is giving simply. Do not over-think this thing. Do not give in order to get something from God. Do not give just for tax purposes.

## ANTICIPATING THE NEXT LESSON

In our next lesson, we see another form of giving and its significance.

—Brian D. Doud.

# PRACTICAL POINTS

1. The money that we give to the church is an offering to God (Exod. 35:20-21).
2. All people can bring an offering to God, regardless of how rich or poor they are (vss. 22-28).
3. God's blessings should make us willing to bring Him an offering (vs. 29).
4. Our willingness to give determines our likeliness to receive (II Cor. 9:6).
5. Giving should come from the heart and bring joy to both receiver and giver (vs. 7).
6. It is wise to give offerings to God, who provides all your needs (vs. 8).
   —Valante M. Grant.

# RESEARCH AND DISCUSSION

1. Is it possible to please God without giving offerings?
2. Is the practice of setting financial assessments for the congregation ordained by God (Exod. 25:1-2)? Discuss.
3. Is it enough to only satisfy financial assessments? Is this a freewill offering? Discuss.
4. Does it matter how much we give or how often we give? Discuss.
5. What should be the motivation for giving (II Cor. 9:7)?
6. Why is it necessary to give offerings to a God who owns everything?
7. How does God measure the value of our offering to Him?
8. What is the comparison between what we give God and what He gives us?
   —Valante M. Grant.

# ILLUSTRATED HIGH POINTS

**Did spin with their hands**

One day, two housewives were relaxing on a park bench. They began discussing what constituted beautiful hands—shape, size, color, or something else. They could not agree.

A male friend happened to come by, and the women asked for his opinion. He looked at their hands long and hard, but knowing that he would be in trouble if he chose one over the other, he wisely answered, "I give up. The question is too hard for me. But ask the poor, and they will tell you that the most beautiful hand in the world is the hand that gives."

**A willing offering unto the Lord**

The beauty of the account of the children of Israel's provision for the tabernacle is in their spirit of willingness. They delighted in providing for the tabernacle where God would dwell in their midst. They gave so generously that they had to be told to stop (Exod. 36:5-7). How many of our churches have this problem?

**God loveth a cheerful giver**

Years ago, a father, desiring to develop his son's character, gave him a penny and a quarter as they were leaving for church. He said, "Son, you put whichever one you want in today's offering."

After the service, the father asked his son which coin he had given. The boy replied, "Well, just before the ushers came around, the pastor said, 'The Lord loves a cheerful giver,' and I knew I would be a lot more cheerful if I gave the penny and kept the quarter."

Perhaps we can sympathize with the young boy. Learning to give graciously and cheerfully takes time as one grows in faith and in the understanding of the Word.
   —David A. Hamburg.

# Golden Text Illuminated

**"Every man according as he purposeth in his heart, so let him give; not grudgingly, or of necessity: for God loveth a cheerful giver" (II Corinthians 9:7).**

Perhaps one of the most frequently heard reasons unbelievers give for avoiding church is the claim "They're always after your money." There may be some truth to this charge; there is at least a long history of pressure tactics used by some preachers and Christian leaders to get people to give more. But what most unbelievers fail to understand is this: God does not want their money!

God does not want our money, either, at least not in the way many imagine. Unsaved people think they can buy God's favor, and too many believers fall into thinking that they can earn more of His favor by giving more. Yet we can do absolutely nothing to earn the great riches of favor and grace that He has already freely given us. Jesus earned that for us; we can add nothing to what He has done.

God does not need our money, for He already owns all that we have and can ever hope to have. Everything we enjoy is a gift from Him.

If God does not want or need our money, why does He ask His people to give a portion to His work? Why was there such emphasis on tithes and offerings, and why do we receive innumerable solicitations for help from churches and Christian ministries?

The relief offering that Paul was raising for famine-stricken believers in Judea provides a clear answer. Paul knew full well that God could have provided for these people's needs any way He desired. The apostle did not need to cajole or beg believers in other regions for help. He did not threaten loss of favor with him or with God for not coming through.

What Paul was doing was offering the opportunity to be part of the blessing God would shower on His needy people.

The words of our text were written to believers who had already determined to be part of God's blessing but who now were having trouble following through with their commitment. Paul was urging them not to fall behind in it. Above all, he wanted them to remember that it was their decision: everyone was to give "as he purposeth in his heart." Paul was not going to prescribe to any of them how much, if any, to give. That was up to them and always had been.

Paul did not want any of them to give because they felt pressured to do so, telling them not to give "grudgingly, or of necessity." The latter term speaks of being under compulsion, of feeling forced to give against one's actual preference. Most of us have felt the stress of a high-pressure pitch for donations; those who succumb to such appeals do so with a mixture of resentment and guilt. That is exactly the opposite of what God wants.

The giving that God invites us to take part in may indeed represent genuine sacrifice, but He does not want to see us chafing under it. On the contrary, "God loveth a cheerful giver." This is more than someone who pastes a smile on his face as the basket goes by. A cheerful giver is one who recognizes the blessing of God in all that he has and enjoys, whether little or much. Further, he has learned that giving itself is a blessed privilege and wants to be part of it. God has set his heart free to be generous.

—*Kenneth A. Sponsler.*

# Heart of the Lesson

My father gave my sister, my brother, and me a dime every Sunday morning when we were children. Every Sunday we dropped our dimes into the offering plate at church. We children had no regular incomes; Dad and Mom did not believe in allowances. But Dad wanted us to learn to be givers. Regularly giving us his dimes taught us a lesson we carry to this day.

Our lesson looks at principles of giving in both the Old and New Testaments.

**1. Gifts of value (Exod. 35:20-24).** After Moses listed the materials needed to build and operate the tabernacle, God's dwelling place with Israel, the people went home to collect goods to donate. They gave goods because "in that day there was no such thing as legal tender" (McGee, *Thru the Bible With J. Vernon McGee,* Nelson).

Giving toward the tabernacle was strictly voluntary. Only those whose hearts stirred them were to give. Both men and women participated.

They gave jewelry: bracelets, earrings, rings, and necklaces. They gave gold. They gave red, blue, and purple fiber; fine linen fabric; goats' hair; and tanned hides. They gave silver, bronze, and wood. Many of these objects were from the plunder they brought out of Egypt.

**2. Gifts of time and talent (Exod. 35:25-26).** Women skilled in spinning spun yarn from the fiber and goat hair the Israelites had donated. Then the women wove the yarn into fabric. This was time-consuming work using primitive tools in temporary housing. Yet they were willing.

**3. Gifts of treasures (Exod. 35:27-28).** Those in leadership brought jewels such as onyx stones for the ephod and breastplate, part of the priestly garments. Twelve precious stones, representing the twelve tribes, covered the breastplate in four rows. The leaders also donated spices and oil for the light, for the anointing oil, and for the incense.

**4. Guidelines for giving (Exod. 35:29; II Cor. 9:6-8).** The choice to give, of what to give, and of the quantity to give was voluntary. Giving an offering to God depended upon each individual's heart.

The Apostle Paul compared giving to farming. A farmer's harvest is directly in proportion to the amount of seed he or she has sown. The farmer who sows little reaps a tiny harvest. The farmer who sows generously reaps a bountiful harvest. Likewise the stingy giver receives little in return. But the generous giver receives much in return in the form of God's blessings. We reap what we sow.

Giving should result from a thoughtful, cognitive choice. We should decide in our own hearts what to give and feel peaceful and happy about the decision.

A grudging attitude of resentfulness for having to give displeases God. Giving because of feeling compelled or pressured also is a wrong reason for giving. God loves cheerful givers—givers who want to help others. They want to share what they have. They want to meet needs.

Giving is an act of faith. If we believe God is able to provide for our needs (and He is), we can give without fear.

In conclusion, giving is voluntary and depends upon our decision to participate. Giving can involve things other than money—we can give goods and services (time and talent). Giving should flow from a delight in sharing rather than from compulsion. Giving causes us to rely on God, trusting Him to care for us. Giving cheerfully is an action God loves.

—Ann Staatz.

# World Missions

Have you ever been part of doing something big for God? Do you remember the excitement, the thrill of knowing what you were doing mattered for eternity?

Have your children and the children in your church had that experience? Today's passage is full of excitement and joy, with people coming and giving, "every one whose heart stirred him up, and every one whom his spirit made willing" (Exod. 35:21).

God wants us giving that way: joyfully, willingly, and cheerfully. Giving can be fun! We should be teaching our children and grandchildren and believers all around us that giving can be a joyful, happy thing. When we give, God gives back. He loves cheerful givers. The Bible says that with the measure we use to give, it will be measured to us (Luke 6:38). Give with overflowing joy, and more overflowing joy will come!

The children in our churches are watching. They learn by our actions more than by our words. Do they see the adults giving with joy and gladness, or do they see us giving grudgingly, complaining, and wishing God did not ask so much?

Perhaps we adults can learn from the children instead.

One set of young brothers wanted to buy a roll of paper for Source of Light Ministries (www.sourcelight.org) to print thousands of Bible lessons. One huge roll is $800! They worked jobs and saved every penny they could. After almost a year, they counted up their money: $53.50. Not giving up, they wrote a simple, handwritten note and sent it, asking people to match their amount. In the end, they were able to give $1,000.01.

Another set of siblings dreamed even bigger. They started with cupcakes at a yard sale to raise $14.00 for chickens for the poor through Samaritan's Purse (www.samaritanspurse.org). Then it was a goat. Then the eldest, thirteen-year-old Gabe, told his mom, "We want to do something that takes a lot of faith." He and his nine-year-old sister decided they wanted to raise $35,000 to renovate a mission hospital in the Congo!

Using skills learned as homeschoolers, they baked and decorated beautiful cakes, selling them for donations to their project. Amazingly, they raised the $35,000 and were even able to go to the Congo for the dedication of the new maternity ward of the hospital.

A young man named Bret was disappointed when his church did not meet their goal for packing shoe boxes for children around the world through Operation Christmas Child (www.samaritanspurse.org/what-we-do/operation-christmas-child/), so he made a plan of his own. He made a goal that for his birthday party, he wanted people to give enough to pack one hundred shoe boxes. His mother tried to tone down his dream. "Let's just try to do thirty or forty," she said, but he kept his goal, not only asking for donations but also working to raise money. On his birthday, friends helped pack 102 boxes.

Let us learn from the children, who give with delight. Let us plan events at our churches and in our homes that give believers a chance to have their hearts stirred and God's work increased. Let us give willingly of our money, our time, and our talents, and then watch with joy when God raises a new generation of cheerful, giving world-changers!

—Kimberly Rae.

# The Jewish Aspect

In this week's lesson, we see the Israelites donating items for use in the tabernacle. In biblical days, giving was an important part of Jewish life. The people gave *korbanot*—sacrifices, offerings, and tithes.

The practice of sacrifices stopped with the destruction of the second temple in A.D. 70. The temple was very important to Judaism. Offering sacrifices in any other place was a sin.

However, while the temple stood, many different sacrifices were offered. Burnt offerings, peace offerings, sin offerings, guilt offerings, food offerings, and drink offerings were presented to God.

In addition to sacrifices, Jews also offered tithes. In biblical days, a tenth of the yield known as the *maaser rishon,* or first tithe, would be separated and given to the Levite. The Levite would then separate a tenth of the first tithe and give it to a *kohen,* or priest, to be treated with sanctity.

A second tithe was given from the remainder that was left of the yield after the first tithe was given. This tenth of the remainder known as the *maaser sheni,* or the second tithe, was to be taken to Jerusalem. The *maaser sheni* would be consumed by the giver and his family with a spirit of sanctity. It was given only on certain years of the seven-year cycle. Every third and sixth year, the second tithe was given to the poor. The tithe given to the poor was known as the *maaser ani* or the "poor man's tithe" (Jacobs, "Tithing," myjewishlearning.com).

Today, Jews give *tzedakah.* The Talmud, the central text of rabbinic Judaism, teaches that *tzedakah* is equal to all the other commandments combined (Bava Bathra, 9b). *Tzedakah,* a Hebrew word meaning "justice" (Telushkin, *Jewish Literacy,* William Morrow) is usually translated a little incorrectly as "charity."

Helping the poor and needy is a duty in Judaism. According to Jewish tradition, "the spiritual benefit of giving to the poor is so great that a beggar actually does the giver a favor by giving a person the opportunity to perform tzedakah" (Rich, "Tzedakah: Charity," www.jewfaq.org). Since giving *tzedakah* is considered the highest of commandments, Jews believe that *tzedakah* is included with repentance and prayer as the three acts that gain forgiveness from sin.

Today, the obligation of *tzedakah* can be fulfilled in many ways. The Jewish person can give money to the poor, to health-care institutions, to the synagogue, or to an educational institution to fulfill his obligation.

The Jewish people believe that according to the Talmud, there are different levels of *tzedakah.* The lowest level is when one gives begrudgingly. Giving cheerfully, even if it is less than you should give, is better than giving begrudgingly.

Giving after being asked is good, but it is better to give *before* being asked. Giving without knowing to whom you are giving ranks high. However, even higher is giving when you know the recipient's identity but he does not know yours. Still higher is giving when neither party knows the other. Finally, the highest level of *tzedakah* is enabling the poor recipient to become self-reliant (Rich).

For Christians, there is one overriding reason to give: Jesus gave His life for us. In giving, we become a little more Christlike.

—*Robin Fitzgerald.*

# Guiding the Superintendent

When it comes to giving, some people stop at nothing. However, many believers like to talk about how much they love to worship God, but they fail to realize that the most concrete way a person can show his love for God is by his giving habits. Our lessons on God and worship now turn to one's giving.

This lesson examines giving hearts, first of the Israelites who built the wilderness tabernacle, and then of the Corinthians who participated in the Apostle Paul's offering for the suffering in Jerusalem.

## DEVOTIONAL OUTLINE

**1. Law of the willing heart (Exod. 35:20-29).** One of the key reasons for ancient Israel leaving slavery in Egypt was to be able to worship their God in the wilderness (8:1). The time had now come for them to construct a worship center. Moses urged the congregation to obey God by giving the materials and talents needed to construct the desert tabernacle (35:4-19).

The people's response was overwhelming. Six times the reader is told that the people gave from a willing heart (Exod. 35:21, 22, 26, 29; 36:2). The people responded with great gifts of their treasures and talent.

This most gracious offering would provide all the materials needed for building the tabernacle and its necessary furnishings, for clothing the priests, and for procuring the spices and oil needed for the incense and the perpetually burning lamps. The women used their talents to help spin the necessary fabrics for the tabernacle tent and courtyard.

So generous was their offering that Scripture records that the people had to be restrained from their giving (Exod. 36:6)! Thus, the law of the willing heart is truly a blessing to behold.

**2. Law of the cheerful heart (II Cor. 9:6-8).** Centuries after the fund-raising for building the tabernacle, the Apostle Paul was in the midst of raising money for the destitute in Jerusalem (chaps. 8—9).

The farmer operates on a very basic principle—the more seed one plants, the more harvest he will reap. The same principle applies to one's giving to the Lord. The law of the willing heart tells us that all giving must come from the heart that desires to give because it is the right thing to do, not because the person is trying to manipulate God in some fashion.

The analogy of the harvest is clear. If one gives a little bit, then he will only reap a little. But if one gives abundantly, then what he gets will be abundant also. The farmer who sows abundantly is like the giver who gives cheerfully. The promise is not necessarily a material return but an "increase [of] the fruits of [his] righteousness" (II Cor. 9:10).

Biblical giving is a heart issue—one needs a willing and a cheerful heart.

## AGE-GROUP EMPHASES

**Children:** No one is ever too young to learn to give biblically. Use this lesson to help your children understand how giving is a vital part of their worship experience.

**Youths:** One's giving reflects one's attitude about God. Use this lesson to help those teens who are struggling with the law of the harvest.

**Adults:** Christian adults want to worship God rightly. Use this lesson to help them see that giving is a vital part of one's worship.

—*Martin R. Dahlquist.*

# Scripture Lesson Text

**LEV. 23:9** And the Lord spake unto Mo'ses, saying,

**10 Speak unto the children of Is'ra-el, and say unto them, When ye be come into the land which I give unto you, and shall reap the harvest thereof, then ye shall bring a sheaf of the firstfruits of your harvest unto the priest:**

11 And he shall wave the sheaf before the Lord, to be accepted for you: on the morrow after the sabbath the priest shall wave it.

**12 And ye shall offer that day when ye wave the sheaf an he lamb without blemish of the first year for a burnt offering unto the Lord.**

13 And the meat offering thereof *shall be* two tenth deals of fine flour mingled with oil, an offering made by fire unto the Lord *for* a sweet savour: and the drink offering thereof *shall be* of wine, the fourth *part* of an hin.

**14 And ye shall eat neither bread, nor parched corn, nor green ears, until the selfsame day that ye have brought an offering unto your God: *it shall be* a statute for ever throughout your generations in all your dwellings.**

22 And when ye reap the harvest of your land, thou shalt not make clean riddance of the corners of thy field when thou reapest, neither shalt thou gather any gleaning of thy harvest: thou shalt leave them unto the poor, and to the stranger: I *am* the Lord your God.

**NOTES**

144

# Bringing Firstfruits

## Lesson: Leviticus 23:9-14, 22

### Read: Leviticus 2:14; 23:9-22

TIME: 1445 B.C.                                   PLACE: Mount Sinai

---

**GOLDEN TEXT**—"When ye be come into the land which I give unto you, and shall reap the harvest thereof, then ye shall bring a sheaf of the firstfruits of your harvest unto the priest" (Leviticus 23:10).

---

# *Introduction*

Believers, more than anyone else, should be thankful people. We have been the recipients of the greatest of all gifts—the gift of eternal life through Jesus Christ.

We have many ways of expressing our thanks to the Lord. Sometimes we directly thank the Lord in prayer for what He has done. Other times we share with others how thankful we are for the Lord's good blessings. Still other times we may meditate on God's blessings and utter a quick prayer of thanks to Him.

The Bible study before us examines a lesser-known feast of Israel that teaches us the lesson of thankfulness in a tangible way. In the Feast of Firstfruits, the Israelites were to bring to the priest each year the first of the harvest. The priest would wave the grain before the Lord as a way to express thankfulness for the harvest and to praise Him for all He had done for them.

We Christians today are not told we need to wave something before the Lord, but we need to be reminded of the lesson of thankfulness. We need to take seriously Paul's command in Ephesians 5:20 to give thanks always.

## LESSON OUTLINE

**I. INSTRUCTIONS FOR THE OFFERING**—Lev. 23:9-13

**II. FURTHER REGULATIONS**— Lev. 23:14, 22

# *Exposition: Verse by Verse*

## INSTRUCTIONS FOR THE OFFERING

**LEV. 23:9** And the Lord spake unto Moses, saying,

**10** Speak unto the children of Israel, and say unto them, When ye be come into the land which I give unto you, and shall reap the harvest thereof, then ye shall bring a sheaf of the firstfruits of your harvest unto the priest:

**11** And he shall wave the sheaf

before the Lord, to be accepted for you: on the morrow after the sabbath the priest shall wave it.

12 And ye shall offer that day when ye wave the sheaf an he lamb without blemish of the first year for a burnt offering unto the Lord.

13 And the meat offering thereof shall be two tenth deals of fine flour mingled with oil, an offering made by fire unto the Lord for a sweet savour: and the drink offering thereof shall be of wine, the fourth part of an hin.

Leviticus 23 describes the Feast of Firstfruits in which the Israelites brought the first of their harvest to the Lord. This passage, however, was not the first to mention the idea of presenting the first of the harvest to the Lord. Exodus 23 describes the feast of harvest and states that "the first of the firstfruits of thy land thou shalt bring into the house of the Lord thy God" (vs.19).

Leviticus 23 then gives a description of how to carry out this command. This text does not give us the time of the Feast of Firstfruits, but from other Scriptures some think it likely took place in conjunction with the Feast of Unleavened Bread described in verses 6-8.

Leviticus 23:11 states that the priest was to wave the sheaf of grain "on the morrow after the sabbath," probably meaning the day after the start of the Feast of Unleavened Bread. This would put Firstfruits in the month Nisan (March-April) and put it on the sixteenth day of the month (vs. 6). If that is the case, then the grain probably was barley, not wheat, since barley was harvested in the spring.

**The Israelites' part (Lev. 23:9-10).** The Lord gave Moses specific instructions for the Israelites' part in the Feast of Firstfruits. Note first that they were

to observe this feast when they entered the Promised Land, or, as God described it: "the land which I give unto you." (These words indicate that the land came from the Lord, not from their own military efforts.) The Israelites, then, were not to observe this feast in the wilderness.

Second, when the Israelites were ready to harvest the grain (probably barley) each year, they were first to cut a few stalks and bring the sheaf to the priest. This offering was the Israelites' way of thanking the Lord for the harvest that year and dedicating the rest of the harvest to Him.

**The priests' part (Lev. 23:11).** When an Israelite brought the sheaf of grain, the priest received it and waved it before the Lord as an expression of thanks and dedication. To wave the offering probably meant the priest lifted it toward heaven and waved it back and forth a few times.

The waving would have been a meaningful action because it would convey the thought *Lord, You have been so good to us this year. Before I harvest the rest of my crop, I present to You this first sheaf to say thanks and to acknowledge that You are the source of all our provisions.*

The last part of Leviticus 23:11 gives the only time reference in the verse. The Israelites were to bring their sheaf "on the morrow after the sabbath," which we said above probably refers to the day after the Sabbath of the Feast of Unleavened Bread (vss. 6-8).

**Additional offerings (Lev. 23:12-13).** In addition to the sheaf of grain, the Israelites were also to bring an animal, fine flour, and wine. The animal was to be "an he lamb without blemish of the first year for a burnt offering unto the Lord." These stipulations were the same as found in Leviticus

1:10-13. The unblemished lamb showed the importance of giving God the best of the flock and reminds us of the Lord Jesus, who was "a lamb without blemish and without spot" (I Pet. 1:19).

The grain offering, or "meat offering," was to be "two tenth deals of fine flour mingled with oil" ( Lev. 23:13). The Scripture uses the word "meat" in this passage, but here the word refers to food in general and not the meat of an animal (cf. John 4:34). The context shows that a grain offering is in view. (We could also call it the meal offering.)

The grain offering, which was probably crushed wheat, was normally one-tenth of an ephah of flour (Lev. 5:11; 6:20), making this offering a double portion. The double portion was the way to show extra thanks for the Lord's blessings. (An ephah was the equivalent of about three-fifths of a bushel, so two-tenths would have been about four quarts.)

The grain offering was to be choice flour mixed with oil, similar to the description in Leviticus 2:1. The flour was to be the finest available, and the oil was likely olive oil. (In Leviticus 2:1, frankincense was added.)

This grain offering was to be roasted, sending a sweet savour to the Lord. The concept of an offering being a sweet savor to the Lord is an anthropomorphic way of saying that the Lord accepted the offering and was pleased (cf. Phil. 4:18).

The drink offering brought to the Feast of Firstfruits was to be one-fourth of a hin of wine. Some think a hin was about a gallon, making this offering about a quart. This drink offering is not mentioned elsewhere in Leviticus but is prescribed in Numbers 6, 15, and 28.

Why were the Israelites commanded to bring the animal, the grain, and the wine along with the sheaf of grain? All these items were part of the regular offerings for the nation, so perhaps God wanted them to remember His additional blessings—the blessings of sins forgiven and pleasing fellowship with Him.

## FURTHER REGULATIONS

**14 And ye shall eat neither bread, nor parched corn, nor green ears, until the selfsame day that ye have brought an offering unto your God: it shall be a statute for ever throughout your generations in all your dwellings.**

**22 And when ye reap the harvest of your land, thou shalt not make clean riddance of the corners of thy field when thou reapest, neither shalt thou gather any gleaning of thy harvest: thou shalt leave them unto the poor, and to the stranger: I am the Lord your God.**

**Regulations for the offering (Lev. 23:14).** The Lord wanted His people to carry out the Feast of Firstfruits as a way of thanking Him, but He had one stipulation. They were not to eat anything from the harvest, "neither bread, nor parched corn, nor green ears," until they first brought their sheaf of grain to the priest. (The term "green ears" probably means fresh grain.)

Why did God make this stipulation? Perhaps because He wanted to be sure His people did not neglect to thank Him before they enjoyed the bounty He supplied.

Leviticus 23:14 ends with the instruction that this feast "shall be a statute for ever throughout your generations in all your dwellings." Note the all-inclusive words in this statement: "for ever," "throughout your generations," and "in all your dwellings." In this way God emphasized the lasting importance of this event.

**Regulations for the harvest (Lev. 23:22).** The Lord wanted His people to thank Him for His agricultural provision, but He also wanted them to express their thanks by leaving some of the grain in the fields after the harvest for the needy.

God instructed His people not to reap the crop out to the very corners of the field and not to go back over the field to pick up grain that had fallen to the ground during the harvest (the gleanings). The reason for this was to give the poor and the foreigners among them access to some food. This procedure showed that the Lord had provided plenty for His people, and He had given them enough to provide for others.

Leviticus 23:22 describes exactly what happened to Ruth and Naomi when they were in need of food. Ruth had apparently learned about this provision in the law and therefore said to Naomi, "Let me now go to the field, and glean ears of corn after him in whose sight I shall find grace" (Ruth 2:2). Naomi consented, and Ruth went to a field to pick up the grain the reapers had left.

In God's good plan Ruth went to the field of Boaz, who knew of Ruth and Naomi and was concerned for them. He was so concerned that he gave two instructions to his reapers that went beyond what he was required to do.

First, he told his men to let Ruth "glean even among the sheaves, and reproach her not" (Ruth 2:15). Apparently, Ruth was allowed to take some of the grain already put into sheaves. Second, he told his men to "let fall also some of the handfuls of purpose for her" (vs. 16). The men were to intentionally let some of the grain they harvested fall back on the ground for Ruth. This account shows an example of someone who obeyed not only the letter but also the spirit of the law given in our passage.

Leviticus 23:22 concludes with the words "I am the Lord your God." By this statement, God emphasized that He was the one who provided for His people, and now they were to follow His model and provide for the poor and needy.

Believers today can follow the principle of the firstfruits in several ways. We can give our tithes and offerings to the Lord from the first of our money, not what may be left over. Giving Him the first part shows our thanks for what He has provided for us and says that all our money is really His.

We can also give the Lord the first part of our day for our private time with Him rather than giving Him the last part of the day when we may be weary. Doing so shows thanks for what He has done for us and affirms that the rest of the day is also His.

We can also give the Lord the first part of our discretionary time to serve Him rather than satisfying ourselves first and giving Him the time we have left over. In every way the principle and practice of firstfruits shows thanks to the Lord and is a means of praising Him.

Before we conclude this study of the Feast of Firstfruits, we want to examine passages by two different New Testament writers that show the principle of firstfruits.

First, Paul wrote in I Corinthians 15 about Christ as the firstfruits of the resurrection. In the first part of that chapter, Paul dealt with those who said there was no resurrection. Then he countered that thinking in verse 20 by writing, "But now is Christ risen from the dead, and become the firstfruits of them that slept."

Just as the Old Testament Feast of Firstfruits pictured the first of the crop and more to come, so Christ, as the firstfruits of the resurrection, signifies that He was the first to rise from the dead and is the guarantee that more will come after Him. This truth assured the believers in Corinth that Christ did indeed rise from the dead and so will all the others who have died in Christ.

Paul further stated that "every man in his own order: Christ the firstfruits; afterward they that are Christ's at his coming" (I Cor. 15:23). This verse adds the thought that this resurrection will take place at the coming of Christ for His church.

Paul had already developed this idea in I Thessalonians 4:16-17: "For the Lord himself shall descend from heaven with a shout, with the voice of the archangel, and with the trump of God: and the dead in Christ shall rise first: Then we which are alive and remain shall be caught up together with them in the clouds, to meet the Lord in the air: and so shall we ever be with the Lord." Thank the Lord for Christ, our firstfruits, who by His resurrection guarantees our resurrection.

The second passage we want to look at is James 1:18: "Of his own will begat he us with the word of truth, that we should be a kind of firstfruits of his creatures." God has promised new heavens and a new earth as described in II Peter 3:10-13. God's work to make us a new creature, or a new creation, in Christ (II Cor. 5:17) means that we lead the way in God's work of redemption. The work He has done in making us new is a guarantee that God will complete His work of making all things new someday.

Paul expanded on this aspect of the firstfruits idea as well in Romans 8:19-23. There he noted that all creation longs for deliverance, waiting for "the glorious liberty of the children of God." Since Adam brought creation under a curse by his sin, it is fitting that the children of Adam would lead the way in restoring creation to freedom and wholeness through our redemption in Christ, as even now we enjoy "the firstfruits of the Spirit."

The firstfruits principle is a blessing to believers today. It shows that we need to give Christ the first and best of what we have as a means of thanking and praising Him for His work.

This principle also guarantees the future for us. Because Christ rose from the dead, we have the confidence that we too shall rise someday. We hope it is today! Because Christ made us new, we have the guarantee that He will make all things new someday.

—Don Anderson.

# QUESTIONS

1. What were the Israelites to bring to the Lord at harvesttime?

2. Why did God want the Israelites to do this?

3. What did the priest do with the sheaf of grain?

4. What were the Israelites to bring along with the sheaf?

5. Why were the people not to eat from the harvest before they brought their sheaf to the priest?

6. What were God's two commands for harvesting a field?

7. Why did God institute this practice?

8. Why does Leviticus 23:22 conclude with the declaration "I am the Lord your God"?

9. In what way is Christ our firstfruits?

10. In what way are individual believers firstfruits?

—Don Anderson.

# Preparing to Teach the Lesson

We can see how weak and fickle the human heart is by the speed and ease with which people forget the Lord and all He has done for them. Unless all the habits and details of our day, week, and year are focused on Him, we can turn aside to secular interests and even pagan and godless thoughts and activities and forget the Lord, as did Israel.

However, God wove into Israel's days and seasons many activities that were designed to remind them of His primacy and centrality in their lives. The firstfruits offering is a perfect example of this principle. Every year at harvesttime, the firstfruits offering was a commemoration of God's blessing and an acknowledgement of His first place in their lives. Any offering that reminds us that God has first place in our lives should be a welcome addition to our routine!

## TODAY'S AIM

**Facts:** to understand the principle of the firstfruits offering.

**Principle:** to understand that God must come first in our thinking, not last.

**Application:** to put God first in every activity of our lives.

## INTRODUCING THE LESSON

Today's lesson is an example of how everyday life and the special seasons of life in Israel were to center on the Lord. God left nothing to chance and human whims when it came to reminders that He had delivered them from slavery and bondage and was giving them the Promised Land with all its blessings. Others had been living in the land and had planted crops. The Israelites were to move in and take over. When the crops matured and were due to be harvested, the people were to harvest them, remembering that the Lord had made this provision for them. God required this firstfruits offering as a reminder of all that He had done and would continue to do for them.

We remember from last week's lesson that we are to bring our offerings to the Lord. Beyond the practical support of God's house and work, this also reminds us that it is the Lord who gives us the ability to earn, and we owe Him thanks for that. If giving to God from what we earn seems to be too much, we should remember that since He has asked us to give, we can be sure that He has given us enough to "make it" with what is left over. God's work done in God's way will never lack God's support.

## DEVELOPING THE LESSON

**1. The principle of the firstfruits (Lev. 23:9-11).** The firstfruits offering was not a tenth of the harvest; it was simply representative of the harvest. It was offered to thank God first; then the rest of the grain with which God had blessed them was harvested. It was a "thank-you," not a discharge of an obligation of a certain amount. While this was to be offered at the first harvest in the Land of Promise, it was also to be done at every successive harvest.

We do not know how long Israel continued this offering, but we do know that when they fell into sin and stopped honoring the Lord, they were carried away captive to other lands from which they had no harvest of their own. They could not then offer a firstfruits offering or any of the other offerings to honor and worship the Lord. They could thank the Lord in prayer or praise, but they could not demonstrate thanks in the practical way that He had prescribed.

**2. Details of the offering (Lev. 23:12-14).** At the same time as this firstfruits offering, there was to be the offering of a yearling lamb without blemish, a grain offering, and a drink offering. The firstfruits offering was not complete in itself. There was also the provision that one was not to eat anything until the firstfruits offering was completed.

A special part of this offering was that it would be carried on perpetually by the nation and individually throughout their future generations wherever they lived. Every household was to be thankful at every harvest that God had blessed them with a bountiful yield.

**3. Additional instructions (Lev. 23:22).** God specified that when they reaped the harvest, the Israelites were not to clean up every last bit of grain but leave some for others. This was to benefit the poor, who had no field to reap, and those who were not of the people of Israel who had no land, or even a place to live. Remember that when Israel left Egypt, some of the Egyptians came with them. It may be that they had not become believers in the Lord, or if they were believers they had not formally joined Israel. They were people without status, something like our poor or homeless people. God in His compassion provided the gleanings for them. By putting in a certain amount of effort, they could share in the bounty of the land. If you recall, this was how Ruth and Boaz met in the fields that were being harvested (Ruth 2:4-8).

## ILLUSTRATING THE LESSON

A thankful heart is a necessity, not just an option.

**GIVE THANKS TO GOD**

God

**HE HAS BLESSED**

## CONCLUDING THE LESSON

The original firstfruits offering took place at the first harvest after the conquest of the Promised Land by Israel. It was to be commemorated perpetually at each subsequent harvest. In much the same way, we can remember that it is the Lord who gives us the ability to earn and blesses our labor. We can bring to Him our offerings to acknowledge His blessing and affirm that He really owns everything we are and have. One could not eat anything until the firstfruits offering was given, so we must remember that God comes first. Whenever there is a decision to be made or work to be done, God comes first. We cannot go wrong by putting Him first in all we do.

We might infer from Leviticus 23:22 that when we are truly thankful for God's blessing upon us, we will readily help provide for those who are less fortunate. It is a wonderful testimony when the people of God are known as those who look out for the needs of needy people.

## ANTICIPATING THE NEXT LESSON

Next week, we study the Year of Jubilee and remember to be glad that our God is the God of liberty.

—Brian D. Doud.

# PRACTICAL POINTS

1. God is our provider, and He deserves the firstfruits of our harvest (Lev. 23:9-10).
2. God appoints stewards over His offering.
3. It is important to follow God's instructions concerning His offerings (vss. 11-13).
4. We should give God the best that we have to offer.
5. God's offering comes before our own expenses (vs. 14).
6. We cannot merely consume everything we earn. God commands us to share with the needy (vs. 22).

*—Valante M. Grant.*

# RESEARCH AND DISCUSSION

1. When giving, why is it important to remember that all things come from God?
2. What is the significance of offering the firstfruits to God? What does this say about God's priority in your life?
3. How does offering the firstfruits to God bless us?
4. What do God's instructions to Moses teach us about giving an acceptable offering to God?
5. Did the children of Israel plant the crop of the first harvest in the land that God gave them? What does this say about God's provision for His people?
6. What are consequences of not giving the firstfruits offering to God?

*—Valante M. Grant.*

# ILLUSTRATED HIGH POINTS

**The land which I give unto you**

The firstfruits offering recognized God as the source of all.

There is a story about an atheist who boasted that he plowed on Sunday, planted on Sunday, cultivated on Sunday, and never went to church on Sunday; yet he harvested more bushels per acre than anyone else, even those who were God-fearing. Obviously, he thought he was the master of his fate.

The answer to this man's boasting is that God does not always settle His accounts at harvesttime. But He does settle His accounts!

**Firstfruits**

On a couple of occasions, a Christian lady in my town brought my family a quart of fresh strawberries. She said she wanted to give the firstfruits of her berry patch to someone in the Lord's work. Although I was not a priest in Jerusalem's tabernacle, I accepted with gratitude and delight.

The Old Testament firstfruits offering was a token offering expressing thanksgiving to God for the anticipated harvest. In a similar way, the church receives offerings on Sunday as an expression of gratitude for God's provisions for the congregation's needs.

**Leave them unto the poor**

Gleaning was part of God's plan for providing for the poor. It was not simply a handout, for the people had to go to the fields and work at gathering what was left of the grain or other crops. The book of Ruth demonstrates the value of gleaning in Bible times.

This old proverb is true: "Give a man a fish and you feed him for a day; teach a man to fish and you feed him for a lifetime."

*—David A. Hamburg.*

# Golden Text Illuminated

**"When ye be come into the land which I give unto you, and shall reap the harvest thereof, then ye shall bring a sheaf of the firstfruits of your harvest unto the priest" (Leviticus 23:10).**

"If I have anything left over after the groceries are bought, the kids are clothed, and the bills are paid, I might think about putting something in the offering plate." While most Christians would never make such a statement out loud, it lies behind the actions of all too many. We live in a world that has a "Give God the leftovers" mentality.

As with so many prevailing attitudes and practices, God's desire for us is precisely the opposite. He wants us to show our trust in His provision by giving right off the top—setting aside a portion for His use as soon as we receive our income.

The main way God established this principle with His people in the Old Testament was through the tithe. The Israelites were to give a percentage of all that they received—whether crops, livestock, or goods—at the outset. They were not to wait to see how much they would actually need and then give. Their giving, though a requirement of the law, was to be an expression of faith in God's goodness and care.

Another vehicle God used to establish the principle of prioritized giving was the offering of firstfruits. When the yearly harvest began, an offering was to be made from the very first gleanings of whatever crop was coming to fruition. This too represented trust that the Lord would provide a full harvest. Giving at the very beginning honored Him.

This principle was not an afterthought from the Lord or something He sprang on them unexpectedly. "When ye be come into the land" looks ahead to Israel's settling in the Promised Land. "Which I give unto you" reminded them that everything they reaped from the ground was by God's gift. They would be giving Him nothing that He had not already given them.

The firstfruits offering was very simple. When harvest began, people were to take a sheaf of whatever grain they were gathering in and bring it as "firstfruits of your harvest unto the priest." It was not a large offering, nor a costly one. But it was very significant, for it showed that God was uppermost in their thoughts even as they began the important task of securing sustenance for another year. They were to remember Him and His gifts to them as they worked.

Throughout the Old Testament, God's people are exhorted not to neglect the bringing of firstfruits to the Lord (cf. Neh. 10:35-37; Prov. 3:9; Ezek. 20:40; 48:14). The practice of offering firstfruits thus became an ingrained part of Israelite life. In the New Testament, the concept of firstfruits takes on a symbolic dimension.

In I Corinthians 16:15, Paul called the household of Stephanas "the firstfruits of Achaia," meaning not only that they were among the earliest believers in that region but also that they were a promise of many more to come. In Romans 8:23, Paul noted that believers possess "the firstfruits of the Spirit." His work in our lives today gives a foretaste of the glory in eternity.

Most significant, Christ Himself is the firstfruits of all who will be raised to glory in Him (I Cor. 15:20, 23). How can we withhold anything from Him?

—*Kenneth A. Sponsler.*

# Heart of the Lesson

I have participated as a craft vendor at a local fall festival twice in recent years. The festival takes place on a historic farm along the Oregon Trail. Volunteers wear pioneer clothing and demonstrate old-time arts such as blacksmithing. Visitors tour the barn and house, listen to live bluegrass music, and squeeze cider. The event celebrates the harvest, particularly of apples.

Ancient Israel celebrated the harvest with a one-day festival of firstfruits on the day after the Sabbath following Passover. During the festival, the people gave God the first of their grain harvest. The first of their crops, cattle, and grapes always belonged to the Lord. Today's lesson explores this time of thanksgiving to God for the harvest and for daily food.

**1. Waving the sheaf (Lev. 23:9-11).** The Israelites watched for the first heading of the barley crop and picked a ripened stalk here and there. They gathered the stalks into a sheaf and brought it to the tabernacle during the festival as a gift to God (McGee, *Thru the Bible With J. Vernon McGee,* Nelson). The priest waved the sheaf before the Lord for His acceptance.

**2. Offering a lamb (Lev. 23:12).** Along with the grain offering, the people sacrificed a defect-free year-old male lamb as a burnt offering expressing their dedication or surrender to God. The person offering the lamb put his hand on the lamb's head, showing he was identifying with the sacrifice. He killed the animal, and the priest sprinkled the blood around the altar. The animal was burned, with the smoke wafting up as an aroma pleasing to God.

**3. Presenting grain and drink offerings (Lev. 23:13-14).** The "meat" (grain) offering accompanied the burnt offering. Israelites brought their best flour mixed with olive oil with salt added. "Salt, as a preservative, was a reminder of God's covenant faithfulness" (Willmington, *Willmington's Bible Handbook,* Tyndale). The priest burned a portion of the flour, releasing a sweet savor to God. The remainder of the flour was food for the priests.

Along with the grain offering, the Israelites presented a drink offering of about a quart of wine. This was poured out, never consumed.

Grain, grapes, and oil were Israel's major crops (Tenney, ed., *The Zondervan Pictorial Encyclopedia of the Bible,* Zondervan). The festival of firstfruits involved giving God all three crops.

The people refrained from eating from their new grain crop until they offered the first of it to God.

The laws that God gave to Moses regarding firstfruits were permanent. All generations of Israelites were to give the first of their harvests to God, wherever they lived.

**4. Remembering the poor (Lev. 23:22).** Firstfruits was a time of celebration. But the poor or sojourner (noncitizen) in Israel had no crops over which to rejoice. God provided for them by requiring that farmers leave grain standing in the corners of their fields. If a harvester dropped grain, he was to leave it on the ground. The poor and the sojourner gleaned this grain. God loved the poor, but He expected them to work for their food.

The people of Israel were to give their first and their best to God. We too should give God our best. All we have comes from Him. Honor God with your firstfruits. Give to Him first out of your paycheck, and trust He will provide for your needs.

—*Ann Staatz.*

# World Missions

In Leviticus 23:22, God's people were instructed to allow the corners of their fields to remained unharvested. They were to leave this portion of their income for the poor.

Might we do the same? We are commanded to give to the Lord, but what if we set aside another portion, beyond our regular giving for the Lord's work?

It has been said that Americans spend more on dog food than they do on missions. Many of us feel money is tight, that we have little to spare, or that if God would bless us with more, we would be able to give.

However, John the Baptist said if we have two coats, we should give one away (Luke 3:11). Very few of us can say money is tight or we have nothing to give when held up to that standard!

People who give find they do not lack. William Colgate tithed on the very first dollar he ever made in business. As his work prospered, he added to that, giving 20, 30, 50, and eventually 100 percent of his income to the Lord. Colgate gave millions to God's work all over the world and remained successful all his life.

Henry Crowell, founder of Quaker Oats, over a period of forty years gave away 70 percent of his income. He also led many business acquaintances to the Lord.

Robert LeTourneau, who became rich through massive machinery, lived most of his career on 10 percent of his earnings, giving 90 percent to the Lord. "The question is not how much of my money I give to God," he said, "but rather how much of God's money I keep for myself."

We may not have millions, but even one dollar can make a difference. Here are some wonderful ways we can use the money God has blessed us with to help the poor and give them the gospel:

Gospel tracts—200 for $1!

Radio program—15 minutes for $45

Bicycle, to enable a missionary to go to many more villages per day than if on foot—$110

Motorbike, can transport two missionaries to even more villages—$1,200

Kerosene lantern for missionary walking at night—$25

Dalit child packet, allowing an "untouchable" child to go to school, eat a meal per day, and have a yearly medical checkup—$50

Flip chart to share gospel with the illiterate—$10

New Testaments—50 cents each!

VBS materials for one child—$5

Battery-powered radio for missionaries in villages—$40

Jesus well, providing clean water and the gospel for an entire community—$1,400

Church building—$10,000-$40,000

Pair of chickens—$11

Camel—$345

Blanket—$12

Fishing net—$25

These are just a few of the many, many opportunities to help reach the world with the tangible love of Christ and hope of the gospel. And this is just one ministry! All of the above can be found and donated to at *Gospel for Asia*, www.gfa.org.

What if we started setting aside an extra 10 percent each month to give to God's work? How exciting and fun it would be for our families to enjoy choosing which ministry to give to! What if we gave 20 percent extra or more?

—Kimberly Rae.

# The Jewish Aspect

This week's lesson is about firstfruits. Many people believe that Jesus rose from the dead on the holiday that has been coined "Firstfruits." Modern Jews are less likely to call the holiday by this name. Instead, they refer to this day as the day that the Omer count begins.

This day was instituted by God in Leviticus 23. In this chapter, God gave instructions for many of the Jewish holidays, including the Sabbath, Passover, Firstfruits, Pentecost, and the Feast of Tabernacles.

In biblical times, when the temple was in existence, a special procession was led by the high priest during the barley harvest. The high priest would go to the Mount of Olives, also called the Mountain of the Messiah (Oakley, *Messiah and the Feasts of the Lord,* Colorado Theological Seminary). Here the firstfruits would be harvested and then carried to the floor of the temple, where it would be threshed with rods. The barley would be roasted and winnowed. The priest would then wave one sheaf before the Lord.

After the temple was destroyed, the holiday changed, becoming less significant. The day became known primarily as the day that the Counting of the Omer, *sefirat ha'omer,* begins.

The Omer, which means a "measure," was the offering given on the day that the high priest waved the first sheaf before the Lord (Strassfeld, *The Jewish Holidays,* William Marrow). Today, most Jewish people begin the Omer count on the next day after the first day of Passover. The count ends on the day before *Shavuot,* Pentecost.

During each night of the Counting of the Omer, this blessing is proclaimed: "Blessed are You, Lord our God, King of the Universe, who has sanctified us with His commandments, and commanded us concerning the counting of the Omer." The blessing is followed by the count of the day. For instance, the Jewish person might say, "Today is the seventeenth day of the Omer," and then the totaled time in weeks toward the seven weeks is stated. The counting is done at night, as each new day begins (Strassfeld).

The Counting of the Omer is a semi-mourning period. During this time, tradition mandates the observance of mourning customs. People are not to cut hair, marry, or attend concerts. Some Jews do not shave during the Omer count (Strassfeld).

The Counting of the Omer is important to the Jewish people because it was commanded by God in the Torah (Lev. 23:15-16) and is a link between Passover, or *Pesach,* which remembers the Israelites' Exodus from Egypt, and Pentecost, which marks the giving of the law at Mount Sinai.

Jews know that there are exactly forty-nine days between Passover and Pentecost. Pentecost actually begins on day fifty.

The thirty-third day of the Counting of the Omer is a minor holiday known as Lag B'Omer. During this day mourning traditions cease for the day. In the place of mourning are outings and joy. Also on this day, bonfires are lit, children customarily play with imitation bows and arrows, and parades take place.

The holiday of Lag B'Omer marks the death of Rabbi Shimon bar Yochai, an eminent second-century A.D. sage. He was the first to teach the mystical ideas of the Torah. Tradition holds that the rabbi instructed his disciples to mark the date of his death as the day of his joy (Zaklikowski, "Celebrate on the Anniversary of Death?" www.chabad.org).

—*Robin Fitzgerald.*

# *Guiding the Superintendent*

God had a great concern. He told Israel, "When thou has eaten and art full, then thou shalt bless the Lord thy God for the good land which he hath given thee. Beware that thou forget not the Lord thy God" (Deut. 8:10-11).

Israel had just come off forty years of wilderness wandering. They were about to go into the Promised Land. In addition to the great land, they would inhabit completely built cities and accompanying crops and orchards. These were all things for which they did not labor. The danger was that they would forget that God had given them all this bounty. To help Israel not forget where it all came from, the Lord instituted a series of feasts and sacrifices to continually remind them that all they had came from God.

The lesson this week looks at two very specific requirements commanded by God to aid Israel in remembering.

## DEVOTIONAL OUTLINE

**1. Firstfruits (Lev. 23:9-14).** God always speaks to people where they are. Leviticus 23 is no exception. Most modern Bible readers give very little attention to the harvest regulations given in the books of Moses. However, for those who pause and examine the regulations, there is much practical truth to be gleaned.

People who work the land and grow crops are familiar with the idea of firstfruits. Even for the home gardener who holds the first tomato in his hands, there is great excitement.

God did not leave Israel to their own designs. He gave very specific procedures for celebrating the harvest. After Israel came into the land and began to harvest their first crops, they were to bring a sheaf of the first grain harvested and present it to the priest. In a special ceremony he was to wave this grain before the Lord. This was followed with the sacrifice of a year-old lamb supplemented with flour and oil. To complete the ceremony, a portion of wine was poured out before the Lord as a drink offering. This all was to be performed on the first day after the Sabbath. On this day all work was forbidden.

For many people today who have no agricultural background, this all might seem strange. However, for agrarian Israel, this was to be a lasting ordinance with a reminder that all the harvest was a special gift from God. "Any claim they had to agricultural wealth was based on God's gift of the land to them. They depended on his favor for the harvest" (Anders, ed., *Holman Old Testament Commentary,* Holman).

The lesson is clear. God does not want leftovers. Only the best and first should be used to give one's thanks to God.

**2. Gleaning (Lev. 23:22).** The ceremony of Firstfruits was not the only regulation that God instituted to teach Israel that all they had was a bountiful gift from God.

Farmers were instructed to leave the corners of the field unharvested and that which fell to the ground during the harvest uncollected. In this way God was providing food for the poor.

## AGE-GROUP EMPHASES

**Children:** This is a good lesson to help your children appreciate the fact that all they have comes from God.

**Youths:** Have the young people discuss how they might be able to give God their firstfruits.

**Adults:** Have your adults discuss this question: In what ways do we give God our leftovers?

—Martin R. Dahlquist.

# Scripture Lesson Text

**LEV. 25:1** And the LORD spake unto Mo'ses in mount Si'nai, saying,

**2 Speak unto the children of Is'ra-el, and say unto them, When ye come into the land which I give you, then shall the land keep a sabbath unto the LORD.**

3 Six years thou shalt sow thy field, and six years thou shalt prune thy vineyard, and gather in the fruit thereof;

**4 But in the seventh year shall be a sabbath of rest unto the land, a sabbath for the LORD: thou shalt neither sow thy field, nor prune thy vineyard.**

5 That which groweth of its own accord of thy harvest thou shalt not reap, neither gather the grapes of thy vine undressed: *for* it is a year of rest unto the land.

**6 And the sabbath of the land shall be meat for you; for thee, and for thy servant, and for thy maid, and for thy hired servant, and for thy stranger that sojourneth with thee,**

7 And for thy cattle, and for the beast that *are* in thy land, shall all the increase thereof be meat.

**8 And thou shalt number seven sabbaths of years unto thee, seven times seven years; and the space of the seven sabbaths of years shall be unto thee forty and nine years.**

9 Then shalt thou cause the trumpet of the jubile to sound on the tenth *day* of the seventh month, in the day of atonement shall ye make the trumpet sound throughout all your land.

**10 And ye shall hallow the fiftieth year, and proclaim liberty throughout *all* the land unto all the inhabitants thereof: it shall be a jubile unto you; and ye shall return every man unto his possession, and ye shall return every man unto his family.**

11 A jubile shall that fiftieth year be unto you: ye shall not sow, neither reap that which groweth of itself in it, nor gather *the grapes* in it of thy vine undressed.

**12 For it *is* the jubile; it shall be holy unto you: ye shall eat the increase thereof out of the field.**

**NOTES**

# Remembering with Joy

## Lesson: Leviticus 25:1-12

Read: Leviticus 25:1-55

TIME: 1445 B.C.                                          PLACE: Mount Sinai

---

**GOLDEN TEXT—"Proclaim liberty throughout all the land unto all the inhabitants thereof: it shall be a jubile unto you; and ye shall return every man unto his possession, and ye shall return every man unto his family" (Leviticus 25:10).**

---

# *Introduction*

In this unit, we have been focusing on giving praise to God. We have noted how generous giving brings praise to God as does bringing Him the firstfruits.

The Old Testament saints had another way of praising God—by observing special holy occasions whether for days, weeks, months, or even years. We are all familiar with the Sabbath Day, which the Jews were to observe in obedience to God. The Sabbath Day regulations stated that the Israelites were to work six days and to rest and worship on the seventh day, which is Saturday on our calendars today.

In our lesson this week, we see how the Sabbath Year (the seventh year) and the Jubilee Year (seven Sabbath Years) also brought praise to the Lord. The Sabbath Year was the seventh year in a seven-year cycle. The Jubilee Year was the year after a cycle of seven Sabbath Years—the fiftieth year. These special times were based on the Lord's Creation week in which He worked six days and rested on the seventh day (Gen. 2:1-3).

## LESSON OUTLINE

**I. REMEMBER THE SABBATH YEAR WITH JOY—Lev. 25:1-7**

**II. REMEMBER THE JUBILEE YEAR WITH JOY—Lev. 25:8-12**

# *Exposition: Verse by Verse*

**REMEMBER THE SABBATH YEAR WITH JOY**

**LEV. 25:1 And the Lord spake unto Moses in mount Sinai, saying,**

**2 Speak unto the children of Israel, and say unto them, When ye come into the land which I give you,** then shall the land keep a sabbath unto the Lord.

**3 Six years thou shalt sow thy field, and six years thou shalt prune thy vineyard, and gather in the fruit thereof;**

**4 But in the seventh year shall be**

a sabbath of rest unto the land, a sabbath for the Lord: thou shalt neither sow thy field, nor prune thy vineyard.

**5** That which groweth of its own accord of thy harvest thou shalt not reap, neither gather the grapes of thy vine undressed: for it is a year of rest unto the land.

**6** And the sabbath of the land shall be meat for you; for thee, and for thy servant, and for thy maid, and for thy hired servant, and for thy stranger that sojourneth with thee,

**7** And for thy cattle, and for the beast that are in thy land, shall all the increase thereof be meat.

**The command for the Sabbath Year (Lev. 25:1-2).** On Mount Sinai, the Lord gave Moses the command concerning the Sabbath Day: "Remember the sabbath day, to keep it holy. Six days shalt thou labour, and do all thy work: but the seventh day is the sabbath of the Lord thy God: in it thou shalt not do any work" (Exod. 20:8-10). God gave this command because "in six days the Lord made heaven and earth, the sea, and all that in them is, and rested the seventh day: wherefore the Lord blessed the sabbath day, and hallowed it" (vs. 11).

In Leviticus 25, we find another special occasion for the Israelites that God gave to Moses on Mount Sinai—the Sabbath Year. The Sabbath Day was primarily a day for the Hebrews to rest and worship. When they entered the Promised Land, they were to observe the Sabbath Year, which was a time for the land to rest for a year in the Israelites' agricultural cycle.

**The six years of work (Lev. 25:3).** Based on the Sabbath Day cycle established at Creation, the Lord wanted His people to plant their fields, prune their vineyards, and take in the produce for six years.

**The seventh year of rest (Lev. 25:4-5).** In the seventh year of the agricultural cycle, the Israelites were to observe "a sabbath of rest unto the land, a sabbath for the Lord." In this year the people of God were not to plant their fields or take care of their vineyards.

In the seventh year, some crops would come up on their own, and the vineyards would continue to produce fruit. The Israelites, however, were not to harvest the crop or pick the grapes of the untended vines. They were to give the land a year of rest.

**Food in the seventh year (Lev. 25:6-7).** The question then arises about what to do with the produce that came up on its own during the seventh year. This food was available for them, their servants, the hired workers, the aliens in the land, and their animals. They were not to harvest it or store it away, but it was available to be eaten as needed by everybody.

Why did God command such a practice? We have come to learn that it was a sound agricultural practice. The seventh year let the land lie fallow so that it could replenish its nutrients for the next six-year cycle of planting.

The Sabbath Year, however, was more than an agricultural issue. It was a year set apart to the Lord. The Sabbath Year undoubtedly was a reminder to the Israelites to take God's Sabbath cycles seriously and to trust Him for food in the year they did not plant.

So what would the people eat in the seventh year? Also, since they were not to plant a crop in the seventh year, what would they eat the next year? Later in Leviticus 25, the Lord promised abundance in obedience to His instruction: "I will command my blessing upon you in the sixth year, and it shall bring forth fruit for three years. And ye shall sow the eighth year, and eat yet of old fruit until the ninth year; until her fruits come in ye shall eat of the old store" (vss. 21-22).

The crop of the sixth year would be so abundant that it would be sufficient for that year and for the next two years. As in the provision of manna (Exod. 16:4-5), God would supply for them if they obeyed Him.

Before we leave this passage, we should consider three other issues relating to the Sabbath Year. First, Exodus 23:11-12 states that the year was instituted to help the poor. "But the seventh year thou shalt let it rest and lie still; that the poor of thy people may eat: and what they leave the beasts of the field shall eat. In like manner thou shalt deal with thy vineyard, and with thy oliveyard."

Second, the Sabbath Year was also to be accompanied by two other actions: releasing people from debt (Deut. 15:1-6) and reading the law to all the people (31:10-13). The canceling of debt every seven years probably prepared the people for the greater cancellation of property transactions and servitude in the Jubilee Year (Lev. 25:8-17).

Third, the Sabbath Year was so important to the Lord that He determined the length of the Babylonian Captivity by the number of times His people failed to observe the seventh year. The Israelites apparently missed keeping the Sabbath Year for 490 years, or 70 Sabbath Years. So the Lord put His people into captivity for seventy years "until the land had enjoyed her sabbaths: for as long as she lay desolate she kept sabbath, to fulfil threescore and ten years" (II Chron. 36:21; cf. Lev. 26:34).

The Israelites did not faithfully carry out the Sabbath Year, but from these Scripture texts we see God meant it to be an important time in the lives of His people. It was to have been a time of joyfully remembering God's provision for them.

## REMEMBER THE JUBILEE YEAR WITH JOY

**8 And thou shalt number seven sabbaths of years unto thee, seven times seven years; and the space of the seven sabbaths of years shall be unto thee forty and nine years.**

**9 Then shalt thou cause the trumpet of the jubile to sound on the tenth day of the seventh month, in the day of atonement shall ye make the trumpet sound throughout all your land.**

**10 And ye shall hallow the fiftieth year, and proclaim liberty throughout all the land unto all the inhabitants thereof: it shall be a jubile unto you; and ye shall return every man unto his possession, and ye shall return every man unto his family.**

**11 A jubile shall that fiftieth year be unto you: ye shall not sow, neither reap that which groweth of itself in it, nor gather the grapes in it of thy vine undressed.**

**12 For it is the jubile; it shall be holy unto you: ye shall eat the increase thereof out of the field.**

God considered the land of Israel to be His land, and His people were in essence tenants (Lev. 25:23; Ps. 24:1). So to regulate the use of the land, the treatment of poorer Israelites, and the economic conditions of the people, the Lord instituted the Jubilee Year.

**Calculating the Jubilee Year (Lev. 25:8).** The Sabbath Year of Leviticus 25:1-7 was the basis for another important celebration in Israel's life—the Jubilee Year. At the end of seven cycles (the number of perfection) of the Sabbath Year (forty-nine years), the people were to set aside the entire next year, the fiftieth year, as the Jubilee Year. In this arrangement, the land would actually have had two consecutive Sabbath Years—the Sabbath Year of the seventh cycle (the forty-ninth year) and the next year, which was the Jubilee Year (the fiftieth year).

**Announcing the Jubilee Year (Lev. 25:9).** The Jubilee Year started with a trumpet blast during the Day of Atonement observance. Leviticus 23:23-25 describes the Feast of Trumpets, which immediately preceded the Day of Atonement, so trumpet blasts were connected to the Day of Atonement and thus to the beginning of the Jubilee Year.

The Israelites were to blow trumpets at the beginning of every month (Num. 10:10). The trumpet blast on the first day of the seventh month (Lev. 23:24) probably signaled the approaching Day of Atonement observance (vss. 26-32). The trumpet blast on the tenth day of the seventh month was given throughout the land and initiated the Jubilee Year.

**Restoration during the Jubilee Year (Lev. 25:10).** The general purpose of the Jubilee Year was to "proclaim liberty throughout all the land unto all the inhabitants thereof." This liberty encompassed two areas of the people's lives—restoring family property and restoring the family itself. First, the Jubilee Year provided liberty, or restoration, for the family property: "Ye shall return every man unto his possession." This restoration of property is then described in verses 13-17. Sometimes the Israelites had to sell their land (really the Lord's land) to pay a debt. Verses 15 and 16 describe the equitable way of transacting a purchase of a piece of property.

During the Jubilee Year, however, all property purchased in the past forty-nine years was to be returned to its original owners (an exception concerning houses inside walled cities is noted in Leviticus 25:29-30). This provi-

sion of the Jubilee Year recognized the Lord's ownership of the land and prevented wealthier Israelites from exploiting, or oppressing, their poorer fellow citizens (vss. 14, 17).

Second, the Jubilee Year provided liberty, or restoration, for the families themselves: Every individual who had been sold into servitude was to be returned to his family. Sometimes an Israelite would become an indentured servant to pay for a debt (Lev. 25:39-40). If this happened, the fellow Israelite was to be released in the Jubilee Year and returned to his family (vs. 41). This provision reminded everyone that all Israelites were slaves to God (vs. 42) and kept some from exploiting their fellow countrymen (vs. 43).

**Agriculture during the Jubilee Year (Lev. 25:11-12).** The agricultural practices during the Jubilee Year were similar to those in the Sabbath Years. They were not to plant crops and were not to harvest anything that grew on its own. The fiftieth year would have been a second straight year of rest for the land, which meant the Lord would have supplied enough food in the crops of the forty-eighth year to last for four years!

The regulations of the Jubilee Year helped the nation's economy and stability, but Leviticus 25:12 goes beyond the physical aspects to say that the Jubilee Year "shall be holy unto you." The Lord wanted to make this year a holy event for them as they reflected on what He had done for them. Like the Sabbath Years, it appears that the Israelites were not faithful in carrying out the Jubilee Years.

Let us take a step back to see how the Sabbath Years and the Jubilee Years were a source of joy to the people. The people would be joyful as they remembered God's provision for them even when they did not plant their crops. They would be joyful as land that had been sold was returned to the owners so that the owners would not be impoverished. They would be joyful as hired servants were returned to their families and not continue in servitude. In every way these events were a joyful and holy time for the people of God.

We have examined two significant events in the Old Testament that were meant to communicate an important message to the Israelites. As New Testament believers, we are not bound by these requirements. Do they have any practical benefit for us? They certainly do.

First, both celebrations remind us of the seven-day cycle of work and rest the Lord intended. We are not bound to obey Sabbath regulations, but one day of rest in seven is a pattern for us to follow.

Second, both celebrations remind us of the Lord's provisions for our needs. The Israelites had to trust the Lord for food when they did not plant a crop. We may not be able to see where the money will come from for a surprise bill, but the Lord promised that if we are obedient to Him, He will meet our needs. "But seek ye first the kingdom of God, and his righteousness; and all these things shall be added unto you" (Matt. 6:33). In Philippians 4:19, the Lord promised to "supply all your need according to his riches in glory by Christ Jesus."

Third, both celebrations (and especially the Jubilee Year) remind us of the need to care for fellow believers. We should not exploit them or oppress them in any way. James wrote about this matter in James 2:15-16: "If a brother or sister be naked, and destitute of daily food, and one of you say unto them, Depart in peace, be ye warmed and filled; notwithstanding ye give them not those things which are needful to the body; what doth it profit?"

Fourth, both celebrations remind us that everyday events should be holy events for us. We should not divide our lives into secular and sacred. Even the physical matters of life, such as how we spend our money or what we do for entertainment, are in the sacred category for us. We must let the Scriptures permeate and direct everything we do.

Fifth, both celebrations remind us that obedience to God brings joy. Some may imagine that a close walk with the Lord leads to a burdensome life. Quite the opposite is true. Obedience brings great joy. As Jesus stated, "If ye know these things, happy are ye if ye do them" (John 13:17). Let us determine to walk in complete obedience to the Lord.

—Don Anderson.

# QUESTIONS

1. How did Israel's agricultural cycle reflect the pattern of the work week and Sabbath Day?

2. What were the Israelites to do every seven years?

3. What were the Israelites to do with the produce that grew on its own every seventh year?

4. Why were they to observe the Sabbath Year?

5. What did God promise to do in the sixth year?

6. How did the Sabbath Year relate to the Babylonian Exile?

7. When was the Jubilee Year to take place?

8. In what way was the Jubilee Year a year of liberty?

9. How were the Sabbath Year and the Jubilee Year to be occasions for joy?

10. What are some practical values of these two events for us?

—Don Anderson.

# Preparing to Teach the Lesson

The Year of Jubilee may seem like a strange concept at first, but it was instituted by God on Mount Sinai and has a significant place in Israel's understanding of who the Lord is and His ways. We serve and worship the same God, and understanding His ways is a vital study to us all.

The Year of Jubilee was grounded in the truths that the Israelites were God's chosen people and the land was the land promised to Abraham and his descendants forever. The Year of Jubilee does not apply directly to us as Christians not living in the Promised Land, but its implications are still instructive to us as God's children. It shows clearly that our God is a God of forgiveness and restoration, of pardon and blessing.

## TODAY'S AIM

**Facts:** to understand the instructions and regulations of the Year of Jubilee.

**Principle:** to realize it is the Lord's way of life for us to rejoice in His possession and provision.

**Application:** to remember daily that Christ has freed us from bondage and servitude to this world.

## INTRODUCING THE LESSON

The Year of Jubilee was not a feast or a special day or ceremony, as were so many of the other religious observances the Lord gave to Israel. It was a time of refraining from doing certain things, of restoration of lands, of release from debts and servitude, and of rejoicing in God's provision for all of life. It really was a special kind of Sabbath, not of resting from work on the seventh day, but of giving the land rest on the seventh year, and then a special

jubilee rest on the fiftieth year, after seven "sevens" of years.

God also reminded Israel that the land He had given them really belonged to Him. Our jobs, our houses, education, and abilities—everything we use and possess—really belong to God. We must look to Him for what we are to do with them.

## DEVELOPING THE LESSON

**1. A rest year (Lev. 25:1-7).** Every seventh year was to be a Sabbath Year of rest for the land. It was to be set apart as unto the Lord. Seeds were not to be sowed in the fields. Over and over again, when the idea of a Sabbath comes up, it is to remind people that the Lord created the world in six days and rested the seventh day. He did not need six days; He set this pattern because human beings need this rest. We also need to be reminded that God is our Creator. If we lose sight of this fact, it becomes very easy for us to deny God's ownership and His authority over us.

God's strength and ability is so immense that He could have easily created the entire universe and all the creatures that exist in a split second. He did not rest the seventh day because He was tired. He never gets tired, nor does His strength diminish because He does something. The pattern of working six days and resting the seventh is, again, to remind us of His creatorship and ownership of everything. If it were not for the fact that He has made promises and wills to keep them, He could simply cancel all of creation, and nothing that we call the created universe would exist. We cannot hold God to His promises; only He can keep His promises for His reasons.

We learn in the New Testament that

the Lord Jesus was the operative agent in creation (cf. John 1:1-3; Col. 1:16-17; Heb. 1:2).

**2. A year of jubilee (Lev. 25:8-10).** The Jubilee Year was a time to "proclaim liberty throughout all the land unto all the inhabitants thereof." As we learn from the rest of chapter 25 of Leviticus, while the fields were to lie fallow, God promised to provide enough produce from the land that there would be enough to last through the Sabbath Year and the Year of Jubilee until—once again—there could be a complete cycle of planting and harvesting.

This should not have been hard for the people of Israel to believe after coming through forty years of wandering in the wilderness. During that time God miraculously provided manna for them to gather and eat every day except the Sabbath. The manna they had gathered on the day before the Sabbath always lasted until time to gather some again.

**3. A holy year (Lev. 25:11-12).** We do not know if the Israelites ever did observe the Sabbath Years or the Year of Jubilee. It is true that when God put Israel under judgment for their sin, He caused others to come and take them captive out of the land. He specifically mentioned then that He would keep them in captivity for seventy years to give the land its Sabbaths (II Chron. 36:21).

The rest of our chapter also gives the regulations for lands mortgaged because of the owner's poverty, and the release of indentured servants in the Year of Jubilee. They could go home to their properties and their families. It was to be a time of great joy and praise to God for the freedom He had given them.

## ILLUSTRATING THE LESSON

We have wonderful freedom in Christ and should be rejoicing in it.

**FREE IN CHRIST**

**NO LONGER BOUND BY SIN**

## CONCLUDING THE LESSON

Our blessed position in Christ is not tied to the Promised Land, or to membership in any specific church or denomination, but rather to the Lord Jesus Himself. We are His possession, and we rest in Him until He returns to take His possession unto Himself. We enter into His rest when we cease our foolish efforts to gain acceptance from God and trust Him fully (cf. Heb. 4:9). We can remember with joy that the Lord Jesus has done everything for our salvation, and salvation does not rest on our ability to live holy lives or please God in some way. We simply receive God's provision for us in Christ.

We might also infer from our background Scripture that we can forgive our brothers and sisters in Christ for any debt they owe us, whether money or a slight or an unkind word. We do not need to wait until a special year but can forgive them and restore in our love at any time. We can live daily in the Jubilee of God's love and provision for us.

## ANTICIPATING THE NEXT LESSON

Next week we look at "Rejoicing in Restoration" from Psalm 34 and Hebrews 2.

—*Brian D. Doud.*

# PRACTICAL POINTS

1. God prepares His people to receive His blessings (Lev. 25:1-2).
2. There is a time to work and a time to rest. They are both important (vss. 3-5).
3. We show appreciation to God by being good stewards over what we have (vss. 6-10).
4. We cannot allow possessions to become more important to us than people.
5. Resting and reflecting on the blessings of God brings joy (vss. 11-12).

*—Valante M. Grant.*

# RESEARCH AND DISCUSSION

1. Why is it important to always remember the things that God has done for you and brought you through?
2. How does gratitude to God for what He has given us impact the way that we care for it?
3. Why is it important to take time to rest and enjoy the things that we have worked for?
4. How can we prioritize the value of people and the importance of possessions in our lives (Lev. 25:10)?
5. How can we apply the concept of the Year of Jubilee to our lives today?
6. What does the Year of Jubilee indicate about forgiveness and God's love for His people?

*—Valante M. Grant.*

# ILLUSTRATED HIGH POINTS

### The land keep a sabbath

There is an eye-care center in my area that specializes in cataract surgery and advertises on television. A rather grim-looking gentleman (obviously the surgeon) declares that the eye-care center really cares about people. One would hope so, even though it is obvious that the establishment is also interested in making money.

The God of Israel manifested His care for the people of Israel, their animals, and even their land by giving them the weekly Sabbath, the Sabbath Year every seven years, and the Jubilee Year every fifty years.

### A sabbath of rest

Today's farmers with air-conditioned tractors have an easier task than the ancients who trudged behind oxen pulling some type of makeshift plow through muddy fields. Harvesting, gathering, and threshing were also done by hand.

The uncertainties of the weather, danger from insects, and other issues tempted farmers to be constantly trying to get ahead. God said to trust Him, to observe His Sabbaths, and to take time to rest. He would supply all one needed.

### A jubile unto you

Sinful man would never have come up with God's program of a merciful Jubilee Year. It goes against the grain of "good business."

Some years ago, I got a personal loan from my local bank. The interest rate at the time was 16 percent. A year later, I asked for a year's extension, and it was granted. Even though the bank officer was a Christian, the bank's policy was to increase the interest by a quarter of a percent. As Proverbs 22:7 says, "The borrower is servant to the lender."

*—David A. Hamburg.*

# Golden Text Illuminated

**"Proclaim liberty throughout all the land unto all the inhabitants thereof: it shall be a jubile unto you; and ye shall return every man unto his possession, and ye shall return every man unto his family" (Leviticus 25:10).**

Students of American history quickly recognize the first part of this week's golden text. It forms the well-known inscription on the Liberty Bell, which hung for years in Philadelphia's Independence Hall and is still a major attraction in its own pavilion across the street. The inscription on the bell became a call to political independence and freedom on the part of the American revolutionaries. The exhortation's meaning in its biblical context is just a little bit different!

The proclamation of the biblical text has to do with the Israelite Year of Jubilee (Lev. 25:8-13). God's people were instructed to set aside every fiftieth year (seven times seven Sabbath Years plus one year) as a year for releasing debts and restoring family holdings. The word "jubile" comes from the Hebrew *yobel,* referring to the trumpet blown to mark the year's consecration.

The Jubilee was intended to be a time of joy and celebration. The liberty that was to be proclaimed at the start of each fiftieth year was a nationwide release from debts and servitude. One of the harsh facts of life in the ancient world was that people could fall into debt to the extent that the only way out of it was to sell off their inherited property. If that did not suffice, they could be forced to sell themselves or their children into servitude—a form of slavery—for a period of time.

The reality was that many people would never be able to work their way out of debt servitude. God, however, did not want a permanent slave class to develop among His people. Nor did He want families to permanently lose the inheritance that He had given them when the nation entered the Promised Land. Jubilee was His prescribed means of preventing these evils.

This release was to have no exceptions; it was to be proclaimed to "all the inhabitants" of the land. Even if someone had gone into servitude or lost his property only a short time before the Jubilee Year, the release was to be applied. Creditors might claim that money or labor was still owed to them, but the Jubilee was to be a complete cleaning of the slate. "Ye shall return every man unto his possession, and ye shall return every man unto his family."

It is not clear how well Israel obeyed the instructions on Jubilee throughout their history—or that they ever did. However, the provisions clearly show us God's heart for His people, especially for the poor and downtrodden. He did not want people to remain trapped in servitude or deprived of their property. The story of Naboth and his vineyard (I Kings 21:1-24) illustrates the importance God placed on preserving family inheritance.

For New Testament believers, the Israelite Year of Jubilee can be a profound reminder that God does not want any of us to live in spiritual servitude. In Christ He has set us free from slavery to sin, under which we were held in darkness. And we do not have to wait till a fiftieth year comes by to experience our freedom. "Ye shall know the truth, and the truth shall make you free" (John 8:32). Our freedom begins now; it will be complete when we see Him.

—*Kenneth A. Sponsler.*

# Heart of the Lesson

My grandpa, a farmer, loved his land. He chopped musk thistles, cockleburs, and hog weeds with a hoe under the withering Kansas sun rather than spray poisons on his soil. A dry-land farmer with no irrigation, he practiced summer fallowing. Periodically, he let his fields rest for a year. Instead of growing crops such as corn or wheat, he sowed a cover crop such as red clover to add nitrogen to the soil and to keep down the weeds.

Regularly allowing one's land to rest was a practice God prescribed for the people of Israel when they entered the Promised Land. Ancient Israel was primarily an agricultural economy. In today's lesson, we will learn how the nation was to care for God's land and prevent long-term poverty among its people.

**1. Keeping a Sabbath for the land (Lev. 25:1-7).** God told Moses on Mount Sinai that when the people of Israel entered the land of Canaan, the land itself was to keep a Sabbath unto the Lord every seven years. For six years the people could sow their crops, prune their grapevines, and harvest their crops. But on the seventh year, they were to allow the land to rest—to be fallow.

They were to harvest no crops that came up on their own and process no grapes on the unpruned vines. They could, however, pick and eat edibles that grew naturally from the fields.

Practically, this gave the land time to rejuvenate—the same reason my grandfather practiced summer fallowing. Spiritually, the Sabbath for the land taught the people faith in God. If they followed Him, He promised a bumper crop the sixth year. They would harvest enough to carry them over to the eighth year's harvest.

The Sabbath for the land also provided the people rejuvenation from the physical demands of agriculture.

**2. Observing the Year of Jubilee (Lev. 25:8-12).** After forty-nine years—seven cycles of Sabbath Years—the people were to observe a Year of Jubilee. The word "jubilee" refers to a ram's horn or trumpet. Rams' horns blew throughout the nation on the Day of Atonement to announce this holy year.

Each tribe and family received a permanent land allotment when they entered Canaan. The people could sell this land and their homes, but the sale was like a long-term lease. Every fiftieth year, land and homes outside walled cities (except homes belonging to Levites) reverted back to the original owners or to their descendants (Lev. 25:29-33). Families were reunited.

The Year of Jubilee guaranteed families would never permanently lose their original land allotments from God. Families that had lost homes and lands because of poverty regained their property and could start over.

This system prevented a few wealthy people from buying up all the land. God cares for the poor and wanted to prevent a permanent underclass of homeless, poverty-stricken citizens in Israel.

The Year of Jubilee was a time of liberty, especially for those who had sold themselves into servanthood because of debt. They were freed during the Year of Jubilee. All slaves were freed. And the land again experienced a Sabbath.

From this passage, we see the importance of taking time for rest. God rested on the seventh day because His work was done. We should follow God's example and set aside the Lord's day as a day of rest. God wants us to be stewards of the land.

—Ann Staatz.

# World Missions

A certain river in South Asia is considered sacred, where worshippers believe they can find forgiveness or healing. Ashes of the dead are often thrown in, in hopes of obtaining blessing for the person who died. People also may wash in the river as they ask what they need or want from the gods.

A man once went to the river to tell people how they could find forgiveness in Christ. As he approached, he heard a terrible wailing. A woman was at the river, beating her chest in anguish.

The woman told him her husband had tuberculosis and had been out of work for a long time. They were out of hope. "The troubles in my home are so great," she said, "and my sins are so many, so I gave the best I had to offer: my first-born son."

The man was horrified to realize she had thrown her baby into the river.

With tears, the man told the woman how she could be forgiven through Jesus. "Why couldn't you have come one half-hour sooner?" she asked in grief. "Then I would not have sacrificed my son" (Yohanan, *Living in the Light of Eternity,* Gospel for Asia Books).

Such a story is not one easily forgotten. So much evil! So much loss!

Jesus said He came to set the captives free (Luke 4:18). We, His people, are to spread the message of deliverance to the captives. This week's passage, Leviticus 25, is about proclaiming liberty to those who are enslaved. They were to be set free to return to their homes. It was meant to be a time of great rejoicing, deliverance, and hope.

We do not read that God's people even once celebrated the Year of Jubilee, and the captives remained enslaved. God's people never fulfilled the goodness He had intended.

It is the same today. God wants all people to be free. People around us may not look like slaves, but there are so many kinds of captivity. People are enslaved to sin in many forms.

God wants them given the message that they can be freed and that they can return to the reality God intended for them from the beginning—peace with God and a right standing with Him for eternity.

Are we sharing the message of freedom, or do we find ourselves also enslaved? Things that keep us from obeying God's call to share the hope of Jesus might be fear, a secret sin, or apathy about the lost. We may tell ourselves we will give when there is more money; we will speak once we are sure of what to say; we will act, but not today.

Again, there are many kinds of captivity—for the lost and for God's children.

Jesus came that we "might have life, and . . . have it more abundantly" (John 10:10). In the upside-down way of the kingdom, what seems like abundant life to the world is really slavery. And what seems like sacrifice is really freedom. If we gave our lives to God's work, we would have less money but more contentment. We would have less stuff but more joy. We might not get praise from men, but we would have rewards in heaven.

The truth would show best when this life is over—when we would stand before Jesus not with empty hands that once grasped things we could not bring with us, but rather surrounded by the people we brought with us, those we helped set free. God would be pleased, and we would have no regrets.

—*Kimberly Rae.*

# The Jewish Aspect

In this week's lesson, we see the Scriptures explaining the Year of Jubilee. Today, modern Jews do not observe most of the Jubilee Year's regulations. However, some of the biblical rules are observed by devout Jews in Israel.

Scholars disagree about when Jubilee regulations stopped being observed. Some believe the regulations stopped being observed when the ten tribes of Israel were deported. Others believe the regulations ended with the destruction of the second temple.

"According to biblical law, the Jubilee is only to be observed when all twelve of the tribes are living in Israel." This means that the rules should be "observed when every tribe is back in the specific part of the land which it was allotted" (Davidson, "When Is the Next Jubilee Year?" www.chabad.org).

When the temple was in existence, and all the tribes were in Israel, the seventh year, called in Hebrew *shemitah,* marked the time that the fields were to be left fallow and debts were to be released. The seven years were marked in cycles (seven times seven) with the fiftieth year being the Year of Jubilee.

The Year of Jubilee is known as *Yobel* or *Yovel.* This name refers to the blast of the shofar that occurs on Yom Kippur announcing the Year of Jubilee.

There is a similarity between the Omer count and the Year of Jubilee. The Omer count is a count of forty-nine days, with Pentecost falling on the fiftieth day. The Year of Jubilee is counted forty-nine years, with the fiftieth being the Jubilee Year. The fiftieth year is a year of freedom and liberty.

There are several reasons why the Year of Jubilee might have been instituted. Practically, allowing the land to rest is an important agricultural principle.

The land in Israel is very important to modern Israelites. Protecting, preserving, and improving the land are central ideas today.

The Jewish National Fund, founded in 1901, has been heavily involved in upgrading Israel's natural environment and farmland. Jews throughout the world collected coins in their blue collection boxes. The Jewish National Fund used this money to purchase land that laid the foundation for the current Jewish state (Scharfstein, *Understanding Israel,* KTAV Publishing House).

The land had been damaged and some of it had been destroyed as a result of wars and Israel's turbulent history. The Jewish National Fund and the Society for the Preservation of Israel have worked hard to restore life to the land and ensure Israel's future.

Since the land and its preservation is important to the people of Israel, trees play an important role in its improvement. They are so important that during some of the wars, the soldiers were warned not to destroy the trees. There is even a special holiday to honor trees called Rosh Hashanah La-Ilanot, or New Year of the Trees.

The land of Israel is God's gift to the Israelite people. As a result, the people see the importance of being good stewards of His wonderful gift.

The Midrash, the rabbis' interpretation of the Torah, teaches that one should be careful not to spoil or destroy the world. Protecting God's creation may have begun with God's command for a Jubilee Year, but it continues in Jewish hearts today.

—*Robin Fitzgerald.*

# Guiding the Superintendent

God had an important lesson for Israel to learn. He instituted two laws concerning land management to teach ancient Israel that all the land was His and that they were only the tenants who used it during their sojourn here in this world (Lev. 25:23-24). Like the laws concerning firstfruits (lesson 11), the Sabbath Year and Jubilee Year laws were intended to be a source of joy (vs. 10) and remembrance.

## DEVOTIONAL OUTLINE

**1. Sabbatical Year (Lev. 25:1-7).** Imagine having an entire year off from many work responsibilities and most expenses paid. Sounds almost too good to be true. But this was not just an idle dream. Ancient Israel was actually commanded to take every seventh year off and not do any planting or harvesting.

As the people were to take the seventh day off from work (Exod. 23:12), so the land was to be allowed to rest every seventh year. The fields were not to be plowed, and the vineyards were not to be pruned (Lev. 25:4).

No sowing, pruning, or harvesting was permitted during the seventh year. The people were to eat only whatever grew of its own accord.

In addition to allowing the land to lie fallow (unplowed and unplanted), any crops the land did produce during the seventh year were to provide food for the common people and animals (Exod. 23:11). Additionally in the Sabbath Year, at the Feast of Tabernacles, the law was to be read to the people assembled to celebrate the feast (Deut. 31:10-13).

One can only imagine what mixed emotions the people of Israel had as they approached the seventh year. However, for those who trusted God to provide food for a whole year, it would have been a time of great faith in their God to supply all their needs.

**2. Jubilee Year (Lev. 25:8-12).** As challenging as the Sabbath Year must have been for Israel, there was still another command from God that was even more challenging of their trust.

Following every seventh Sabbath cycle (that is, every fifty years) there was to be a time of Jubilee, of celebration. Liberty was to be proclaimed throughout the land. Regarding land that had been bought or sold over the last fifty years, God said, "Ye shall return every man unto his possession, and ye shall return every man unto his family" (Lev. 25:10). All land would be returned to its original owner, and every slave was to be set free. As in the Sabbath Year, there would be no sowing of crops. There could not be a better way to teach this truth: "The earth is the Lord's, and the fulness thereof" (Ps. 24:1).

Sadly, the Sabbath Year and Jubilee Year were all theory for Israel. As far as we can tell, they never followed this regulation. One of the reasons given for the Babylonian Captivity of Israel was to give the land the rest it never got (II Chron. 36:20-21).

## AGE-GROUP EMPHASES

**Children:** Most children are just starting to grasp the idea of ownership. Use this lesson to teach them the importance of seeing God as the ultimate Owner of all.

**Youths:** Have the teens discuss what interests them most about the Sabbath principle.

**Adults:** The Sabbath and Jubilee Years were to help Israel learn to totally trust God. Have the adults talk about times when they had to totally trust God and what they learned from it.

—Martin R. Dahlquist.

# Scripture Lesson Text

**PS. 34:1** I will bless the Lord at all times: his praise *shall* continually *be* in my mouth.

**2 My soul shall make her boast in the Lord: the humble shall hear *thereof*, and be glad.**

3 O magnify the Lord with me, and let us exalt his name together.

**4 I sought the Lord, and he heard me, and delivered me from all my fears.**

5 They looked unto him, and were lightened: and their faces were not ashamed.

**6 This poor man cried, and the Lord heard *him*, and saved him out of all his troubles.**

7 The angel of the Lord encampeth round about them that fear him, and delivereth them.

**8 O taste and see that the Lord *is* good: blessed *is* the man *that* trusteth in him.**

9 O fear the Lord, ye his saints: for *there is* no want to them that fear him.

**10 The young lions do lack, and suffer hunger: but they that seek the Lord shall not want any good *thing*.**

**HEB. 2:17** Wherefore in all things it behoved him to be made like unto *his* brethren, that he might be a merciful and faithful high priest in things *pertaining* to God, to make reconciliation for the sins of the people.

**18 For in that he himself hath suffered being tempted, he is able to succour them that are tempted.**

---

**NOTES**

---

# Rejoicing in Restoration

## Lesson: Psalm 34:1-10; Hebrews 2:17-18

Read: Psalm 34:1-22; Hebrews 2:5-18

TIMES: about 1000 B.C.; about A.D. 67          PLACES: Palestine; unknown

---

**GOLDEN TEXT**—"O taste and see that the Lord is good: blessed is the man that trusteth in him" (Psalm 34:8).

---

# *Introduction*

All of us who know the Lord—even those of us who have walked with Him for decades—find ourselves at times needing to come back to Him. We may have let an area of our Christian life slip either because of laziness or deliberate sinful intent. No believer is beyond the the need for spiritual renewal.

The two Scripture passages in this week's study give us some practical direction on what we should do to be restored to the Lord. We should not, however, forget what needs to take place before we even get to Psalm 34. We need to confess our sin and acknowledge our need for a return to the Lord. Apart from such acknowledgement, we will never come back to Him.

This unit of study has reminded us of the joy that comes from a right rela-tionship with the Lord. We all know from experience the heartache that comes from walking in disobedience in an area of our lives. We also know the joy that comes when we return to Him.

If you find you need to restore any area of your Christian life that you have let slip, do so this week before you meet in class.

## LESSON OUTLINE

I. **MAGNIFY THE LORD—Ps. 34:1-3**

II. **LOOK TO THE LORD—Ps. 34:4-7**

III. **TRUST THE LORD—Ps. 34:8-10**

IV. **FIND HELP IN THE LORD—Heb. 2:17-18**

# *Exposition: Verse by Verse*

**MAGNIFY THE LORD**

**PS. 34:1** I will bless the Lord at all times: his praise shall continually be in my mouth.

**2** My soul shall make her boast in the Lord: the humble shall hear thereof, and be glad.

**3** O magnify the Lord with me, and let us exalt his name together.

Before we examine these verses, let us consider two features of Psalm 34—the heading of the psalm and the acrostic nature of the psalm.

The heading for this psalm reads "A Psalm of David, when he changed his behaviour before Abimelech; who drove him away, and he departed." The heading makes reference to I Samuel 21:10-15, which speaks of when David fled from Saul to Gath and pretended to be mad to escape reprisal from the Philistines. As David escaped from Abimelech, he penned the words to this psalm of praise to the Lord for His deliverance. (Abimelech is a title, not a proper name, and evidently refers to Achish.)

The second interesting feature about this psalm is its acrostic format. The Hebrew alphabet has twenty-two letters. Starting at the alphabet's beginning, the first word of each verse in this psalm begins with the next letter in the Hebrew alphabet, accounting for the twenty-two verses. The acrostic format of this psalm would have helped in memorizing it. (Psalm 119 is another example of an acrostic psalm. There the first words in each group of seven verses begin with the successive letter in the Hebrew alphabet. Many copies of the Bible print the Hebrew letter before each section.)

**Magnify the Lord at all times (Ps. 34:1-2).** Running throughout the first three verses is the theme of magnifying, or exalting, the Lord. "O magnify the Lord with me, and let us exalt his name together" (vs. 3). To magnify something means to make it larger. To magnify the Lord means to make Him larger and more important in our minds and in the minds of others. We do so by praising Him, exalting Him, and lifting Him up. Verse 1 specifically calls on us to "bless the Lord." We frequently ask the Lord to bless us, but here we

are told to bless Him.

To bless the Lord is another way of saying we should magnify and praise Him. Take a moment to look up the other times we find this instruction in the Psalms and note why we are to bless the Lord (16:7; 26:12; 103:1, 2, 20, 22; 104:1; 115:18; 134:2; 135:19, 20). We recognize that God's blessings on us are undeserved, but He deserves every blessing and praise we give to Him.

The believer who wants to restore a right relationship with the Lord needs to magnify the Lord at all times, not just occasionally. Exalting the Lord should be a daily practice for us. David said in the second part of Psalm 34:1, "His praise shall continually be in my mouth." We would each do well to set aside a time each day to bless Him.

Another way of expressing the thought of blessing the Lord is found in David's affirmation that his soul would make his boast in the Lord. We are never to boast in ourselves, but we are to boast about the Lord to Him and to others. Let us continually tell the Lord how great He is and what great things He has done. The unbeliever will not understand what we are doing, but the humble person will hear it and rejoice.

**Magnify the Lord's name (Ps. 34:3).** David continued his theme of exaltation in verse 3 by urging us to magnify God's name. Many of our names have meaning, but there is no guarantee that any of us will live up to our name.

The Lord's name is different. Our Lord's name stands for His character. He completely embodies everything in His name. God's name is so special that David instructs us to "sing forth the honour of his name: make his praise glorious" (Ps. 66:2). Take a few minutes to look up the different names of the Lord and to meditate on them.

## LOOK TO THE LORD

**4 I sought the Lord, and he heard me, and delivered me from all my fears.**

**5 They looked unto him, and were lightened: and their faces were not ashamed.**

**6 This poor man cried, and the Lord heard him, and saved him out of all his troubles.**

**7 The angel of the Lord encampeth round about them that fear him, and delivereth them.**

**Look to the Lord for deliverance from fears (Ps. 34:4-5).** Another essential part of returning to the Lord is turning away from ourselves and looking to Him. In verses 4-5, David spoke of his fears, which may be what he faced in Gath as recorded in I Samuel 21. David affirmed that when he sought the Lord, the Lord heard him and delivered him from all his fears. We have the confidence that when we seek the Lord, He will hear us and deliver us from our fears.

In Psalm 34:5, David expanded the focus from himself to all Israel ("they looked unto him"). When God's people looked unto Him, they were not disappointed and did not suffer shame. Rather, their eyes were "lightened," or made radiant, showing the joy they experienced by looking to the Lord and finding His deliverance.

**Look to the Lord for deliverance from troubles (Ps. 34:6-7).** In verses 6-7, David praised the Lord for delivering him from troubles. Again, he may have had in mind the troubles in I Samuel 21, but in a greater sense he may have thought about all the troubles he faced in his lifetime. David referred to himself as a poor man to show his need for the Lord to deliver him.

In Psalm 34:7, David wrote about "the angel of the Lord," who delivers those who fear Him. The angel of the Lord in the Old Testament was probably a preincarnate appearance of the Lord Jesus Christ. We determine this to be true by looking in the contexts where the angel of the Lord is mentioned. In Exodus 3:2, the angel of the Lord appeared to Moses, but Exodus 3:4 states that God was the one calling to Moses in the bush. (We see the same connection in Stephen's speech in Acts 7:30-34.) In Judges 6:12, the angel of the Lord appeared to Gideon, but verse 14 tells us this person was the Lord Himself.

Psalm 34:7 assures us that the angel of the Lord, probably the Lord Jesus Christ Himself, encamps around, or surrounds, us to deliver us from our troubles. This thought reminds us of Hebrews 13:5, where we learn that the Lord promises He will never leave us or forsake us. (See II Kings 6:15-18 for an example of the Lord surrounding His own.) In all our troubles, we know the Lord is with us.

## TRUST THE LORD

**8 O taste and see that the Lord is good: blessed is the man that trusteth in him.**

**9 O fear the Lord, ye his saints: for there is no want to them that fear him.**

**10 The young lions do lack, and suffer hunger: but they that seek the Lord shall not want any good thing.**

**Trust God because He is good (Ps. 34:8).** The theme of verses 8-10 is trust. "Blessed is the man that trusteth in him [God]." The believer can trust in God first because He is good. To say God is good means He is always upright in His character (25:8), He always has His children's best interests in mind (31:19), and He always directs His actions to accomplish what is good for those who love Him (Rom. 8:28).

How do we learn we can trust the Lord? By tasting and seeing that the Lord is good. The idea of tasting here is of sampling some food, particularly with the intention of putting it to the test. We may try a bite of food to see whether we like it. To taste the Lord is to put Him to the test to see how good He is. Peter echoed the same thought when he wrote, "If so be ye have tasted that the Lord is gracious" (I Pet. 2:3). The Lord never fails to pass the test for being good.

**Trust Him for your needs (Ps. 34:9-10).** We can trust the Lord because He meets our needs. In verse 9, David challenges all of us ("ye his saints") to fear, or reverence, Him because those who do so will lack nothing. This thought reminds us of Psalm 23:1, where David wrote, "The Lord is my shepherd; I shall not want."

David then contrasted the animal kingdom with the Lord's provision. Young lions may lack sufficient food, but those who seek the Lord "shall not want [lack] any good thing" (Ps. 34:10). Paul made a similar statement to the Philippian church: "But my God shall supply all your need according to his riches in glory by Christ Jesus" (Phil. 4:19). We can trust the Lord because in His goodness He meets all our needs. That reality should cause us to come back when we walk away from Him.

## FIND HELP IN THE LORD

**HEB. 2:17 Wherefore in all things it behoved him to be made like unto his brethren, that he might be a merciful and faithful high priest in things pertaining to God, to make reconciliation for the sins of the people.**

**18 For in that he himself hath suf-fered being tempted, he is able to succour them that are tempted.**

Our examination of Psalm 34 helped us focus on the Lord's character that leads us to worship Him and trust Him. In Hebrews 2:17-18, we find practical help as we return to the Lord. He can help us return to Him as we face temptations and the pull of the flesh.

**Christ's humanity (Heb. 2:17).** In this verse, the writer of Hebrews affirmed Christ's sinless humanity, which qualified Him to be our "merciful and faithful high priest in things pertaining to God."

We find Christ's humanity expressed in verses such as I Timothy 2:5. "For there is one God, and one mediator between God and men, the man Christ Jesus." In His incarnation, Christ took on humanity so that in one person He was both fully God and fully man.

He became human like us in every respect except one—He was (and still is) sinless. "For we have not an high priest which cannot be touched with the feeling of our infirmities; but was in all points tempted like as we are, yet without sin" (Heb. 4:15). His sinless humanity means He knows what we experience and can be a merciful and faithful High Priest.

At the end of Hebrews 2:17, the writer stated that because of Christ's sinless humanity, He was able to "make reconciliation for the sins of the people." Christ made reconciliation by satisfying the just demands of the wrath of God so that we do not have to bear that wrath. Theologians refer to this work as Christ's propitiation for us (Rom. 3:25; I John 2:2; 4:10).

**Christ's help (Heb. 2:18).** Because Christ fully took on humanity, He knew what it was like to suffer and be tempted. In the physical sense, He suffered

176

the normal experiences of humanity—hunger (Mark 11:12), thirst (John 19:28), and weariness (John 4:6). Because He was "touched with the feeling of our infirmities" (Heb. 4:15), He can now help us in our times of similar weaknesses.

In a greater sense, however, Christ knew what it was like to face temptation to sin. He could never give in to sin because He had no sin nature, but still He experienced the full force of temptation. Matthew 4:1-11 shows us one example of Christ's temptations. Satan first tempted Christ to command the stones to become bread—a temptation to satisfy His physical appetite.

Second, Satan tempted Christ to jump off the pinnacle of the temple—a temptation to notoriety. Third, Satan tempted Christ to fall down and worship him—a temptation to power and glory. In all three temptations, the Lord Jesus quoted Scripture to resist the appeals of Satan.

The reality of Christ's temptations is seen in Hebrews 4:15 quoted above. He "was in all points tempted like as we are, yet without sin." The writer made it clear that Christ was tempted not just in a few points like us but "in all points." So we can never say, "The Lord does not know what I am going through."

Because Jesus experienced the full force of temptation, He is able to help us in our temptations. He can help us as we follow His example in Matthew 4 of resisting temptation by appealing to Scripture (vss. 4, 7, 10). We find the same principle in Psalm 119:11, where the psalmist said, "Thy word have I hid in mine heart, that I might not sin against thee."

We can also ask Him for His help as we face temptations. Hebrews 4:16 invites us to "come boldly unto the throne of grace, that we may obtain mercy, and find grace to help in time of need." When we do so, we have the promise that "God is faithful, who will not suffer you to be tempted above that ye are able; but will with the temptation also make a way to escape, that ye may be able to bear it" (I Cor. 10:13).

If we find ourselves struggling with temptations that have kept us from a closer walk with the Lord, we can find help in Christ, who gives the strength to overcome those temptations. Then we will experience the joy that comes from returning to Him. He will not give us the cold shoulder when we do but, like the father of the prodigal son, will welcome us with open arms.

—Don Anderson.

# QUESTIONS

1. What does it mean to magnify the Lord, and how do we do that?

2. How often should we magnify the Lord?

3. How can we be delivered from our fears?

4. What does Psalm 34:7 assure us about "the angel of the Lord"?

5. What does it mean to taste and see that the Lord is good?

6. In what ways did Jesus become like us? In what one way did He not?

7. What is propitiation, and how did Christ provide it?

8. What can Jesus do for us because He was tempted?

9. How does Jesus help us resist temptation?

10. What are some key Scriptures we can turn to when we find we need to return to God?

—Don Anderson.

# Preparing to Teach the Lesson

Almost every truly born-again person can recall the time when he first trusted the Lord and was saved. Most will testify that they experienced great joy in the Lord at that time. Many, if not all, will also admit that there have been times when they faded away from that joy and the fellowship they enjoyed with the Lord. I have heard only one person testify that she "never lost the joy of the Lord."

Sometimes this is expressed as back-sliding or slipping back into sin. We find in I John 1:9 the New Testament way of being restored to fellowship: "If we confess our sins, he is faithful and just to forgive us our sins, and cleanse us from all unrighteousness." We will then be brought back into the joy of the Lord and fellowship with Him.

This principle is found in the Old Testament as well, and today we look at an example of a psalm written by David that encourages people to seek restoration to fellowship with God.

## TODAY'S AIM

**Facts:** to understand that the Lord can restore us to joyful fellowship with Him.

**Principle:** to understand we can be restored to the joy of the Lord at any time, from any type of decline.

**Application:** to live with the knowledge that God desires to restore us to fellowship daily.

## INTRODUCING THE LESSON

The subject of the believer in decline and subsequent restoration to joyful fellowship with God may have been covered in many sermons and lessons, but today we look at this subject in mainly an Old Testament setting.

We human beings are very weak spiritually; indeed, the Bible declares that before we trust in Christ and are born again, we are spiritually "dead in trespasses and sins" (Eph. 2:1). Once we have been born again and have the ministry of the Holy Spirit within us, we have spiritual strength. However, even then it is sadly possible for us to forget the teachings of Scripture and ignore the promptings of the Holy Spirit and sin against the Lord. We then lose the joy of the Lord and need to be restored to fellowship.

Although being in a right relationship with God is not described in the Old Testament as a "born-again" experience, there are many mentions of people getting out of fellowship with Him and then being restored. We look at a passage about this today.

## DEVELOPING THE LESSON

**1. Praise for deliverance (Ps. 34:1-7).** David, under the inspiration of the Holy Spirit, began with personal application of the concept.

We know from what the superscription tells us that this psalm is from the time when David was hiding from the persecution of King Saul. On this occasion David feigned insanity before the king of Gath (I Sam. 21:10-15). We read, "This poor man cried, and the Lord heard him, and saved him out of all his troubles" (Ps. 34:6).

We need not be sunk in despair over untoward circumstances. We need not feel that surely God does not hear our prayers because we are not really on good terms with Him. A child of God should feel that he can come to the Heavenly Father, regardless of the circumstances.

**2. Refuge in God (Ps. 34:8-10).** This psalm also has application to a congregation or a smaller fellowship of believers, say in a home church or Bible study. A group can get out of fellowship with the Lord, and then its members will quite probably be out of fellowship with one another. The beauty of corporate fellowship and what can be described as "the presence of the Lord" can be lost under these circumstances.

What is needed is for all to acknowledge the problem and go to the Lord in prayer, confessing the sin and praying for restoration. When a group is thus restored to fellowship with God and each other, there is a glory and a joy that is wonderful in the lives of the believers and a powerful testimony to the unsaved. It is probably true that our emotions are not a good barometer of where we are spiritually, and yet we should feel "bad" when we are out of fellowship with the Lord. There is an old saying, "When God seems far away from you, guess who moved." Christians in right fellowship with God should be the happiest people in the world.

**3. Jesus our High Priest (Heb. 2:17-18).** The Lord Jesus is the Second Person of the Trinity, and as such He is just as truly God as are the Father and the Holy Spirit. When He took on the form of man by the operation of God, as recorded in Luke 1:35, He set aside many of His rights or prerogatives as God. He lived a perfect life as a man. He went to the cross, where He died for our sins and rose again, and then He went back to the Father. During His earthly ministry, however, He set aside part of the glory He had with His Father in heaven.

We do not understand this entirely because we are only human. However, we see in His great high-priestly prayer of John 17, especially verse 5, that He desired and longed for restoration to the glory He had with the Father before the world began. So although the Lord Jesus never did sin, and His fellowship and joy with the Father was never broken, still by the experience of becoming human, He understands our need to be restored to fellowship with our Father in heaven. He stands ready to forgive and restore any of us and all of us when we call on His name and trust in Him. The Lord Jesus was made like us in order that He might mercifully and faithfully reconcile us from a state of decline. He can give us comfort because He understands us.

## ILLUSTRATING THE LESSON

The blessings of fellowship with God are wonderful indeed.

**THE BLESSINGS OF FELLOWSHIP ARE WONDERFUL**

## CONCLUDING THE LESSON

The conclusion is unescapable that individuals and groups can be restored to the joy and rejoicing of fellowship at any time. If pride or self-seeking ambitions are present, joy is lost and prayers hindered. We cannot then "taste and see that the Lord is good" (Ps. 34:8). The blessing of God on us is as sure today as it was on David years ago. We have the advantage of the testimony of Scripture and the many examples given there.

## ANTICIPATING THE NEXT LESSON

Next quarter will be concerned with justice in the New Testament. Start by reading Matthew 12:1-14.

—*Brian D. Doud.*

# PRACTICAL POINTS

1. Our salvation is reason enough to bless the Lord for the rest of our lives (Ps. 34:1).
2. We should testify of God's goodness and rejoice together (vss. 2-3).
3. If we seek the Lord, He will deliver us (vs. 4).
4. God is good and will not withhold any good thing from His people (vss. 5-10).
5. God is merciful and wants to reconcile us to Himself (Heb. 2:17).
6. Jesus is there to help us resist temptation, just as He did (vs. 18).

—*Valante M. Grant.*

# RESEARCH AND DISCUSSION

1. How do we express gratitude to God for His restoration power?
2. What can we expect to find when we seek the Lord?
3. Why is it important to always bless the Lord and praise Him?
4. Is it necessary to come together to praise God for what He does for all of us? Why?
5. What is the connection between restoration and rejoicing?
6. When we exalt the name of the Lord, what results do we see in our lives?
7. How is it evident that God hears our prayers? Discuss.
8. Is there anything on earth that can tempt us beyond the reconciling power of Jesus (Heb. 2:18)?

—*Valante M. Grant.*

# ILLUSTRATED HIGH POINTS

**O magnify the Lord**

Many in the world change the words of Psalm 34:3 to "O *minimize* the Lord with me, and let us *despise* his name together." Some do it deliberately; others do it ignorantly.

Some high school girls in Arizona had posed for their senior picture day in T-shirts that spelled "Best You've Ever Seen Class of 2016." Then six posed for another picture, which went viral, to spell a degrading word. People were upset, and rightly so, calling for their expulsion from school. One indignant person was quoted as saying, "We need to understand that words matter!"

True! But what about our Lord's name, which is so often used thoughtlessly and in vain?

**And were lightened**

Another rendering of Psalm 34:5 reads, "Those who look to him are radiant." Indeed, our countenance as Christians should express our inner joy. Anxious and confused looks belong to unbelievers.

**O fear the Lord**

Psalm 34:9 expresses the same principle as Matthew 6:33 and Romans 8:28. God knows what is best and graciously provides it for His children. We need to accept the fact that if we do not get what we think we need, God knew it was not good for us.

Two teardrops met in the river of life. "Who are you?" one asked the other. "I am a teardrop from a girl who loved a man and lost him. Who are you?" "Well," replied the first, "I am a teardrop from the girl who got him."

Life is often like that. Learn to trust God in *all* things, recognizing His love and grace toward us.

—*David A. Hamburg.*

# Golden Text Illuminated

**"O taste and see that the Lord is good: blessed is the man that trusteth in him" (Psalm 34:8).**

How do you tell a person who has never eaten an apple what an apple tastes like? How do you describe the flavor of pumpkin pie to someone unfamiliar with that dessert? You can start with generalities—an apple is sweet (or maybe tart) and juicy; pumpkin pie is sweet and smooth. You can add further details, but soon you are faced with the reality that no words you use are sufficient to give a clear idea of how these foods taste. To really know, the person will simply have to taste them himself.

That is the approach that David took in trying to convey to people what God is like. He could have written a lot *about* God (which, in fact, he and other Bible writers did in many passages), but in our text he invites people to find out for themselves, saying, "O taste and see."

David, who in the context of the psalm in which our golden text is found was rejoicing in God's deliverance from foes, was not interested in having people simply know the right things about God. David had experienced God's goodness to him firsthand; he was eager to see others experience that goodness for themselves.

When we proclaim the gospel of Christ to others, we are not hoping that people will merely change their beliefs about Him or agree with our statements. We want to see them trust Him with their whole being and experience Him in a full-fledged personal relationship. We want them (and ourselves) to taste His goodness, to know it on an intimate, heart level.

This is not to endorse a contentless, free-floating experience-based approach to knowing God as some mystics and cults do. All that we know of God is based on solid truth as taught to us in the Scriptures. We are to taste and see "that [He] is good." God's goodness is an objective, true reality that we can understand (to a degree) with our minds. But it is also a personal reality that we need to perceive within.

God's great goodness leads naturally to the next major truth in our text: "Blessed is the man that trusteth in him." The Hebrew word for "blessed" is the same one that begins the very first psalm: "Blessed is the man that walketh not in the counsel of the ungodly." It can sometimes be translated "happy," but it speaks of a deep, inner joy that is not affected by changing circumstances. It carries the same idea of the "blesseds" that Jesus pronounced in His Sermon on the Mount (Matt. 5:3-11).

The picture behind "the man that trusteth in him" is that of a warrior or valiant man who takes refuge in the Lord. Of course, the verse applies to all people of any age and either gender, but David was deliberately setting the bar high. If even a valiant warrior finds blessing in taking shelter in God, how much more the rest of us! We may think strong individuals do not need God, but that is not true.

This text seems a particularly appropriate one with which to wrap up a quarter's studies. It is a very simple truth, but it carries a profound significance that can never be exhausted. My prayer is that every reader will have tasted and found—and will keep tasting and finding—that the Lord indeed is good!

—*Kenneth A. Sponsler.*

# Heart of the Lesson

My pastor walks through the congregation carrying a wireless microphone at the end of every Sunday service. Many people use the microphone to share prayer requests, and the pastor or an elder prays for each one. But many people also use the microphone to praise God for answered prayer and for Him working in their lives. Thanking and praising God privately is important. But thanking and praising God in a corporate setting honors God publicly and is a testimony to others of God's faithfulness.

David, Israel's second king, wrote the praises in Psalm 34, the text for today's lesson, when he was running from King Saul. David took refuge in Gath among Israel's enemies. When the king's servants recognized David, he feigned insanity. David's actions so repulsed the king that he sent David away.

**1. David's praise to God (Ps. 34:1-3).** David said that he would bless God at all times. Words of adoration would continually flow from his mouth. God was his reason for boasting; he desired to celebrate what God had done for him. As a result, those who were discouraged would be encouraged. David urged those listening to him to join him in praising God.

**2. David's testimony of deliverance (Ps. 34:4-6).** David said he had sought God—he had prayed. God heard those prayers and freed David from his fears. David assured his listeners that those who ask God for help with a problem will go away with a radiant, joyful countenance. They will not go away looking ashamed for having asked God for help.

David repeated that he had cried to God about his problems. He had felt desperation and even referred to himself as being a "poor man" (Ps. 34:6). David then affirmed that God had heard and delivered him. We too can tell others how God has worked in our lives. This is one of the most winsome and irrefutable ways to share our faith.

**3. God's goodness to His people (Ps. 34:7-10).** David explained that the angel of the Lord encamped around and rescued those who feared Him. God watches over His people and protects them. He meets their needs.

David invited his listeners to taste and see that God is good. In Scripture, to taste often suggests full participation in the thing enjoyed (Richards, *The Bible Reader's Companion,* Cook). David wanted others to fully experience God's goodness.

David noted that even the young, powerful lions that roamed Israel grew hungry between hunts. But people who fear the Lord and seek Him lack nothing—God supplies their needs.

**4. Jesus' high priestly role (Heb. 2:17-18).** David wrote from the perspective of one who loved God before Jesus' coming. From David's descendants came the Messiah, Jesus, who took on the physical limitations of a human except for a sin nature. He experienced suffering and temptation. He was "made like unto his brethren" so he could become our compassionate, trustworthy high priest.

In the Old Testament, the priest represented the people before God and offered animal sacrifices for their sins. But Jesus, our High Priest, was Himself the sacrifice for our sins. By shedding His blood, He satisfied God's righteous demands, restoring us to Him.

Jesus identifies with us, having lived as a human. He sympathizes. Because He suffered and was tempted, He can help us endure suffering and temptation.

—*Ann Staatz.*

# World Missions

If none of those who trust in the Lord will be desolate (Ps. 34:22), it is understood that those who do not trust in the Lord will be. Indeed, Psalm 34 specifies numerous troubles that a person can face and be delivered from with the Lord's goodness: fear, afflictions, broken hearts, troubles, lack, and shame. Jesus takes our suffering upon Himself and gives us strength and hope.

Those who do not know Jesus have trials and difficulties, but they have no Deliverer—no one to give them strength, comfort, and help.

People have said they do not know how anyone gets through cancer, a death in the family, losing a child, or other tragedies without the Lord. The sad truth is that many people do *not* get through. Over 44,000 people committed suicide in the United States in 2011. That averages to one person dying every twelve minutes, and that is just in America. Factoring in the whole world, it goes down to one person every forty seconds.

God holds out hope for those in despair, but how can people taste and see He is good if they do not know about Him or if what they know about Him is wrong?

One evangelistic association began an Internet ministry, determining that though many countries are difficult to reach for political or cultural or even physical reasons, almost every country in the world is accessible via the Internet. With the world culture changing from being relational to digital, when people are seeking answers, they often go to their computer rather than a friend or confidant. This ministry, www.PeaceWithGod.net, is using that new dynamic to turn the entire world into their mission field. Over five hundred volunteers answer questions from seekers all over the globe. Here are some of the questions they have received. How would you answer?

"I'm at the end of the road and I have no one to turn to. I don't want to live like this any more."

"I want to see Jesus when I die. I try to live right and go to church, and I do believe I am a good person. What else do we need to do to be ready?"

"I am at the end of my rope, and suicide seems like my only alternative."

"Are my prayers pointless? Who am I to be heard?"

"I'm eleven years old, and I'm mean to my six-year-old brother. I hurt him sometimes, like slap him when he aggravates me. And I'm very scared that I'm going to die and end up in a lot of pain and harm and burn up in hell. I asked for forgiveness like two or three times while sobbing. I'm so scared. Where will I end up?"

"My family is Muslim, and most of the people in my country are Muslim. If they can know that I am converting, they will kill me. So then what will I do?"

People need to know that God is good, He cares for them, and He offers them salvation. At the Peace With God ministry, people are responding to the gospel every minute. Over seven million people have already made decisions for Christ!

To find out how to become a volunteer and share the gospel with seekers on the Internet, go to www.SearchforJesus.net. They ask for a commitment of two hours per week. You can be a missionary right from your own home and tell people how they can taste and see that God is good.

—*Kimberly Rae.*

# The Jewish Aspect

This week's lesson includes a portion of Psalm 34. Psalm 34 is an acrostic poem, with each verse beginning with a different letter of the Hebrew alphabet arranged in order. To Jews it is an important psalm, and among some it is recited every Sabbath.

The Sabbath, one of the most important days for Jews, is a day set aside to refresh and renew. It is a day when worries are cast aside and toil ceases. It is a sanctuary of time when one stops usual duties and obligations for a minivacation.

The Jewish Sabbath starts on sundown of Friday evening and ends on Saturday night. It ends when there are three stars present in the sky that can be seen with the naked eye.

Sabbath keeping was included in the Ten Commandments and is therefore considered an obligation of the Torah. However, the day is supposed to be one of joyful rest. The atmosphere of the home on that day is bright and cheerful. The best food is prepared, and the finest clothing is worn.

The first Sabbath meal occurs on Friday night. The table is covered with premium white linen and china. Two loaves of challah, the special Jewish braided bread, lie covered on the dinner table along with the Sabbath candles.

On Saturday morning after the synagogue service, the family gathers once again for another Sabbath meal. Again, the atmosphere is one of joy.

The Sabbath is a beautiful gift of God to mankind. It is believed that the Sabbath is a major contribution of the Jewish people to the world. It is a day of rest, peace, and deliverance.

The last part of the Sabbath day includes the *havdalah* ritual. Havdalah, which means "separation," marks the formal conclusion of the Sabbath and the returning to the work week. During havdalah, while standing, the wine, spices, fire, and then havdalah itself is blessed. Sabbath ends with everyone saying, "Shavua Tov" or "Good Week" to each other (Perelson, *An Invitation to Shabbat,* UAHC Press).

Since biblical law forbids work on the Sabbath, Judaism has sought to define specifically the kinds of things that are forbidden. For example, driving or even turning on a switch to light a stove is prohibited. Spending money or handling money is also prohibited. The objects that are forbidden to be handled are called *muktzeh.*

On the Sabbath, objects can be carried inside a home, but they cannot be carried outside a private domain (Telushkin, *Jewish Literacy,* William Morrow). In some buildings, there are special Sabbath elevators that operate automatically. The elevators stop on every floor since operating an electric switch on Sabbath is forbidden (Harris, "For Jewish Sabbath, Elevators Do All the Work," NewYorkTimes.com).

Although there are a number of Sabbath regulations, the true idea of Sabbath is to create an island of peace in one's life. The day is meant to nourish the soul. Sabbath separates the observer from the frenzy of the world and allows him to focus on the important things of life. It is a day of turning one's focus toward the divine.

Rest, an important concept in the Jewish Sabbath, also plays an important part in Christianity. Jesus said, "Come unto me, all ye that labour and are heavy laden, and I will give you rest" (Matt. 11:28).

Jesus stands as the Christian's Sabbath rest. His death and resurrection shelter the believer from the world.

—Robin Fitzgerald.

# Guiding the Superintendent

When troubles come into the life of the believer, he is never left to his own devices. In the midst of great personal struggle, David said to "taste and see that the Lord is good: blessed is the man that trusteth in him" (Ps. 34:8). Taste, see, trust—all words of great encouragement.

The author of Hebrews informs us that Jesus Christ is always ready "to succour [help] them that are tempted [tested]" (Heb. 2:18). The bottom line is this: God is always ready to help and restore those who turn to Him.

## DEVOTIONAL OUTLINE

**1. Focus on the Lord (Ps. 34:1-10).** In this psalm, young David had just escaped from the hands of the enemy— the Philistines. David broke out into a song of praise to God for his deliverance. It would seem that David exhausted the dictionary for words that could be used for praise to God.

David began with a call to bless the Lord. His starting point was the Lordship of God. Even in the most terrifying of circumstances, one's focus should always be the Lord.

Related to blessing the Lord is boasting in the Lord. David focused entirely on the Lord.

Blessing leads to boasting, which in turn leads to glorifying the Lord. David's high view of God shone brightly. The Lord was the most important thing in his life.

David testified that when he sought the Lord, the Lord heard him. Others looked to Him and were not disappointed. The Lord heard David when he was oppressed.

When a man praises God, God acts. The Lord's response is to save "him out of all his troubles" (Ps. 34:6), not *from* his troubles but *out of* his troubles. The promise is clear. The angel of the Lord (in the Old Testament often the preincarnate Christ) will deliver him.

David was not finished. Next, he called on people to "taste and see that the Lord is good" (Ps. 34:8). Tasting here means more than a brief glance. It means to embrace the Lord with all one's being.

When one looks inward, all he sees is self. When one looks outward, he lacks nothing. Psalm 34 calls this fearing the Lord. Fearing the Lord is closely linked to seeking the Lord. Those who have the Lord have no need for anything else.

When troubles come, one's eyes should always be on the Lord.

**2. Focus on Jesus Christ (Heb. 2:17-18).** Within the mystery of God becoming man, we are told that Jesus Christ became a human so that He would understand the struggles we are going through.

We never need to feel that Jesus Christ does not understand what we are experiencing in life. He has experienced it too, so we can trust Him to understand. When troubles and problems come, we should turn to the Lord, not ourselves. The biblical response to struggles is praise to God for deliverance.

## AGE-GROUP EMPHASES

**Children:** Children always enjoy eating. Ask them what come to mind when they hear "taste and see that the Lord is good" (Ps. 34:8).

**Youths:** For most words of praise in Psalm 34, there is a corresponding promise from God. Have the teens identify these promises.

**Adults:** Have your adult class members tell how God blessed them when they focused on Him, not on their struggles.

—*Martin R. Dahlquist.*

telling us that Jesus Christ is the one who fulfilled the tabernacle system of the Old Testament. He opened up a new way to God by keeping the entire Mosaic Law perfectly and paying for our sins through His death, burial, and bodily resurrection (Rom. 10:4; Heb. 10:1-21).

Although His divine glory was veiled while He ministered on earth, it was evident that Jesus was God in human form, for He said that the one who sees Him sees the Father (John 14:9).

Today the glory of Christ is focused in the gospel (II Cor. 4:4). Believers in the gospel have the privilege of the very glory of Christ showing through their lives (vs. 6) as they obey the Word of God by the power of the indwelling Holy Spirit.

First Corinthians 10:31 says, "Whether therefore ye eat, or drink, or whatsoever ye do, do all to the glory of God."

Take some time to think about that. The God of glory came to earth in His eternal Son to show us the glory of God, centered in Christ's work on the cross and His bodily resurrection. Through faith in Him, believers can show God's glory in all the daily things they do. How practical is that? In God's timing, all believers will experience God's full glory in eternity.

The Lord's glory is often missed because believers are not following Jesus. It has been said that God is most glorified in His children when they are closely following Him.

Is your life reflecting the glory of Christ? If not, then it is easy to be a "glory hound." If Jesus' glory satisfies your life, you will not strive to receive your own glory. Rather, in whatever you think, say, or do, Christ will be glorified in and through you.

# The Only Way to Go

PAUL R. BAWDEN

One time my family and I traveled to a major city about ninety miles from where we lived. Once we arrived in the city, we had to find our way to a specific church to be part of a wedding ceremony. We knew how to get to the city, but finding the church was a greater challenge.

How did we find the way? I put the address of the church into Google Maps on my smart phone, and we were directed exactly to where the church was. In fact, the voice providing the directions on the phone told us ahead of time when we were to turn at a light and which way, right or left. Technology is truly amazing. I am sure you have used Google Maps (or equivalent) as well.

What is rather astounding and sad at the same time, however, is that many

people who use Google Maps to find their way to a specific, physical place , do not take time to consider the reality that there is help for them in the Bible to find the way and destination for their souls.

The consequence of not considering the direction and destination the Bible provides for an individual's spiritual life is being lost in a chaotic world where any idea of man goes or any opinion about God or outright denial of God's existence is totally acceptable. Such a person flounders around in his own reason and misses out on what the unchanging revelation of the eternal God has for him. However, Scripture makes it clear that the God of the Bible is personal and actively involved in the lives of people, especially those who respond to Him in faith.

In the Old Testament, Abraham (when his name was still Abram) discovered this when God appeared to him in what is today the country of Iraq. Abram was living under polytheism, which is a belief in many gods concocted by man, when the eternal God appeared to him, and Abram responded to Him in faith. Abram left his country and went to the land that God led him to, the Promised Land, which the nation of Israel has a part of today.

Hebrews 11:8 gives the New Testament commentary on Abraham's faith journey. "By faith Abraham, when he was called to go out into a place which he should after receive for an inheritance, obeyed; and he went out, not knowing whither he went."

In responding to God, Abraham was trusting Him for His direction and the destination to which He would lead him physically. But there was more than just direction toward a physical destination. Abraham had faith in God for his eternal destination as well. Hebrews 11:9-10 puts it this way, "By faith he sojourned in the land of promise, as in a strange country, dwelling in tabernacles with Isaac and Jacob, the heirs with him of the same promise: for he looked for a city which hath foundations, whose builder and maker is God." Verse 10 tells us that Abraham had faith in God for his spiritual direction and destination.

The greatest challenge in Abraham's life was when God directed him to take his son Isaac to Mount Moriah to offer him as a sacrifice (Gen. 22:1-18). Abraham's obedience to God was really the highlight of his faith walk with God. Abraham's answer to Isaac's question about where the lamb for the burnt offering was displayed this faith. He told Isaac, "My son, God will provide himself a lamb for a burnt offering."

Did God provide the lamb for the burnt offering? Definitely! God honored Abra-

ham's faith, which trusted God for both guidance in his life on earth and a destination after his life.

But there is more here. Abraham's offering of his son Isaac and God's provision of the lamb as a substitute for Isaac is a picture of how the Father provided His one and only Son, the Lord Jesus Christ, the Lamb of God, to be the sacrifice for the sins of the world. That is why John said this about Jesus: "Behold the Lamb of God, which taketh away the sin of the world" (John 1:29).

During His ministry, Jesus said, "God so loved the world, that he gave his only begotten Son, that whosoever believeth in him should not perish, but have everlasting life" (John 3:16). In John 14:6, Jesus declared, "I am the way, the truth, and the life: no man cometh unto the Father, but by me." What was Jesus saying? He was the only one who could provide true direction and a real destination after this life—He was the only way to go.

Why could Jesus say that? He would die on the cross to pay the penalty for our breaking God's law, be buried, and conquer the grave bodily for us to demonstrate that redemption had been accomplished, our sins have been paid for eternally, God's justice has been satisfied, and reconciliation with God is available for all.

What each of us has to do to experience what Jesus has accomplished for us through His death, burial, and bodily resurrection is ask Him by faith to be our Lord and Saviour (Rom. 10:9-13).

Have you asked Christ to be your Lord and Saviour? I trust you have. If not, I encourage you to consider Him and what He has done for you. If you know the Lord personally, live for Him in the power of the indwelling Holy Spirit (Gal. 5:16), giving evidence of His fruit in your life (vss. 22-23).

In the Old Testament, Abraham believed God, and the Lord declared him righteous (Gen. 15:6). Abraham, then, had faith in God according to the revelation that he was given. Yet, as Jesus said in John 8:56, "Your father Abraham rejoiced to see my day: and he saw it, and was glad." This tells us that Abraham's faith brought him to his destination in the Lord's presence, where he saw the eternal Son, Jesus Christ, before He became incarnate. Abraham had experienced fully that the Lord Jesus was the only way to go.

Through His death, burial, and bodily resurrection, Jesus Christ is the full revelation of God. The believer in Christ is given His indwelling presence in the Holy Spirit and the sure promise of being in God's presence forever.

People look to Google Maps for directions and a right destination. The believer looks to the Bible to find true direction for living here and receives heaven as his destination. The believer in the Bible, God's map, knows that Jesus is the only way to go.

# TOPICS FOR NEXT QUARTER

# PARAGRAPHS ON PLACES AND PEOPLE

## THE MIDDLE OF THE COURT

The account of the dedication of the temple is found in II Chronicles 6 through 7 as well as I Kings 8. It was timed to coincide with the Feast of Tabernacles. The people were assembled in Jerusalem for a total of fourteen days (II Chron. 7:8-9). The number of animals sacrificed during this celebration was staggering—a total of 142,000. The meat was shared with the people during this two-week feast.

The scope of the sacrifice required Solomon to consecrate part of the court surrounding the temple for sacrifices since the bronze altar constructed for this purpose was insufficient for the immensity of the task. The court was divided into sections, with separate areas for priests, women, and Gentiles.

## IN THE SEA

An amazing passage in Revelation 5 describes the throng of worshippers surrounding the throne in heaven. The narrative focuses first on the twenty-four elders, then the angels, then all creatures in creation. The praise culminates in Revelation 5:13, where "every creature which is in heaven, and on the earth, and under the earth, and such as are in the sea" praise God.

The statement by John is unambiguous. Praise emanates from every created being, everything in which life resides. How is it possible for every creature, including every aquatic dweller (whale, lobster, octopus, and more) to give praise to God? The full understanding of this may yet remain a mystery, but there can be no question—every creature will praise its glorious Creator in some way.

## THE WOMEN THAT WERE WISE HEARTED

Exodus 35 contains the account of the collection of materials taken up for the tabernacle. An enormous amount of resources was necessary for its construction, including gold, silver, bronze, wood, linen, and animal skins. Both men and women donated precious stones and metals. Verse 25 says that "all the women that were wise hearted did spin with their hands."

The amount of fabric needed for the curtains enclosing the tabernacle proper and the courtyard was immense—over three hundred square yards. The curtains were made either from linen or goat's hair. The fabric was woven, either by hand or on looms—a huge undertaking. Yet the women, "whose heart stirred them up" (Exod. 35:26), were willing to undertake such a task for the God of Israel.

## THE STRANGER

The nation of Israel has always been welcoming to the "stranger," the term the Bible uses for what we today would call an immigrant or resident alien. There were always those living among the Jewish people who were non-Jewish. Their reasons for doing so would have varied. Some were permanent residents. Others were living in the country temporarily or only passing through.

God made provision for the poor and the stranger, who, being non-Jewish, had no land inheritance. The corners of Israel's fields were to be left unharvested, and gleaning (harvesting of crops left in the field after the reaping) was not to be done. The nation was to exhibit generosity and compassion.

—*James Parry.*

# Daily Bible Readings for Home Study and Worship

(Readings are for the week previous to the lesson topics.)

**1. March 4.   The Lord Will Provide**

M.—Remember What the Lord Has Done. Deut. 8:11-20.
T.—Jesus Tested in the Wilderness. Matt. 4:1-11.
W.—Prayer and Strengthening. Luke 22:39-46.
T.—Help from the Sanctuary. Ps. 20:1-9.
F.—Provision Received by Faith. Heb. 11:17-22.
S.—Blessing in Response to Obedience. Gen. 22:15-19.
S.—Abraham's Obedient Faith. Gen. 22:1-14.

**2. March 11.   A Prayer of Dedication**

M.—God's Promise to David. Ps. 132:8-12.
T.—The Lord Has Chosen Zion. Ps. 132:13-18.
W.—Jesus, Heir of David's Throne. Acts 2:29-36.
T.—Completion of the Temple. II Chron. 6:1-11.
F.—A Place for Prayer. II Chron. 6:28-33.
S.—Prayers from Captivity. II Chron. 6:36-40.
S.—Solomon's Prayer of Dedication. II Chron. 6:12-21.

**3. March 18.   Worshipping in God's Temple**

M.—A New Worshipper of Jesus. John 9:24-38.
T.—Worshippers Among the Gentiles. Isa. 19:19-25.
W.—Worship Commanded by the King. II Chron. 29:25-30.
T.—Deliverance from Many Troubles. Ps. 107:1-9.
F.—Healed and Forgiven. Ps. 107:17-22.
S.—Solomon's Blessing. I Kings 8:54-61.
S.—Dedication of the Temple. II Chron. 7:1-9.

**4. March 25.   Seeking His Face**

M.—The Fast the Lord Wants. Isa. 58:6-12.
T.—The Fruit of Righteousness. Jas. 3:13-18.
W.—Compassion and Justice. Exod. 22:21-29.
T.—Choose Life. Deut. 30:15-20.
F.—Walk Before Me in Uprightness. I Kings 9:1-5.
S.—Evil from Unfaithfulness. I Kings 9:6-9.
S.—The Choice Before Us. II Chron. 7:12-22.

**5. April 1.   He Has Risen (Easter)**

M.—Suffering, Death, and Resurrection Foretold. Mark 8:31—9:1.
T.—Resurrection on the Third Day. Matt. 20:17-19.
W.—Risen as He Said. Matt. 28:1-6.
T.—I Go and Will Come Again. John 14:1-6.
F.—Women at the Empty Tomb. Luke 24:22-24.
S.—Jesus on the Emmaus Road. Luke 24:13-21.
S.—The Lord Is Risen Indeed. Luke 24:1-12, 30-35.

**6. April 8.   Appearance of the Risen Lord**

M.—The Risen Jesus in Their Midst. Luke 24:36-49.
T.—Witnesses to the Resurrected Christ. I Cor. 15:1-8.
W.—Continue in What You Have Learned. II Tim. 3:14-17.
T.—An Ethiopian Told of Jesus. Acts 8:26-35.
F.—Jesus' Charge to Peter. John 21:15-23.
S.—A Reliable Testimony. John 20:30-31; 21:24-25.
S.—It Is the Lord! John 21:1-14.

**7. April 15.   Follow Me**

M.—Peter's Three Denials. John 18:15-18, 25-27.
T.—From Doubt to Faith. John 20:24-28.
W.—Sent to Proclaim the Good News. Matt. 10:5-15.

T.—The Lord of the Harvest. Matt. 9:35-38.
F.—The Shepherd and His Sheep. John 10:11-18.
S.—Losing Life to Find It. Matt. 10:34-39.
S.—Follow Me; Feed My Sheep. John 21:15-25.

**8. April 22.   The Lord God Almighty**

M.—Great Is the Lord. I Chron. 16:23-34.
T.—Limits on Satan's Power. Job 1:6-12.
W.—The Voice of the Lord. Ps. 29:1-11.
T.—Looking unto Jesus. Heb. 12:1-6.
F.—Vision of Four Living Creatures. Ezek. 1:5-14.
S.—The Lord God Omnipotent. Rev. 19:1-8.
S.—Heavenly Worship. Rev. 4:1-6, 8-11.

**9. April 29.   Blessing, Glory, and Honor Forever**

M.—Glory at His Appearing. I Pet. 1:3-9.
T.—All Things Under His Feet. I Cor. 15:20-28.
W.—Sanctified by His Glory. Exod. 29:38-46.
T.—If God Be for Us. Rom. 8:31-39.
F.—The Scroll of God's Words. Ezek. 2:8—3:11.
S.—The Lion of Judah. Rev. 5:1-5.
S.—All Creatures Worship the Lamb. Rev. 5:6-14.

**10. May 6.   Giving from a Generous Heart**

M.—Give Willingly from the Heart. Exod. 25:1-9.
T.—Give Alms Quietly. Matt. 6:1-4.
W.—Be Ready with Your Gift. II Cor. 9:1-5.
T.—Holy to the Lord. Lev. 27:30-33.
F.—Blessings on the Righteous. Ps. 112:1-10.
S.—Gifts for the Tabernacle. Exod. 35:10-19.
S.—Give Cheerfully and Generously. Exod. 35:20-29; II Cor. 9:6-8.

**11. May 13.   Bringing Firstfruits**

M.—Honor God with Your Firstfruits. Prov. 3:1-10.
T.—Martyrs, Firstfruits for God. Rev. 14:1-5.
W.—Gifts, a Pleasing Sacrifice to God. Phil. 4:15-20.
T.—Preparing Grain Offerings. Lev. 2:1-10, 14.
F.—Offerings Without Blemish. Lev. 22:17-20.
S.—Sabbaths and Feasts. Lev. 23:1-8.
S.—Giving to God First. Lev. 23:9-14, 22.

**12. May 20.   Remembering with Joy**

M.—Blessings from Obeying God. Lev. 26:1-6.
T.—Lands and Houses Shared with All. Acts 4:32-37.
W.—Bearing One Another's Burdens. Gal. 6:1-5.
T.—Promised Blessings. Lev. 26:9-13.
F.—Honest Dealings. Lev. 25:13-17.
S.—Helping One Another in Hardships. Lev. 25:35-38.
S.—Sabbath Years and the Jubilee. Lev. 25:1-12.

**13. May 27.   Rejoicing in Restoration**

M.—Atonement for the People. Lev. 16:15-19.
T.—The Lord Hears the Righteous Cry. Ps. 34:11-18.
W.—But We See Jesus. Heb. 2:5-9.
T.—Salvation Through Suffering. Heb. 2:10-13.
F.—Destroying the Devil's Power. Heb. 2:14-16.
S.—Jesus, Our High Priest Forever. Heb. 7:18-28.
S.—Jesus, Our Redeemer and Deliverer. Ps. 34:1-10; Heb. 2:17-18.

# REVIEW

**What have you learned this quarter?**

**Can you answer these questions?**

### Acknowledging God

### UNIT I: Follow in My Ways

## March 4

### The Lord Will Provide

1. In what way did God "tempt" Abraham?
2. What special things about Isaac made it especially difficult for Abraham to obey God's command?
3. What did Abraham evidently believe God would do to Isaac?
4. What indications do we have that Isaac also was obedient to God's will?
5. What provision do you need to trust God for today?

## March 11

### A Prayer of Dedication

1. In what ways did Solomon show his humility and reliance on God?
2. How do we understand both God's immensity and His awareness and concern for our lives?
3. What was the important truth about the place where God would put His name?
4. What was Solomon's main petition to the Lord?
5. What are the steps you can take to dedicate yourself to the Lord?

## March 18

### Worshipping in God's Temple

1. Why is fire a fitting symbol for the Lord?
2. What was the glory of the Lord that filled the temple?
3. What was the people's response to the fire and the Lord's glory?
4. What did the large number of animal sacrifices show about the people's worship?
5. In what sense were the sacrifices a "sweet savour"?

## March 25

### Seeking His Face

1. What were the Israelites to do when they faced difficulty?
2. Why does II Chronicles 7:14 not apply directly to Christians today?
3. What anthropomorphic expression do we find in this verse, and what does it mean?
4. What would happen to the temple if the people turned from God?
5. How do we seek the Lord's face in our lives today?

### UNIT II: All Glory and Honor

## April 1

### He Has Risen (Easter)

1. Why did the women come to the tomb?
2. Why were the women perplexed when they came to the tomb?
3. What was significant about the arrangement of the graveclothes in the tomb?
4. What do we learn about the resurrected body of Christ from this passage?
5. What part does the resurrection play in our salvation and Christian life?

## April 8

### Appearance of the Risen Lord

1. What might Peter have meant when he said, "I go a fishing" (John 21:3)?
2. Why did Jesus ask the disciples if they had caught any fish?
3. What did the large catch of fish reveal to the disciples?

4. In what way did Jesus' actions re-assure His disciples?

## April 15
### Follow Me
1. What are the two possible meanings of the phrase "more than these" in John 21:15?
2. What did Jesus tell Peter to do when he affirmed his love for Him?
3. What prophecy did Jesus make about Peter's death?
4. What did Jesus say to Peter's question about John?

## April 22
### The Lord God Almighty
1. Why is the appearance of God compared to precious stones?
2. Who is pictured by the seven lamps of fire?
3. What three attributes of God are emphasized by the angelic worship?
4. What does casting crowns before God represent?

## April 29
### Blessing, Glory, and Honor Forever
1. How do we see the three Persons of the Triune God in Revelation 5?
2. Why is Jesus worthy to take the book and open its seals?
3. What three aspects of Christ's work are highlighted in the elders' song?
4. How does Christ's eternal nature impact our worship?

### UNIT III: Give Praise to God
## May 6
### Giving from a Generous Heart
1. What words describe the Israelites' spirit in giving?
2. What agricultural analogy did Paul use to encourage giving?
3. What kind of giver pleases the Lord the most?
4. What is promised to those who give generously?
5. What is the real issue in generous giving?

## May 13
### Bringing Firstfruits
1. What were the Israelites to bring to the Lord at harvesttime?
2. Why were the people not to eat from the harvest before they brought their sheaf to the priest?
3. What were God's two commands for harvesting a field?
4. Why does Leviticus 23:22 conclude with the declaration "I am the Lord your God"?

## May 20
### Remembering with Joy
1. How did Israel's agricultural cycle reflect the pattern of the work week and Sabbath Day?
2. What were the Israelites to do every seven years?
3. How did the Sabbath Year relate to the Babylonian Exile?
4. How were the Sabbath Year and the Jubilee Year to be occasions for joy?

## May 27
### Rejoicing in Restoration
1. How often should we magnify the Lord?
2. How can we be delivered from our fears?
3. In what ways did Jesus become like us? In what one way did He not?
4. What can Jesus do for us because He was tempted?
5. How does Jesus help us resist temptation?